THREE WORLDS OF
CHRISTIAN-MARXIST ENCOUNTERS

THREE WORLDS OF
CHRISTIAN-MARXIST ENCOUNTERS

Edited by
NICHOLAS PIEDISCALZI
and
ROBERT G. THOBABEN

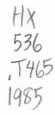

FORTRESS PRESS   **PHILADELPHIA**

Library of Congress Cataloging in Publication Data

Main entry under title:
Three worlds of Christian-Marxist encounters.

Includes bibliographical references.
1. Communism and Christianity—Addresses, essays, lectures. I. Thobaben, Robert G. II. Piediscalzi, Nicholas.
HX536.T465   1985   261.2'1   84–48724
ISBN 0–8006–1840–8

1273L84   Printed in the United States of America   1–1840

For our wives
Janet Thobaben
and
Sibyl Piediscalzi
Our mentors in dialogue

CONTENTS

CONTENTS

THIRD WORLD ENCOUNTERS

CONTRIBUTORS and EDITORS

MAURICE BOUTIN is professor of philosophical theology at the University of Montreal. He received his Ph.D. from the State University of Munich, West Germany. He is editor of the book *Christianisme-Marxisme: Positions et Questions* and coeditor of the book *L'homme en mouvement: Le sport, le jeu, la fête*.

PAUL DEATS is Walter G. Muelder Professor of Social Ethics at Boston University, School of Theology. Deats received a B.A. from Southern Methodist University, an M.Div. from Union Theological Seminary, and a Ph.D. from Boston University. He is a minister in the United Methodist Church. In 1980 and 1982 he visited in Cuba. He is editor of the book *Toward a Discipline of Social Ethics*.

EDWARD J. GRACE is executive director of the Italian Ecumenical Center and executive editor of *The Bridge* (Italian Ecumenical News Agency). He received a B.A. from Catholic University, a B.A. from Gregorian Pontifical University (Rome, Italy), and an S.T.L. (Masters) in Theology from Gregorian Pontifical University. He has lived in Rome for many years. His articles have appeared in *Christianity and Crisis*, *The Ecumenist*, and *Concilium*. He is the author of many articles each year for *The Bridge* on Italian religious, political, cultural, and labor issues.

ALICE L. HAGEMAN is copastor of the Church of the Covenant (Presbyterian– UCC) in Boston and an attorney with the Community Law Practice in Boston. She received a B.A. from the College of Wooster, an M.Div. from Union Theological Seminary, and a J.D. from Northeastern University Law School. Hageman has visited Cuba eight times since 1969 and was a visiting lecturer in the Seminario Evangelico in Matanzas, Cuba, during the spring of 1982. She is editor of the book *Sexist Religion and Women in the Church: No More Silence* and coeditor of the book *Religion in Cuba Today*.

STEPHEN P. HOFFMAN is assistant professor of political science at Taylor

University in Upland, Indiana. Hoffman received a B.A. from Rutgers University and a Ph.D. from Princeton University. He was a foreign service officer with the U.S. Department of State from 1977 to 1981, serving from 1977 to 1979 in Stuttgart, West Germany, and from 1979 to 1981 in Baghdad, Iraq. He recently published an article in *Fides et Historia* and contributed a chapter to a book entitled *Evangelical Perspectives on the Bishops' Pastoral Letter.*

GEORGE MATHEW is assistant director of the Christian Institute for the Study of Religion and Society (CISRS) in New Delhi, India, and general secretary of the People's Union for Civil Liberties in New Delhi. He received a B.A. from Kerala University, a B.D. from Serampore University, and the M.A., M.Phil., and Ph.D. from Jawaharlal Nehru University. During the 1981–82 academic year he was a visiting fellow at the University of Chicago, Committee on South Asian Studies. He is the author of two books, *A Day with Paulo Freire* and *Shift in Indian Politics.*

ARTHUR F. MCGOVERN, S.J., is a professor in the philosophy department and faculty director of the honors program at the University of Detroit. McGovern received an A.B. from Georgetown University, an M.A. from Loyola University in Chicago, an St.L. from West Baden College in Indiana, and a Ph.D. from the University of Paris. He is the author of a book entitled *Marxism: An American Christian Perspective.*

PAUL MOJZES is professor of religious studies at Rosemont College outside of Philadelphia. He is also coeditor of the *Journal of Ecumenical Studies* and editor of the *Occasional Papers on Religion in Eastern Europe.* He attended Belgrade University Law School in Yugoslavia and received an A.B. from Florida Southern College and a Ph.D. from Boston University. He is the author of *Christian-Marxist Dialogue in Eastern Europe.*

NICHOLAS PIEDISCALZI is a professor in the department of religion and director of the Master of Humanities degree program at Wright State University in Dayton, Ohio. Piediscalzi received a B.A. from Grinnell College, a B.D. from Yale University Divinity School, and a Ph.D. from Boston University. He coedited and contributed the concluding chapter of *From Hope to Liberation: Towards a New Marxist-Christian Dialogue.* He also coedited and contributed to *Contemporary Religion and Social Responsibility, Teaching About Religion in Public Schools, Public Education Religion Studies: An*

Overview, and *The Bible in American Education.* He served as editor of the C.A.R.E.E. *Christian-Marxist Newsletter* from 1980 to 1984.

ROBERT G. THOBABEN is professor of political science at Wright State University. He received a B.Sc.C. from Ohio University, an M.A. from Miami University, and a Ph.D. from the University of Cincinnati. During the 1980–81 academic year he was an associate member of Clare Hall at Cambridge University, England. He coedited and contributed an introductory essay to the book *From Hope to Liberation: Towards a New Marxist-Christian Dialogue.* His articles have appeared in such journals as *The Forum, Journal of Ecumenical Studies, Cross Currents,* and *Peace and the Sciences.*

NORMAN E. THOMAS is Vera B. Blinn Professor of World Christianity at United Theological Seminary, Dayton, Ohio. He received an A.B. from Yale University, an M.Div. from Yale University, and a Ph.D. from Boston University. He is the author of *Christianity, Politics and the Manyika* and editor of two other books, *Rise Up and Walk* and *Self Reliance in Zambia.*

JAMES E. WILL is Henry Pfeiffer Professor of Systematic Theology at Garrett-Evangelical Theological Seminary. He is also director of the Peace and Justice Center at the same institution. Will received a B.A. from North Central College, a B.D. from Evangelical Theological Seminary, and a Ph.D. from Columbia University. He is the author of *Must Walls Divide,* and his articles have appeared in such journals as *Encounter, Journal of Ecumenical Studies,* and *Dialectics and Humanism.*

PREFACE

This volume grew out of our participation in dialogues and our fifteen-year-old team-taught, interdisciplinary course, Christian-Marxist Dialogues—the only one of its kind in the United States.[1] At first, we taught solely from printed materials. Eventually, we included a dialogue in our course, an effort which resulted in the publication of *From Hope to Liberation: Towards a New Marxist-Christian Dialogue*.[2] Next we began to participate in international dialogues on a regular basis. Finally, we served as the codirectors of two North American dialogues which were sponsored by Christians Associated for Relations with Eastern Europe. Our involvement in all of these activities introduced us to the wide variety of encounters taking place in the world and to many of their leaders. As a result, we came to see a need for a single text that would present and assess the different types of Christian-Marxist relationships now operative and that would be intelligible to scholars, students, and educated lay persons. With the invaluable advice and help from many individuals whom we met from and in different parts of the world, we were able to produce this volume. To all of these individuals we express our appreciation. We single out for special recognition the following groups and individuals: the Wright State University Research Council chaired by Dr. Donald C. Thomas, dean of the School of Graduate Studies, and the Liberal Arts Research Committee chaired by Dean Perry D. Moore, both of which provided generous grants to attend dialogues, conduct interviews, and type and reproduce the manuscripts which eventually resulted in the completion of this volume for publication. Professor Thobaben is deeply appreciative of the faculty and graduate students of Clare Hall (Cambridge University, England) for providing a stimulating academic atmosphere for writing, and Professor Piediscalzi is especially grateful for the insights and documents he received from leaders he interviewed in Japan, Hong Kong, the People's Republic of China, India, Italy, Switzerland, and Great Britain during a 1981 research tour. Finally, we want to thank Joanne Ballmann, Veda Horton, Kathy Mettler, and Eileen Sestito who shared in the typing of the early and final copies of this text; Lisa Houck Neff and Douglas Slaton, graduate assistants, who tracked down sources and performed other valuable services on our behalf; and Christine M. Hastings and Davis Perkins of Fortress Press for their editorial advice and assistance.

N.P.
R.G.T.

NOTES

1. For a complete description of this course, see Robert G. Thobaben and Nicholas Piediscalzi, "Teaching a Course on the Marxist-Christian Dialogue," in Paul Mojzes, ed., *Varieties of Christian-Marxist Dialogue* (Philadelphia: Ecumenical Press, 1978), 178–96. Also published in *Journal of Ecumenical Studies* 15:1 (Winter 1978): 178–96.

2. *From Hope to Liberation: Towards a New Marxist-Christian Dialogue* (Philadelphia: Fortress Press, 1974).

INTRODUCTION
Nicholas Piediscalzi

Prior to the 1950s most Christians and Marxists viewed themselves as enemies locked in mortal combat. Since that time, select individuals and groups within each camp have exchanged their combative stances for those of peaceful coexistence or mutual cooperation. In many parts of the world today these Christians and Marxists join in informal discussions, formal dialogues, or joint reform projects. The purpose of these encounters is to overcome the barriers to peaceful coexistence and to establish a foundation for the cooperative building of a more just and humane world.

The causes of this dramatic change are many. First, both Christians and Marxists began to realize that neither institution would soon fade away and that it would be impossible for either one to eliminate the other. Out of this insight arose the recognition that both Christians and Marxists share a common responsibility for the future of humanity and that it is necessary for them to face this future as partners rather than enemies.

Second, Christians and Marxists discovered that together they confront global problems that neither can solve alone: the threat of nuclear annihilation, pollution of the atmosphere, the depersonalizing and destructive consequences of industrialization and urbanization, and stagnating economies.

Third, they learned that they share similar institutional problems: dogmatic approaches to knowledge and truth which prevent accurate analysis of the present world situation; stagnant and self-entrenched bureaucracies which hinder rather than foster the solution of problems; and cults of personalities which stifle initiative.

Fourth, changes within the Marxist camp provided new opportunities for a reassessment of each group's hostile stance toward the other: Khrushchev's speech before the 20th Party Congress of the Soviet Union introduced a period of de-Stalinization which opened the Communist system to limited forms of self-criticism. It also led to a relaxation of the party's strict control over intellectuals and artists and a more-relaxed and open stance toward religious groups. As a result, for example, young Marxists in Czechoslovakia called attention to what for them was a serious problem—that the establishment of a Socialist society did not automatically produce the "new man" of socialism. According to Jan M. Lochman, they raised a series of pointed questions:

> Is it not high time that the problems of man were urgently faced? What is the meaning of life? What is the purpose of history—and not only the universal historical process, but my personal history? Can individuals, even whole generations, be satisfied with the answer, that the coming communist society will bring its own solution for these things? And what about the question of evil once the structure of society has been revolutionarily changed and a new social order built? . . . Can one ignore the question of truth in the face of the official teaching of the party? Is it enough simply to accept and await the explanation of the party when faced by the grim realities of a political trial? Is the call: "Comrades, believe the party" really a satisfactory answer for the party member?[1]

In their search for answers to these questions, these thinkers turned to non-Marxist literature and philosophies, for example, to existentialism and, eventually, to the Bible. Out of their searching came Vítězslav Gardavsky's *God Is Not Yet Dead* in which he claims that the Bible and selected Christian thinkers have a great deal to contribute to Socialist thinkers and society;[2] and Milan Machoveč's *A Marxist Looks at Jesus* in which he extols Jesus' openness to the future, humility, identification with the oppressed, and nonviolent methods.[3] Machoveč also claims that "Communists have the greatest right to regard themselves as the authentic perpetuators of Old Testament messianism and early Christian desires for radical change."[4]

At the same time, leading Communist figures in the West, for example, Herbert Aptheker in the United States, Roger Garaudy in France, and Palmiro Togliatti in Italy, began to call for a reevaluation of the Marxist analysis of religion and of the Marxist treatment of the churches.[5] A Swiss Communist, Konrad Farner, asserted during this period that communism as a socioeconomic system is not incompatible with the basic tenets of Christianity. This is the case because the Christian tradition in its earliest days practiced a form of communism. Furthermore, during its two-thousand-year history Christianity has not been tied permanently to any one property system. Likewise, neither communism nor socialism as a socioeconomic system, unlike Marxism's dialectical materialism, is an all-encompassing world view. Each only proposes the establishment of a particular social order on the foundation of a specific system for the distribution of property. Because it is not a world view, communism is compatible not only with Marxism but also with Christianity, Islam, Buddhism, Hinduism, or any other world view.[6]

At the same time, Communist governments in some Eastern European countries, for example, Poland and Hungary, were forced to acknowledge the power of the churches in their domains and their inability to rule effectively without their support. Hence they entered into dialogues and cooperative ventures with the major religious groups in their nations.

Fifth, similar changes with comparable results took place within the Christian community. The late Joseph Hromádka of Czechoslovakia insisted that socialism and Christianity are not necessarily inimicable and that there are many areas of concern, for example, social justice and equality, which they hold in common. Moreover, Marxism seeks to correct many of capitalism's serious problems, many of which have been ignored by Christianity. For these reasons he called all Christians to view Marxism with seriousness and urged Czechoslovakian Christians to work with the government for the establishment of a just and humane Socialist society.[7] Other Eastern European church leaders agreed.

The World Council of Churches along with other Western European and North and South American church bodies called for a new approach to communism. They asked their members to view not only the "evils" of communism but also its "achievements." They pointed to the different types of Marxism emerging in the world and suggested that some of them should be recognized and respected as forces for the achievement of freedom, equality, and justice.[8]

The 1966 Geneva World Conference on Church and Society adopted the following recommendation:

> A direct dialogue is possible between Christians and advocates of non-Christian ideologies. Specifically we urge that the World Council of Churches seek to initiate an informal dialogue with Marxists on an international basis, in each region of the world. We believe this will increase possibilities of cooperation between Christians and non-Christians, irrespective of their ideologies, for the furtherance of peace and progress for all mankind.[9]

In 1967 the Central Committee of the World Council of Churches accepted this recommendation and instructed the Department of Church and Society to conduct a dialogue between Christians and Marxists. This encounter took place in Geneva from 8 to 11 April 1968.[10]

Significant changes also took place within the Roman Catholic community. These were embodied in the papacies of John XXIII and Paul VI and the actions of the Second Vatican Council. Both popes and the council ceased pronouncing anathemas against communism, and each called for a sympathetic and reconciling approach toward Socialist systems in order to lay a foundation for constructive dialogue.[11] They also encouraged establishing contact with Communist leaders. As a result, during his reign, John XXIII for the first time in papal history received a Communist official, Alexi Adzubei. Paul VI followed John XXIII's lead in 1967 when he received the president of the Soviet Union, Nicolai Podgorny. And in 1973 the Vatican made a public overture for dialogue with the People's Republic of China on "the basis of Roman Catholic recognition that the thoughts of Chairman Mao Tse-tung reflect also Christian values."[12] One year later, Dom Helder Pessoa Camara, archbishop of Olinda Recife in Brazil, lecturing at the University of Chicago's celebration of St. Thomas Aquinas's Seventh Centenary, called upon the Christian community in general and the University of Chicago in particular "to try to do with Karl Marx today, what in his day St. Thomas did with Aristotle."[13] According to Dom Helder, the thought of Marx contains many truths of value for the Christian community to ponder and utilize. Furthermore, Marx "leads Christians to rediscover the biblical view of man as co-creator" and faith as *praxis* instead of intellectual assent to a system of beliefs.[14]

Sixth, Christians and Marxists in Third World countries discovered that they face a common enemy—oppressive regimes which refuse to provide a modicum of political freedom, economic justice, and equality for their citizens. They concluded that their dedication to the achievement of political reform and economic justice transcends their ideological differences and provides ample justification for their working together rather than separately to achieve these common goals. Within this new situation, Marxists discovered that it is necessary to distinguish between reactionary and revolutionary Christians and that they have much in common with the latter. They also came to appreciate and admire the dedication and courage of Christians engaged in transforming society. On the other side, Christians in search of socioeconomic theories to analyze the failure of "development" programs to solve their economic and political problems discovered helpful analytical tools in Marx's writings. At the same time, they came to the conclusion that it is possible to separate Marxist ideology from Marxist socioeconomic analysis and that it is possible, further, to use the latter effectively without subscribing to Marx's atheism and materialism. (For this reason, some of them refer to themselves as Christian Marxists.) Like their Marxist counterparts, these Christians developed an appreciation and admiration of the Marxist concept of solidarity, the courage displayed by Marxists in threatening situations, and their dedication to achieving political and economic reforms in the face of adversity.[15]

The informal discussions, formal dialogues, and action projects tend to reflect the economic, social, political, and cultural conditions of the areas in which they arise. This being the case, it is proper to consider these developments according to the widely used First, Second, and Third Worlds' typology developed by social scientists. The First World is composed of the United States and its Western allies. The Soviet Union and Eastern European nations comprise the Second World. The developing nations of Latin America, Asia, Africa, and the Near East form the Third World. A description of the different types of encounters which take place in these worlds follows.

THE FIRST WORLD

For the most part, First World dialogues have been conducted by intellectuals within the Communist Party and Christian churches. Most of these dialogists are not official representatives of their parties or ecclesiastical bodies. They hold that present world tensions and conflicts which could produce a nuclear holocaust need to be defused. One way to accomplish this is through rational dialogue. They also admit that each system confronts serious internal contradictions and problems that require resolution if the "high humanism" of both Christianity and Marxism is to be realized. Dialogues may produce the occasion for self-examination and mutual criticism which can provide the insights necessary for overcoming institutional barriers to the realization of human fulfillment in both Christianity and Marxism. For this reason, these dialogists affirm the humanistic roots and concerns common to Christianity and Marxism and contend that peaceful evolutionary change is preferable to violent revolutionary change.

The earliest of these dialogues began by defining the nature and purpose of dialogue. Special emphasis was placed upon eschewing conversion tactics. Herbert Aptheker declared that Christians and Marxists seek "dialogue, not to score points or win over an opponent, but to comprehend each other, learn from each other, and undertake to discover likenesses, as well as differences, the better to help create a less destructive human order."[16] They also addressed such topics as freedom, subjectivity, alienation, transcendence, hope, and love. As a result of these dialogues, some Marxists developed a keen interest in the questions of both personal and social ethics according to Wieland Zademach. They pursued with seriousness and sensitivity the issues of institutional authority versus personal freedom; the nature of human personality; the goal of happiness; and the meaning and significance of suffering and death. On the other side, some Christians gave more attention to the Marxist concept of "the future" and, as a result, rediscovered the "future-orientation" of the Bible. Out of this came the "theology of hope." Others turned to the political dimensions and ramifications of the Judeo-Christian tradition and developed "political theologies" and the "theologies of liberation."[17]

Dorothee Sölle holds that Christians who participated in dialogues during this period "taught Marxist philosophers to look anew for a 'theory of subjectivity which is not subjectivist and a concept of transcendence which is not alienated.' Transcendence here means . . . the capacity of creatively overcoming the given set of conditions in a historical situation." At the same time, Sölle continues, Marxists helped Christians to relearn "the meaning of *incarnation*. . . . By being confronted with philosophical materialism, Christians learned to take existence more seriously . . . [both in the] sense of body and society. Hence, hunger and joblessness, the industrial-military complex and its consequences for everyday life, advance into theological themes."[18]

There are exceptions to this typological description of First World dialogues. Three will be mentioned here. Italy's unique history and culture have produced an entirely different type of encounter. Italian Communists are inheritors of both a "free-thinking" tradition derived from the Enlightenment and staunch anticlericalism, especially in Northern Italy. This legacy prompts them to reject not only the dogmatism and monarchical episcopacy of the Roman Catholic Church but also the absolutism and totalitarianism of Leninist-Stalinist Marxism. After the Kremlin attacked the Italian Communist Party in 1983 for its wayward behavior, Giancarlo Pajetta, foreign policy spokesman for the party, wrote in *L'Unita*, the party paper, "The Soviets cannot dictate to the rest of the Communist world. . . . There's no such thing as a Communist Vatican. . . . Nobody can excommunicate us. . . . the idea of a Communist party as a 'center' or 'leader' for other parties was an idea whose time was past."[19] This national trait and the collaborative efforts of Italian Catholic Communists and Marxist Communists against Fascism and Nazism created a wealth of mutual admiration and trust which eventually led to the disbanding of the Catholic Communist Party and the transformation in 1948 of the Italian Communist Party into a nonideological organization. From that time on, it has not been necessary for an individual to adopt Marxist philosophy to become a member of the party. As a result, some of the leading figures in the Italian Communist Party today are prominent Roman Catholic lay persons.

Following in the footsteps of the Italian Communist Party and the spirit of Eurocommunism, the Executive Committee of the Spanish Communist Party in February 1975 declared their party pluralistic, Socialist, and democratic. They made known that they wanted Christians to join their party. They also assured Christians that some of them would be elected to the Central Committee and positions of leadership. At the same time they called for a reevaluation of traditional Marxist criticism of religion. They also announced that they were departing from Communist orthodoxy by separating Marx's scientific and analytic method from his materialist philosophy and that it was no longer necessary for a Communist to be an atheist. Furthermore, they affirmed that each individual possesses a realm of personal freedom which is not subject to party authority. The Executive Committee concluded by calling for Christians and Communists to join forces in working for the creation of a new and just society.[20]

For a short period (1972–77), a small group in the United States joined in action-oriented dialogue. Their goal was not to resolve theoretical differences; rather, they sought ways to condemn and overcome the injustices engendered and perpetuated by the American capitalist system. Arthur McGovern discusses this group in detail later in this volume.

THE SECOND WORLD

Christian-Marxist encounters in the Second World, with the exception of Albania, Bulgaria, Romania, and the U.S.S.R., have moved from open hostility and conflict to limited toleration of and cooperation with religious bodies. De-Stalinization was responsible for part of this change. Also, in some Second World countries the church serves as the focal point of national identity and unity; a large part of the population maintains active church membership. Moreover, their ecclesiastical authorities do not have a history of accepting a subservient position to political authority. Hence, the Communist parties have come to the realization—usually reluctantly—that in order to rule effectively and in order to achieve a Socialist society, they must recognize the church, allow for its continuation, and establish a working relationship with it. The churches in these countries have abandoned their anti-Communist stances. They admit that socialism will not fade away and that it has established more just and equitable economic orders in their societies. They also agree neither to challenge the authority of the government nor to impede the further development of socialism. Like their political counterparts, the church authorities agree to a cooperative mode of relating.

In his comprehensive study of Christian-Marxist dialogues in Eastern Europe, Paul Mojzes offers a useful typology for understanding Second World encounters.[21] He classifies these dialogues according to the stances adopted by governments toward dialogue. Mojzes admits the limitation of his typology: each type is applicable only to specific historical periods, and practically all Eastern European countries have moved back and forth between the first and second types. Furthermore, in some individual cases there are encounters that could fall into a category other than the prevalent pattern. With these limitations acknowledged, Mojzes presents six types of Second World dialogues. Since the sixth type is his vision of an ideal form of dialogue for Eastern Europe that does not exist, only the first five will be considered here.

First, there are countries—Albania, for example—where the Communist government seeks to abolish all religious institutions and, therefore, prohibits all dialogues.[22] A second type is found in such countries as the U.S.S.R., Bulgaria, and Rumania where the governments prohibit dialogues within their own borders but permit Christian churches to function within specific limits set by the state. In some instances they have made accommodations that provide a modicum of tolerance for the churches and at times a limited degree of cooperation.[23] The U.S.S.R., for example, will permit international organizations to conduct dialogues within their borders. They control the topics of these dialogues and generally include only one representative from the Russian Orthodox Church—usually a patriarch—in their delegation. This representative presents a general statement on the Russian Orthodox Church's position on social justice, peace, or disarmament and does not engage in dialogue as a Christian with Marxists from his country or other nations. (The Soviet government follows this same pattern in forming and sending delegations to dialogues outside its borders.)

The third type—"dialogue despite official disclaimers"—was conducted until very recently in the German Democratic Republic. Under these circumstances, the government invites the churches to declare their solidarity with the aims of the Socialist state and to cooperate with the government in achieving its goals. However, since the government believes that Marxism is all-sufficient, it does not expect the churches to provide the state with any new or constructive insights. Thus, at least in the public domain, there is not need for dialogue on specific issues and problems.[24] More recently the government has abandoned its "official disclaimers" policy for a more receptive public stance toward the churches. Stephen P. Hoffman discusses this change in detail in a later chapter.

"Carefully managed dialogues"—the fourth type—are held in Hungary and Poland. Their goal is to foster a *modus operandi* for the party and the church. Neither group believes that dialogue is desirable. However, it is accepted as a necessity because each group holds and exercises significant power and is unable to pursue its aims and goals without recognizing and collaborating with the other. Because the stakes are high, each is unwilling to cooperate unconditionally with the other. Hence dialogue is pursued for the purpose of setting the purpose, goals, and limitations of cooperation. As a result, caution is one of the major characteristics of these dialogues.[25]

The fifth type—"critical involvement in dialogue"—occurred in Czechoslovakia from 1964 to 1968 and takes place at times under very limited conditions in Yugoslavia. Participants in these dialogues do not present themselves as the official spokespersons of either their party or their churches. Rather, they view themselves as responsible critical thinkers who expect to be enriched by the dialogue while remaining deeply rooted in their own traditions. For this reason, these dialogues are marked by a "pluralism of expectations" that at times have resulted in criticism of their establishments. As a result, they have been rejected by their governments.[26]

THE THIRD WORLD

José Míguez Bonino asserts that First and Third World Christian-Marxist dialogues seek to eliminate barriers to the formation of more equitable and humane societies by establishing a basis for cooperation. However, they differ significantly in their approaches. First World dialogues begin by accepting Christianity and Marxism as two self-contained and self-sufficient world views which are in conflict over differing major presuppositions. By discussing their areas of convergence and divergence, the dialogists hope to establish the parameters within which cooperation may take place.[27] In Third World nations, Christians and Marxists come together not for theoretical discussions; instead, they join together in revolutionary projects which are motivated and justified by a Marxist analysis of their oppressive conditions. Thus, these cooperative ventures are not the products of intellectual dialogues, but practical, immediate, remedial reactions against existing conditions, namely, the intolerable suffering of the masses who are exploited by a small minority who control their nations' wealth and governments.[28] Reflecting on these developments, Bonino develops two theses, one regarding Christians and a second concerning Marxists.

Thesis One: Christians who are dedicated to overcoming the grave injustices which exist in their societies have found in Marxist theory the only adequate explanation for the failure of the many reform and development programs inaugurated in their countries. These Christians share four common characteristics. First, they do not come from the proletariat. They are professionals, religious leaders, and university students who may be classified as members of the *petite bourgeoisie*.[29] Their goal is to redistribute wealth and power in their societies, not because they are poor and downtrodden, but because they identify empathetically with the suffering masses and because they understand the root causes of their exploitation. Second, these Christians have also discovered that traditional reform movements and acts of individual and institutional philanthropy are irrelevant and ineffective in their situations. Instead, radical changes in their economic and political structures are required. Third, the inability of Christian democratic parties to effect any significant and lasting changes in their societies convinces these Christians that they must adopt a revolutionary approach to their problems and that Marxism is the only viable means available to them at this time. Fourth, because these Christians are dedicated to practical change, they are not interested in adopting new dogmas. For this reason, they display a great flexibility in their use of Marxism. They are open to revising their models and approaches whenever their situation calls for change, and they are eager to seek new solutions to their problems. Moreover, they separate Marxist analysis from Marxist ontology and utilize only the former.[30]

Thesis 2: In their efforts to raise a revolutionary consciousness among the proletariat, Marxists have discovered Christians engaged in the same activity. This has introduced them to a revolutionary dimension of Christianity unknown to them heretofore. As a result, Marxists are revising their attitude toward Christianity. They no longer denounce all Christians as impediments to revolution. Furthermore, because Christians are able to raise the consciousness of the proletariat and organize them into political action groups, Marxists have been forced to revise their absolute devotion to dialectical materialism and their militant opposition to all forms of religion. They have learned that religious faith is capable of forming a revolutionary consciousness. Hence they are compelled to accept Christians as necessary and equal partners in their efforts to conduct a successful revolution.[31]

Both Christians and Marxists in Third World nations realize that there are major philosophical and theological differences separating them. However, they feel that the crisis situations in which they find themselves do not allow the luxury to discuss and resolve these differences. They must put them aside as they join forces in fighting exploitation and oppression. Eventually, they may be able to sit down to discuss their differences, or eventually they may form nonideological parties like the Italians and Spaniards, which permit a plurality of world views.

For the most part, neither the Marxist officialdoms nor the Christian hierarchies in the Third World sanction these cooperative activities. In India, for example, where the party's privileged position with the proletariat has been threatened by the success of radical Christian groups, these joint encounters have been condemned and forbidden by party leaders. As in the First and Second World encounters, the most successful ventures are conducted by those not at the center of party or ecclesiastical power but, rather, by those who are more interested in reforming their own institutions and nations than in obtaining or preserving privileged positions for themselves and their institutions.

An exception to this Third World typology is found in black Africa. Several Christians have achieved political power and have adopted Marxist analyses and strategies in their own thinking and political programs. As Norman E. Thomas discusses in detail later in this book, Léopold Senghor of Senegal, Kenneth Kaunda of Zambia, and Julius Nyerere of Tanzania—all avowed Christians—have blended traditional African and Christian values with those of Marxist socialism in the formation of their own ideologies. In Zimbabwe both President Canaan Banana and Prime Minister Robert Mugabe hold that one may be both a Christian and a Marxist. Both also encourage Christians to become as revolutionary as Marxists. Despite these differences from other Third World encounters, African encounters remain *praxis*-oriented.

One other significant form of dialogue that takes place between representatives from First and Second World nations—the International Scientific Symposia on Peace which began in 1971 and continue to the present— merits consideration here. These symposia are cosponsored by the Institute for Peace Research of the University of Vienna and the International Institute for Peace which is also located in Vienna. The latter receives its basic funding from the Soviet Union whose officials appoint the institute's executive director from their own ranks. Originally limited to representatives from Eastern and Western European countries, the symposia expanded to include representatives from North America when the Institute for International Understanding (now called the Institute for Peace and Understanding) which is located on the campus of Rosemont College in Pennsylvania became a third cosponsor in 1977. Three years later in 1980 a Jewish representative and a Muslim representative were invited to participate in the proceedings, and in 1981 a delegate from Latin America was admitted. Since their inception in 1971 symposia have been conducted annually on a rotating basis in Austria, the Soviet Union, West Germany, Sweden, Spain, the United States, and Italy. The number of participants generally is limited to forty with attempts to have equal representation from Eastern and Western European countries and North America. The major goal of the symposia is to analyze "scientifically" the causes of international tensions and conflicts and to explore ways to eliminate them.

The symposia follow a common format and pursue themes which are determined by the institutes' leaders in Vienna. A major position paper on the conference's theme is read by an Eastern European representative—usually someone from the Soviet Union—and another by a Western European or North American delegate. After these are discussed by the group, a series of shorter papers are presented by delegates from Eastern and Western countries, and they in turn are discussed by the group. Genuine dialogue usually does not occur at the formal sessions; instead, fairly long polemical position statements are presented. On the other hand, meaningful discussions take place at mealtimes and during free periods. There is no real evidence that these symposia have had any significant influence on the societies from which the delegates come. However, the symposia do offer the delegates an occasion to become fairly well acquainted and an opportunity to understand the dynamic context out of which their counterparts operate. In turn, the delegates overcome some of their distrust of each other. Paul Mojzes, a leading figure in these dialogues, has suggested that they allow individuals from countries who place strict limits on dialogues to probe these limits with the sanction of their superiors. This appears to be of special significance to Eastern Europeans—especially those who feel the need to control dialogues.[32]

There are some who believe that the Soviet Union cosponsors these symposia in order to have a platform to espouse their own official position and to have it endorsed by its satellite countries. Others hold that the Soviet Union joined in this venture in 1971 to counteract the negative publicity it received for invading Czechoslovakia in 1968, disbanding dialogues in Czechoslovakia, and forbidding participation in the Paulus-Gesellschaft dialogues on the pretext that both fomented dissension and counterrevolutionary activity. Having denounced and rejected open forums and thereby having gained the reputation of being against dialogue, the Soviet Union seeks to prove, through the International Scientific Symposia on Peace, that it seeks and supports constructive dialogue with non-Marxists.

In addition to describing the different types of Christian-Marxist encounters which have emerged in different parts of the world, the foregoing paragraphs establish that, like the Christian tradition, Marxism is not a monolithic structure. It, too, has varied manifestations in the world that have been conditioned in part by different historical, continental, cultural, social, and economic conditions and by the power relations in their respective areas. Therefore, an adequate study of these encounters requires a careful analysis of all of these factors. The following chapters seek to provide such an analysis which will enable the reader to develop an accurate understanding of the variety of Christian-Marxist encounters now operative in the world and to assess the significance of these encounters for both the present and the future. A brief summary of each chapter follows.

Edward J. Grace traces the unique history of Christian-Marxist encounters in Italy from 1941 to the present. He explains how and why the Catholic Communist Party of Italy was instrumental in transforming the Italian Communist Party into a pluralistic and democratic political institution, and he shows the long-range liberating influence of this change on Italian political and religious life.

Maurice Boutin describes and assesses the European dialogues sponsored by the Paulus-Gesellschaft during the time periods 1965–67 and 1975–78. He argues that these dialogues were practical and action-oriented, and not theoretical and impractical as many claim.

After analyzing why there is a national aversion to Marxism in the United States, Arthur F. McGovern traces and evaluates the different types of encounters which have taken place in the United States between 1965 and 1972, 1972 and 1977, and 1977 and the present. He concludes that encounters in the United States lack organized institutional support and are dependent upon the efforts of dedicated individuals for their survival.

James E. Will recounts the passage of Christian-Marxist encounters in Poland through four major stages. Despite innumerable ongoing conflicts Will concludes that these encounters have produced positive results in Poland, for example, the resolution of specific conflicts by means of negotiation. This is a unique achievement in the Eastern Communist world.

Paul Mojzes describes and analyzes the several different periods of dialogue which have transpired in Yugoslavia. He points out that the government recently has retreated from a formal participation in dialogues so as to prevent any ethnic group from using them to encourage feelings of independence and separation. He also explains why the encounters in Yugoslavia have been limited primarily to discussions between Roman Catholic theologians and Marxist philosophers.

Norman E. Thomas examines and assesses two different forms of encounter which have emerged in black Africa—one centers around African Socialism and a second focuses on revolutionary Marxism. He concludes that because black Africa is liberating itself from European colonial domination it stands in a unique position to forge a new form of *praxis*-oriented encounter.

After presenting a brief history of the introduction of Christianity and Marxism to India, George Mathew traces the uneasy development of Christian-Marxist encounters in India. He concludes that Christian-Marxist cooperation in India has been minimal and that more Christians than Marxists have made an attempt to understand the other's position.

Alice L. Hageman and Paul Deats review the major changes in Christian-Marxist encounters in Cuba over the past twenty years. For the most part both groups have abandoned a mutual suspicion, distrust, and overt hostility in favor of developing a mutual respect and trust. Still, many obstacles to cooperation exist.

In the concluding chapter, Robert G. Thobaben plots the ebbs and flows of Christian-Marxist encounters over a twenty-year period. He presents issues that should be discussed by Christians and Marxists and suggests how a serious study of Christian-Marxist encounters can make valuable contributions to the discipline of political science.

After reading these chapters, the reader may come to conclude, as K. C. Abraham has, that Christian-Marxist encounters occur on at least three different planes—"personal, socio-political and cultural"[33]—and that four different types of encounter have emerged. First, there are "unreflective partnerships" in which the participants do not see any necessary conflict between Christianity and Marxism. The latter is viewed as an effective tool for overcoming socioeconomic injustices and the former as a source of "spiritual" orientation and strength. "Partnerships in struggle" is the second type of encounter recognizable in the world today. Here the participants contend that the urgent moral need to transform corrupt societies through joint revolutionary activity transcends the basic theoretical differences that separate Christians from Marxists. Third, there remains the "opposite camps" approach in which each group views the other as a dangerous rival who eventually must be converted or eliminated. Finally, partnerships in "critical involvement" have emerged. These partners believe that Christians and Marxists can be of significant help to each other through dialogues that produce constructive self-criticism.[34]

This author believes that the most promising type of encounter for the future would be one which combines "partnerships in struggle" with "critical involvement." This would enable Christians and Marxists to work together toward achieving their common goal—building a more just and humane world—while allowing each an opportunity to transcend internal weaknesses by drawing upon the strengths of the other.

NOTES

1. *Encountering Marx: Bonds and Barriers Between Christians and Marxists*, trans. Edwin H. Robertson (Philadelphia: Fortress Press, 1977), 33.

2. *God Is Not Yet Dead* (Harmondsworth, Eng.: Penguin Books, 1973).

3. *A Marxist Looks at Jesus* (Philadelphia: Fortress Press, 1976).

4. Ibid., 193.

5. See Herbert Aptheker, "What May Man Really Hope For?" in *From Hope to Liberation: Towards a New Marxist-Christian Dialogue,* ed. Nicholas Piediscalzi and Robert G. Thobaben (Philadelphia: Fortress Press, 1974), 30–35; Roger Garaudy, *From Anathema to Dialogue* (New York: Herder & Herder, 1966), 100ff.; and Palmiro Togliatti, "On International Working-Class Unity," *Political Affairs* 43:10 (October 1964): 44–45.

6. "The Christian and the Marxist: A Marxist View of Dialogue," *Background Information for Church and Society* (World Council of Churches) 39 (April 1968): 17–18.

7. *Theology Between Yesterday and Today* (Philadelphia: Westminster Press, 1957), 83–84.

8. See Harvey G. Cox, "Let's End the Communist-Christian Vendetta," *Christian Century* 83 (9 November 1966): 1375–79.

9. *World Conference on Church and Society: Official Report* (Geneva: World Council of Churches, 1967), 206.

10. For a summary of this dialogue see Ans J. van der Bent, "Marxist-Christian Dialogue in Geneva," *Study Encounter* 4:3 (1968): 143–46.

11. See Pope John XXIII, *Mater et Magistra* and *Pacem in Terris*; Pope Paul VI, *Octogesima Adveniens* and *Gaudium et Spes*; all in Joseph Gremillion, ed., *The Gospel of Peace and Justice* (Maryknoll, N.Y.: Orbis Books, 1976).

12. As reported in the *International Herald Tribune,* 19 April 1973, 2.

13. "What Would St. Thomas Aquinas, the Aristotle Commentator, Do If Faced With Karl Marx?" *Resource Service* (Chicago: Jesuit Project for Third World Awareness) I:12 (October 1974): 7.

14. Ibid.

15. See Shepherd Bliss, "Latin America—Where the Dialogue Became *Praxis,*" in *From Hope to Liberation,* 77–101; and Jóse Míguez Bonino, *Christians and Marxists: The Mutual Challenge to Revolution* (Grand Rapids: Wm. B. Eerdmans, 1976).

16. Aptheker, "What May Man Really Hope For?" 28.

17. "On the Christian Marxist Dialogue: An Attempt to Define a Position," *Journal of Ecumenical Studies* 20:3 (Summer 1983): 419.

18. "The Christian-Marxist Dialogue of the 1960s," *Monthly Review* 36:3 (July–August 1984): 22–23.

19. *Journal Herald* (Dayton, Ohio), 26 January 1982, 2.

20. Gonzalo Arroyo, S.J., "Christus ins ZK: Öffnung der spanischen KP," trans. Klaus Pitter, *Neues Forum* 24 (August–September 1977): 24–25.

21. Paul Mojzes, *Christian-Marxist Dialogue in Eastern Europe* (Minneapolis: Augsburg Publishing House, 1981), 38–182.

22. Ibid., 40–41.

23. Ibid., 41.

24. Ibid., 49ff.

25. Ibid., 66.

26. Ibid., 110.

27. Bonino, *Christians and Marxists*, 29. While Bonino's analysis centers on Latin America, the author is convinced that his categories and theses are also applicable to all other Third World countries.

28. Ibid., 16.

29. Ibid., 19.

30. Ibid., 19–20.

31. Ibid., 23–28.

32. Mojzes, *Christian-Marxist Dialogue in Eastern Europe*, 108–9.

33. "Marxism and Christianity in India," in *A Vision for Man: Essays in Honour of J. R. Chandran*, ed. Samuel Amirtham (Madras: Christian Literature Society, 1978), 391.

34. Ibid., 397–403.

SUGGESTIONS FOR FURTHER READING

Aptheker, Herbert, ed. *The Urgency of Marxist-Christian Dialogue: A Pragmatic Argument for Reconciliation*. New York: Harper, Colophon Books, 1970.

Garaudy, Roger. *From Anathema to Dialogue: A Marxist Challenge to the Christian Churches*. Translated by Luke O'Neill. New York: Herder & Herder, 1966. Reprinted: New York: Random House, Vintage Books, 1968.

Lochman, Jan Milič. *Encountering Marx: Bonds and Barriers Between Christians and Marxists*. Translated by Edwin H. Robertson. Philadelphia: Fortress Press, 1975.

Mojzes, Paul, ed. *Varieties of Christian-Marxist Dialogue*. Philadelphia: Ecumenical Press, 1978. Also published as a special edition of the *Journal of Ecumenical Studies* 15:1 (Winter 1978).

Oestreicher, Paul, ed. *The Christian Marxist Dialogue: An International Symposium*. London: Macmillan, 1969.

"Religion and the Left" (a special double issue on Christian-Marxist Encounters), *Monthly Review* 36:3 (July–August 1984).

FIRST WORLD ENCOUNTERS

ITALY

Edward J. Grace

Christian-Marxist Encounter (CME) is an integral part of Italian life. Occurring on individual, group, and national levels since the 1940s, it significantly influences Italy's religious, political, and cultural life. In 1979, five million baptized Catholics who attend Mass regularly voted for parties that have Marxist origins.[1] An estimated 25 percent of these would identify themselves as both "Catholic" and "Communist," "Socialist" or "Independent." Many are both active members of their parishes and their respective parties. Some of these are members of the central committees of the Communist and Socialist parties.[2] Well above 60 percent of the members of the various Protestant churches in Italy (Waldensian, Methodist, Baptist, and Pentecostal) vote for "leftist" parties. Some of the ordained pastors of these churches are heads of Communist or Socialist Party sections (local party chapters).[3]

The ability of Italian Christians to join the Communist Party and to serve in positions of leadership may be traced in part to the founding of the Unifying Cooperative Party in 1941 and the Catholic Communist Party in 1942. Their members and leaders were held in good standing by both the Vatican and the Italian Communist Party leaders at that time. During World War II these people were imprisoned along with Marxist Communists by the Fascists, and they also fought side by side with Communists in the Resistance movement. These experiences, which occurred basically during the period from 1937 to 1945, taught both Italian Christians and Marxist Communists that there was more that united than separated them. This lesson eventually moved the Italian Communist Party to declare itself "secular" and "nonideological" thereby removing the acceptance of Marxist ontology as one of the party's membership requirements. The late Lucio Lombardo Radice, one of the Party's leading theoreticians, recorded part of this movement in an article he published in 1977:

> I collaborated, conspired with the movement of the Communist Catholics between the spring of 1942 and that of 1943. . . . We were "picked up" because the clandestine newsletter we, Communist Atheists, wrote together with Commu-

nist Catholics had been uncovered. The important intuition of the Communist Catholics already back in the 1940s was that of the compatibility of Christian faith not only with class struggle but also with Marxism understood as an indispensable tool for class struggle and the construction of a society without classes. The key concept was the distinction between *historical materialism* understood as a political methodology, i.e., as a tool for historical interpretation and analysis of social structures, and *dialectical materialism*, seen as a comprehensive atheistic and deterministic vision of the world. Already then these Communist Catholics maintained that dialectical materialism was not only dispensable but actually damaging to the development of a correct and effective revolutionary politics.[4]

In response to a question asking how many of these Catholic theoretical formulations had been accepted by the Italian Communist Party, Lombardo Radice said, "I would dare to answer: *everything* pertaining to the relationship between the political party and Marxist teachings."[5] Thus, a clear understanding of today's significant CME in Italy requires knowledge of the period of gestation which took place between 1937 and 1945.

THE BEGINNING:
CHRISTIANS MEET COMMUNISTS IN THE
ANTI-FASCIST RESISTANCE

The first issue on the agenda of the Catholic left was very concrete: how to draw other Catholics into the struggle to overthrow Fascism. This was not an easy task because the majority of the Roman Catholic hierarchy, priests, and politically active laity was either in alliance with the Fascist regime or adopted a stance of neutrality. The first identifiable nucleus of these anti-Fascist Catholics came almost entirely from the Catholic Action branch of the southern division of the diocese of Rome. They promoted their basic position in an underground flyer: "Clandestine political struggle with all its means and risks (jail, torture, etc.) alone can save Catholics from the serious responsibilities for racism and war. . . . [Therefore, we must] destroy the myth of the political unity of all Catholics, exploited and exploiters, and promote a Left Christian movement."[6] *This small beginning provided an important legacy of practice and theory for future CME.*

This group along with other Catholic forces who actively opposed Fascism formed the Unifying Cooperative Party (Partito Cooperativista Sinarchico [PCS])[7] in 1941. Their manifesto contains their emerging views on the Roman Catholic Church, church-state relations, dialectical materialism, and their attitude toward the Italian Communist Party (PCI).[8] The manifesto asserted that the Roman Catholic Church, because of the inexhaustibility of the Gospel teachings, possesses many relevant insights to share with humanity: for example, "love of neighbor"; "the common good"; and "the ultimate worth of each individual." However, it warned that these insights will not be accepted by society unless the church rids itself of its conservative and, at times, reactionary spirit which prevents "the clergy and Christian culture from aligning itself with the advance of civilization in these last centuries."[9]

At the same time, the manifesto called for a separation of church and state in the new society that its authors hoped to establish. Because their religious values affirmed and guaranteed individual liberties, they opposed any alliance of church and state that, as they experienced under the alliance of the Vatican with the Fascist regime, eliminates personal freedoms. They also viewed with suspicion any move toward the "nationalization" or "collectivization" of property and industry. They believed that these "solutions" contain serious threats to individual freedom, one of their important religious values. As an alternative, they called for the transformation of medium- and small-sized industries and large- and medium-sized farms into worker-owned cooperatives. According to them, the formation of such cooperatives would ensure and protect individual liberties and promote democracy.[10]

Simultaneously, these Catholics expressed their willingness to work with the PCI but called for the suspension of the party's antireligious propaganda and anticlericalism, describing both as a "classical infantile disease of communism."[11] On what they believed to be Marxist principles, they argued that "clearing the terrain of these ahistorical prejudices . . . [would serve as] a very important and revolutionary act."[12]

Their manifesto declared that human dignity, individual liberties, religion, and education are "ontologically superior" to the economic realm. Their intention was to "avoid every form of materialism and safeguard the rights of the human person, freeing them from the superstructure of the Leninistic state."[13]

The PCS changed its name in 1942 to the Communist Christian Party (CCP) in order to demonstrate its clearly chosen class consciousness.[14] In its first published document, the CCP reasserted the PCS's affirmation of the positive dimensions of Gospel teachings still found in Roman Catholicism and its rejection of all reactionary elements in the churches. It also reissued its call for the categorical exclusion of every antireligious, atheistic policy of the PCI and reaffirmed the principle of human liberty.[15]

This first document was brief because of the demands of the ongoing armed struggle. The life of the CCP was equally brief: four hundred members were arrested in Rome in May 1943. Although they were released shortly after the Italian armistice was signed with the Allied Forces in July 1943, their prison experiences convinced the Christian Communist leaders that they would be more effective as a movement (the Communist Catholic Movement [CCM]) than as a political party. There were two major reasons for this change. First, the only real distinction between them and the PCI was religious-philosophical (the PCI then required philosophical adherence to dialectical materialism for membership). Second, they came to believe that religious affiliation was an insufficient basis for a separate political party.[16]

The German Nazi reoccupation of Italy in September 1943 forced the Communist Catholic Movement (CCM) underground. However, they continued their theoretical work and presented a systematic exposition of its position in a booklet entitled *Communism and Catholics*. This document begins by describing the existing relationship between religion and politics. It states that the task of religion is to "indicate the moral ends of humanity, the ultimate meaning of the human person. No human activity is able to escape these ends." Conversely, the role of political activity is to provide justice for all citizens by establishing the best possible environment for their spiritual and physical well-being. While the achievement of this goal is the responsibility of the state, this does not mean that religion is excluded from the political sphere. Religion, the booklet continues,

> will deplore the deviations from justice and will denounce abuses, excesses, and social evils. However, to suggest technical policies [for achieving justice] is to go beyond its task inasmuch as the question is temporal and historical, thus changing according to time, place, and situation.[17]

Within the text itself, it is important to note the concerted effort to establish the proper relationship between religion and politics and the insistence that this is one of the first tasks of any Christian who wants to engage in political activity.[18] This position views religion, politics, church, and state as independent entities, each performing a unique service for the community. To be sure, they interact and influence each other, but they should not be confused with each other and they should be kept separate constitutionally. This has been and continues to be one of CME's basic policies.

In recent years, the majority of the other political parties in Italy and the Roman Catholic and Protestant churches have accepted this position. The new Concordat signed between the Vatican State and the Italian government on 14 February 1984 and the Intesa (Accord) ratified by both the Waldensian Table (which represents both itself and the Methodist Church) and the Italian government on 17 February 1984 affirm this position. In the former, the Roman Catholic Church surrenders its position as possessor of the state's sole religion. On the other hand, both the state and the Roman Church affirm their sovereignty and independence, accept responsibility for their domains, and agree upon a "reciprocal collaboration for the promotion of the human person and the good of the country."[19]

The Intesa grants the Methodist and Waldensian churches equal status with the Roman Catholic Church, including full dignity, equality, and liberty. These two Protestant churches recognize the separate but interrelated roles fulfilled by church and state and agree to a set of regulations for the areas where the two overlap.[20] This is a dramatic reversal of a position adopted by the Protestant churches in 1946.[21] The remaining Protestant churches in Italy may join in similar accords with the government when they so choose.

In *Communism and Catholics*, the Communist Catholic theoreticians further refined their arguments in favor of historical materialism over dialectical materialism—their key contribution to CME according to Lombardo Radice. They "accepted Marxism as a methodology for action, but rejected it as the philosophy of humanity. [They also] *accepted Communist politics but refused the Communist religion.*" The "political truth of Marxist methodology" was accepted when they understood that "the philosophical position upon which it is based is superficial to the application of the methodology."[22] One of their arguments was based on their own experience: if many Catholics "fight for a Communist idea, they bear witness to the fact that the dialectical-materialistic ideology is not indispensable . . . to the political energy of the proletariat," and to the fact that "religion . . . is not a bourgeois ideology, a brake on political action."[23]

After the publication of *Communism and Catholics*, Franco Rodano, a young intellectual in CCM, sought to apply this thesis to atheistic Marxists as well as Christians who utilize Marxist theories and methods in their analyses of society. He argued that historical materialism is not related necessarily to economic determinism. He quoted passages from Marx, Lenin, and Gramsci that reveal their opposition to any form of fatalism and their affirmation of human action as the necessary and final catalyst. "Mechanistic contradictions within the productive forces were not sufficient to change the face of society . . . the intervention of the free energy of human beings was necessary." After a series of other examples Rodano concluded:

> Hence the history of Marxism is in reality the history of its progressive liberation from the most materialistic of all conceptions: that of fatalism which is in turn the foundation of every materialistic philosophy. . . . *Historical materialism* is, therefore, the road for us Catholics, for all of us who have the interest of the human person at heart, as it is our duty to struggle against fatalistic and determinis-

tic deformations and concepts which deny the person by destroying his/her liberty.[24]

To understand this fundamental distinction, it is helpful to look briefly at a polemical exchange between *Il Segno*, a traditional Catholic magazine, and *Voce Operaia*, CCM's clandestine newspaper. When *Il Segno* attacked this new position, *Voce Operaia* rebutted:

> *Il Segno* does not pay attention to the political science of *historical materialism*. . . . It notes only the Communist *Weltanschauung*, the Communist religion, which we just as clearly reject. . . . The belief in *dialectical materialism* as the concept of a political solution for all humanity and for all morality is a contingent, suprastructural factor which is not at all essential. [On the contrary, today it can be] damaging to the realization of Communist policies and even in contradiction to its proposed ends. With respect to Catholic doctrine, one can admit historical materialism with the same tranquillity as the materialism of physics or chemistry. [For, the discovery that] the events of political history (not of all human history) are impelled by class interests does not in fact exclude the autonomy of the human conscience nor its transcendence.[25]

It is evident that at this time the Communist Catholics were clearly addressing themselves to both the Italian Catholic Church and the PCI. While there has been continual development of this thesis over the years, many of the pillars of today's CME were firmly set in this period. None, however, is more important than the Communist Catholic's distinction between Marx's philosophy (dialectical materialism) and his sociology (historical materialism). For this group, historical materialism is a scientific, empirical, political methodology for action which studies the economic structures of society and its resulting classes (social divisions and conflicts caused by the economic organization of society). They consider it the best tool or method to date, to analyze and explain the existing social conflicts in society and, hence, the best foundation upon which to formulate political programs aimed at overcoming these conflicts. According to the advocates of historical materialism, it was not Marx's philosophy but his methodology that led him to identify the working class as the social force capable of overcoming the social conflicts within capitalism at that historical moment. As a result, these advocates see Marx's methodology as a science, differing from other sciences only in that its object of study is the economic structure. Moreover, since it is a limited science, historical materialism cannot provide a world view. This distinction, coming as it did in the context of an armed struggle against Fascism, is absolutely fundamental for any understanding of today's Italian CME.

THE OFFICIAL CHURCH AND CME OF
THE LATE 1940s

When World War II ended, the Vatican did not have an official position on the "political unity of Catholics." Inside the Vatican there were high level discussions about whether it would be better to have: 1) conservative, moderate, and left Catholic parties since all these political tendencies existed among Catholics in Italy (Cardinal Ottaviani's position); 2) the political unity of Catholics, with the Catholic party seen as the secular arm of the church (Father Cordovani's and Pius XII's position); or 3) the political unity of Catholics with the Catholic party seen as autonomous in its political choices (Cardinal Montini's position).

While these discussions were in process, the Communist Catholics were neither formally attacked nor condemned.[26] In fact, during a papal discussion in February 1944, Pius XII referred benevolently but anonymously to the movement. His position at that moment consisted in recalling a passage from *Quadragesimo Anno* (1932) which states that Catholics who choose to be apostles among the Socialists must "profess fully the Christian truth and demonstrate, also to Socialists, that insofar as their stated aims are just, they can be defended much better by the principles of Christian charity."[27] This statement only affirms the Vatican's belief in the superiority of its social doctrines over Socialist doctrines. Not long after Italian Liberation Day, however, as the new world alignment began to make itself felt within the Vatican State and with the prospect of democratic elections in Italy just around the corner, the Cordovani–Pius XII position was accepted. The possibility of more than one Catholic party or Catholics belonging to more than one party was thereby excluded. After this decision was made, dramatic actions were taken. On 2 July 1945, Pius XII declared, "no one can be a good Catholic and a true Socialist." In an article in the *Osservatore Romano* on the same day the CCM was upbraided for its "lack of knowledge of Christian social doctrine." The article concluded that "no one can be a good Catholic and a Communist at the same time."[28] This attack and its timing was amazingly similar to those launched by the Vatican against Democrats and Republicans in the preceding century.[29]

The reply of *Voce Operaia*, the newspaper of the CCM, was calm but to the point. The will of the CCM is "to remain profoundly rooted in orthodoxy. [Moreover, we do] not conceive history materialistically." In their defense, they used a passage from the 1943 Christmas message of Pius XII which recognized the material conditioning of every spiritual activity.[30]

The leaders of the CCM also sent a letter to the pope in which they declared themselves to be "obedient children ready to make public retractions about each clearly indicated theoretical error" and about "every point of the political program which was proved to be against the teachings of the church or even to move away from them in a dangerous manner."[31] This precise request never received a reply. "The orthodoxy of the CCM, or that of the individual members, was never the object of that precise examination which they had asked of the Holy See, for it was not the Vatican's real target."[32]

This pressure applied against the Communist Catholics prompted them to merge with other left Catholic groups to form the short-lived Christian Left Party (Partito della Sinistra Cristiana [PSC]). The formation of the PSC ignored the Communist Catholic's previous rejection of religion as the foundation stone for a political party or a political program. Behind this momentary compromise lay the hope that the PSC might be able to defeat the Vatican's attempt to force all Italian Catholics to vote only for the Catholic Party, now called the "Christian Democratic" Party (DC).[33]

The first national congress of the PSC was held in Rome, 5–6 July 1945. A series of supporting arguments were set forth in favor of historical materialism as a most effective method to reform society. Among these was a reference to Engels, the father of dialectical materialism, who "was forced to speak of the 'high moral and spiritual drive which [is a significant element in] every revolutionary victory.'" Also noteworthy was the Congress's firm opposition to the PCI's retention of dialectical materialism as its ideology. Fedele d'Amice, another leading intellectual in the movement who supported Rodano's stance, declared that granting Catholics permission to join the PCI only means "that . . . [the PCI] does not ask them to note—when they join—their theoretical contradiction."[34]

Less than six months later, in December 1945, the PCS disbanded. There were several reasons for this, the most important of which was the strong conviction of the Communist Catholics who believed that the very existence of a political party based on a religion was—whatever the short-range goal— ultimately detrimental to the essence of both religion and the political process. This was a victory for those Christians who had insisted upon a clear separation between religion and politics. Nevertheless, the CME suffered a setback in the official Roman Catholic world by the successful political strategy of the DC and the Vatican which united religion and politics.

THE ITALIAN COMMUNIST PARTY AND CME

After the PSC disbanded, the Italian CME was threatened momentarily when Palmiro Togliatti (secretary of the PCI) recommended that militant Catholic leftists, especially those from the CCM, should join the DC, if they wanted to continue to work as a Catholic political force. One scholar of this period states that the tension was great. A solution had to be found to prevent the dissolution of seven years of CME. The Communist Catholics were presented an impossible alternative: "All their preceding theoretical developments excluded their joining the DC," a party using religion as one of its main supports. Notwithstanding Togliatti's initial statement, these "young revolutionaries were firmly convinced—and this was their strong point— that the PCI could and had to change; that is, it could and had to develop a fully secular concept of politics."[35]

Consequently they asked Togliatti and the PCI to reconsider their position. Togliatti, who was convinced that the only path to socialism in the industrialized West was through democracy, citizen participation, and consensus, was then in the process of organizing a new, broad-based party. He reflected seriously upon the request. Both *praxis* and critical Marxist theory appeared to be on the side of the Communist Catholics.[36] The rigor of their arguments from Marxist "canons" and the prestige which they had gained by their participation in the Resistance movement were two of the key factors that moved Togliatti and the PCI to change their stance. This positive response came when the PCI's Fifth Party Congress approved a modification of Article 2, in the PCI's Constitution (January 1946). Belief in dialectical materialism was no longer required as a prerequisite for party membership, thereby firmly weaving the thread of CME, begun in 1937, into the fabric of practical politics. This revised Article 2, which is still in force, reads:

> All citizens who have attained eighteen years of age and who, regardless of race, religious faith or philosophical convictions, accept the party's political program and pledge themselves to work in a party organization, may join the Italian Communist Party.[37]

As soon as this article was adopted, the leaders of the PSC recommended membership in the PCI to their disbanded members who numbered approximately twenty-two thousand. Many of them joined the PCI.[38] One of the PSC leaders, Antonio Tatò, a practicing Roman Catholic, has served on the PCI Central Committee since 1972 and is head of the public relations department of the PCI. He also served as personal political secretary to the party's former general secretary, the late Enrico Berlinguer. Reflecting on Article 2 during a Temple University Study Seminar in 1978, Tatò confirmed Lombardo Radice's observation:

> Article 2 of the Statute was a first, but decisive step of the PCI; it was an irreversible step by which the PCI opened itself to all secular and Catholic forces, to all currents of human thought, and to all cultures. It was concrete proof of the desire and the decision of the PCI to abandon "dogmatism" and "scholas-

tic" formulations. All the fruit which in substance has been gathered comes primarily from that turning point of the PCI in 1946.[39]

The elimination of dialectical materialism as the required philosophical faith for party membership meant that CME was not only an external possibility but an internal way of being for the Communist Party. This needs to be stressed: CME was being affirmed and ratified internally by a Communist party. Second, not only was a Communist party (not just an individual Communist) explicitly separating atheism from socialism (in 1946) but it was also rejecting the aggressive promotion of atheism, even terming subtle antireligious propaganda as a classical infantile disease of communism and counterproductive to the building of socialism. Third, Article 2 represented a statutory confirmation of the PCI's basic character. As such it was a sound foundation open to new, more democratic forms of organization and theoretical development.

In short, the PCI rejected nineteenth-century positivistic dogmatism and adopted a new pluralistic approach. The PCI opened itself to all persons regardless of race, religious creed, and philosophical convictions. This was CME's most notable achievement. It now should be evident why Lucio Lombardo Radice noted the valuable contributions which the Communist Catholic experience made to the PCI's adoption of a new stance toward Christianity in particular and religion in general; and why knowledge of these nonmessianic, nondogmatic roots of CME in Italy is essential to understanding the widespread phenomenon of CME in Italy today; and why lack of knowledge of this experience outside Italy leads to the mistaken portrayal of Italian CME as mere pragmatism or rationally unfounded and contradictory behavior.

THE DEVELOPMENT OF THE CME IN POSTWAR ITALY

The PCI's postwar effort to create an atmosphere of dialogue and cooperation was directed not only toward individual believers, as evidenced by Article 2, but also toward the institutional church. This was clearly demonstrated by the PCI's position and voting record on Article 7 of the new Italian Constitution which was adopted in December 1947.[40]

Article 7 regulates the Italian state's relationship with the Italian church and the Vatican State. Until the 1948 Concordat was ratified, it duplicated the 1929 Concordat which provided financial support to the Italian Catholic Church and the Vatican State, required the teaching of Catholicism in the public schools, and declared Catholicism to be the religion of the state. The Vatican State pressed for the continuation of these privileges. If the Concordat had not been reaffirmed as Article 7, the Vatican immediately would have become an international organization on Italian soil rather than an independent state. The Christian Democrats, who favored Article 7, commanded only 35.2 percent of the popular vote. The Socialist Party (20.7 percent), the Republican Party (4.4 percent), and the Liberal Party (6.8 percent) all opposed it. While the DC was aided by the Monarchy Party's 3 percent, without the support of the PCI and their 18.9 percent of the popular vote, Article 7 would not have passed.

The dividing of the world into East-West blocs after World War II fed the Vatican State's fear of communism while the 1948 DC electoral victory (48.5 percent) fed their political aspirations. Thus they ignored the PCI's support for Article 7 and the openness of the PCI to Roman Catholics. In 1949, Pius XII excommunicated everyone who "is member of, votes for, or in any way aids Communist political forces."[41] This went well beyond condemnation of philosophical atheism and, in Italy, had clear political overtones. The excommunication made it difficult to develop CME in Italy, particularly with the institutional Italian Catholic Church. Moreover the awareness of the separation of the adjective "atheistic" from the noun "Communist" made by the Communist Catholics and then by the PCI had not penetrated very far into the Catholic or Communist communities. Hence the general climate was extremely tense and ideologically charged. But it did not, according to Tatò, "make us change our political policies. On the contrary, the excommunication even reinforced our conviction that it was necessary to continue this dialogue which the entire PCI had made its own at the beginning of 1946."[42]

In summary, the Italian CME was in a precarious position in 1949. Some scholars feel that, if it had not been for Article 2, Togliatti, and the Communist Catholics, CME might have been expunged from the PCI. Nevertheless, the foundations had been securely laid. Rodano and other Catholics who had joined the Communist Party continued to support CME. Some of them published their reflections and analyses in two important theoretical journals, *Lo spettatore italiano* (1952–56) and *Il dibattito politico* (1955–59). Almost unnoticed and with varying results, they continued to provide a point of reference and reflection for politically sensitive Catholics. They worked side by side with nonbelieving PCI members and leaders on various political issues, thereby fulfilling the original intention of the revised Article 2. At the same time, they maintained their contacts with certain ranking Vatican officials.

These contacts eventually impressed upon the Vatican State the need for it to improve its relations with Eastern European countries. The arguments for this change were published in *Il dibattito politico* from 1955 to 1959.[43] The first step in this move occurred when Togliatti and Monsignor Giuseppe De Luca, a close friend of both Pope John XXIII and Rodano, met in Rodano's home. They explored ways to improve relations between the Vatican and Eastern European countries and the Vatican and the PCI. One of the results of this encounter was a telegram of good wishes that Khrushchev sent to John XXIII. This act enabled the Vatican to seek new relations with the Eastern European nations. John XXIII prepared the way for this event while he was the archbishop-patriarch of Venice. During this reign he sought to establish cordial relations with non-Catholics. One of these gestures occurred in 1957 when he sent his greetings to the Socialist Party Congress being held in Venice.[44]

Another visible example of the influence of the ideas developed by pre– and post–World War II CME is Pope John XXIII's encyclical *Pacem in Terris*. Lombardo Radice maintains that the "distinction between philosophical materialism and practical-theoretical perspectives" of the Communist Catholics is reflected in Pope John's distinction "between false philosophical doctrines and their economic, social derivations which can be considered in a positive light."[45] Tatò likewise was convinced that

> our [the Communist Catholics and then the PCI's] fortitude in carrying forward the dialogue against enormous outside opposition bore its fruits. . . . [Our] distinction between religion and politics and between historical movements and the ideologies which inspire them was almost completely incorporated in *Pacem in Terris*.[46]

That the climate had changed substantially was confirmed by John XXIII's entire pontificate and by Vatican II. During this period the church took concrete steps to ease tensions between itself and the PCI. The PCI now had external reasons to support the theory and practice it had followed since 1946. At its Tenth Congress in 1962, the PCI adopted a resolution which stated that "the aspiration for a Socialist society not only can grow in a person who professes a religious faith, but it can even be stimulated by a deeply felt religious conscience faced with the dramatic problems of the contemporary world."[47] Few scholars doubt that this statement was inspired, if not actually written, by Catholics in the PCI. However, this declaration also reflects theoretical contributions from the large number of atheistic and other non-Christian intellectuals who were members of the PCI at that time.

THE DIALOGUE ERA AND CME IN ITALY

Vatican II indirectly contributed to the well-known springtime of CM dialogue. In Italy, as in other First and Second World countries, Christian and Marxist intellectuals and academics developed many thoughtful essays on metaphysics, epistemology, ethics, and aesthetics.[48] What is less well known (and so frequently misunderstood) is the position of the PCI on such dialogue initiatives in this and subsequent periods. While the PCI welcomed the new dialogues and followed them attentively, as they had Vatican II, the party did not promote or directly participate in them. The reason for this position lies in the evolution of the theory and practice of Article 2 and the experiences surrounding it. Having become a pluralistic secular party, the PCI no longer viewed itself as the promoter of any single world view. Therefore, it wanted to avoid any activity that would compromise its position. Hence it would not officially participate in initiatives that would or could be perceived as advocating a faith system. Indeed, the positive experience of the last twenty years in developing practical political programs aimed at changing society in a Socialist direction had strengthened the PCI's conviction that considering Marxism as a faith system was, in fact, detrimental to the creation of a socially just and "classless" society. For this reason, the PCI refused to participate officially in any dialogue in which Christianity and Marxism are viewed as two different faith systems.

One of the most important public clarifications of this position occurred in 1966, when Luigi Longo, interim PCI general secretary, stated that the PCI supports "a state that is effectively and absolutely secular. . . . Just as we are against a confessional state so we are against state atheism."[49]

This statement is notable for two reasons. First, it clearly overcomes the ambiguity of the 1947 privileged status the PCI had granted the Catholic Church for reasons of political expediency. Second, it rejects state atheism as sectarian and detrimental to the advancement of socialism. The statement is very clear: "We are opposed to a state that attributes any sort of privilege to any ideology, religious faith, culture, or artistic trend to the detriment of others."[50] This statement also has gained broad support among mainline and evangelical Protestants, cultural and ethnic minorities, and a large number of Catholics. The concept of the secular nature of the state was first elaborated by Communist Catholics who had entered the PCI in the pages of *Il dibattito politico* (1955–59). The above political thought had been cross-fertilized by PCI members of other philosophical and religious convictions. But, as one researcher states, credit must be given to those early tenacious advocates of CME who "worked so hard" to apply the implications of Article 2 so that the Marxism of the PCI "really developed toward a political science which did not remain blocked by the metaphysical pretensions" of being an all-inclusive global interpretation of reality. To do so "in the climate of the hard ideological conflict of the 1950s meant to meet strong . . . resistance" by a good portion of the older party base and even some of its intellectuals, not to mention being isolated or rejected by the majority of the Catholic church leadership. "But that is what they did although they had to pay a heavy personal price."[51]

An article written by Ossicini in 1975 reflects the major theoretical differences between this CME and Christians for Socialism (CFS) which sprung up in Italy in 1974. The article takes issue with the members of CFS who believe it is possible to join Christianity and Marxism into a dialectical unity. Christianity ceases to be "a faith," he wrote, "if it shuts itself totally in history which is the fatal error of the so-called Christian Marxists."[52] Marxism, on the other hand, "ceases to be a scientific analysis of history . . . [when it replaces its scientific discipline with an] escape into metaphysical or super-structural belief in 'Marxist ideology.'"[53] Such an escape is a form of alienation which removes Marxists from history and hinders them from actualizing their concrete Socialist goals to transform society's economic structures.[54]

Another important issue raised in this debate was the relationship of the institutional church to capitalism. CFS claimed that the Roman Catholic Church compromised its mission by aligning itself with a reactionary economic system: "The church is an integral part of the capitalist system due to the financial interests and the power it must defend."[55]

This attack was interpreted by the advocates of CME as an erroneous analysis of the Catholic Church and a barrier to the establishment of a Socialist society in Italy. According to them, "the church . . . resists the mechanical classical schemes which tend to explain history as a struggle between rigidly counterposing interests, between the property owning bourgeois block and the proletarian block."[56] This is the case because over the centuries the church—judged empirically—acts as a primary institution of society not wedded permanently to any economic system. In the past nineteen centuries, the Catholic Church has lived with and sanctioned for limited periods many different types of economic and political systems which have passed out of existence. Furthermore, the church has never expressed a preference for capitalism as an ideal system. Moreover, it reserves the right to reject *any* economic system that it judges to be in conflict with its ultimate mission and contingent interests.

It is important to grasp this historical analysis because it has influenced the PCI's policy on church-state relations. The PCI does not reject the church as a reactionary institution; often it cooperates with its leaders on what it believes to be mutually beneficial economic, political, and cultural programs.

CME SHIFTS TO OFFICIAL PUBLIC DEBATE
BETWEEN THE CHURCH AND THE PCI

The fact that the PCI received 34 percent of the national vote in the 1976 election was partly the result of their continued effort to promote and develop a concrete and clearly stated position on CME. This electoral victory served as a catalyst to open a new dimension of CME, which took place in an exchange of formal, public letters between Bishop Luigi Bettazzi (diocese of Ivrea) and the PCI general secretary, the late Enrico Berlinguer.[57]

Bettazzi initiated the dialogue by sending a "public" letter to Berlinguer. He began by stating that his letter grew out of his "concern for a more Christian and more humane Italy." His tone communicated a desire for true dialogue. He asked Berlinguer whether the PCI would follow a Leninist-Stalinist course if it came to power and whether it would adopt an antitheistic and antichurch policy. (Like Gozzini ten years earlier, Bettazzi exhibited an almost unexplainable ignorance of Article 2 and the pluralistic nature of the PCI.)[58]

Berlinguer replied by informing the bishop that the members and leaders of the PCI have "different cultural backgrounds and different ideological, philosophical, and religious convictions." This is not "a product of chance . . . [but is due to] Article 2 . . . and its daily application."[59] Furthermore, "the Italian Communist Party as a party . . . as a political organization, does not profess Marxist ideology as a materialistic and atheistic philosophy."[60]

Berlinguer also pointed out the PCI's nondogmatic use of Marxist theory: "Without a Marxism understood and used critically as a lesson, not accepted and read dogmatically as an unchangeable text, the positions the PCI holds today and the growth of its organizational and electoral strength would be completely unexplainable."[61]

Bettazzi's pointed question "[Will not] the legitimate effort for a Socialist renewal of the collectivity . . . degenerate into an atheistic dictatorship as it had elsewhere?"[62] prompted Berlinguer to formulate an unequivocal policy statement:

> The PCI is not only determined to build here in Italy a party that is secular and democratic, and, as such, neither theist, nor atheist, nor anti-theist, but also, as a direct consequence, it desires a secular, democratic *state* that is likewise *neither theist, nor atheist, nor anti-theist*.[63]

This clear statement by the general secretary of the PCI which committed the PCI to the establishment of a secular, democratic, and pluralistic state was well received in both religious and secular circles and advanced the cause of CME in Italy.

Another fundamental concern voiced by Bettazzi—the PCI's position on the future role of churches and church organizations in our society[64]—pushed the PCI to a new level of concrete expression. Berlinguer responded by affirming two important principles:

> 1) All of the various forces that are willing and able to satisfy the needs of our families and citizens must be allowed to work within the education, health, and welfare structures set up by the public authorities with full rights and with their own ideas and cultural patrimony. . . . [Therefore, there will be] a great deal of room for the participation of members of religious orders and institutions and also for the initiatives of ecclesiastical bodies and authorities.[65]
>
> 2) The free contribution of Christian organizations and church institutions, in fields of activity concerned with satisfying new needs toward the construction of a democratic, free, more just new society, will be guaranteed.[66]

Besides restating the PCI's support of a secular, pluralistic, and democratic society, Berlinguer's reply contained a new set of specific guidelines for the PCI's working relations with religious institutions which were derived from the two principles recorded above. The PCI also applied these guidelines to its relations with philosophical and cultural institutions. Berlinguer's affirmation of religious freedom and his recognition of religion's ongoing positive contributions to the "common good" of society were acclaimed publicly at the time of his death (11 June 1984) by Pope John Paul II, other Italian bishops, and Italian Protestant leaders.

A HEURISTIC CME

Those involved in the Italian CME constantly raise critical questions about its nature, purpose, and goals. For example, a recent book by Ossicini on CME in Italy sold over two hundred thousand copies. An internationally acclaimed psychologist and vice-president of the Italian Senate, Ossicini strives constantly to prevent those involved in CME from transforming their tentative working theories and principles into abstract dogmas. Positively, he wants to keep everyone open and receptive to the development of new knowledge and new approaches to solving societal problems. For this reason, Ossicini, in his new book, encourages all involved in CME to address three important problems. First, they must work incessantly to insure and safeguard the open and free subjectivity of political choice. Second, they must guard against the reductionist tendency to identify political science solely with the "scientific method." Political science is a human science which, in order to do justice to its central subject—human beings in community—

must use a variety of methods. Also, political science must be viewed not as a value-free but value-ladened discipline. Third, those concerned about the development of CME must recognize the limited validity of distinguishing between *Weltanschauung* and ideology, and, in particular, the limited value of classifying religion as a *Weltanschauung*.

Ossicini also writes appreciatively of the positive influence CME has had upon the Italian Catholic hierarchy. He reports that he was deeply moved when he heard a Roman Catholic bishop confess in a public debate his

> respect and esteem for those Catholics who for a long time . . . [have been pioneers in raising] the problem of the Christian presence in revolutionary politics [and which has been] promoted over a long arch of time and with many sacrifices by Italian Communists.[67]

This bishop also suggested that

> the limited testimony of some of us has not only permitted encounter, but has favored the possibility of facing the problem of CME in the clearest manner possible; that atheistic Marxists have come to understand the nonalienating role of religion and even the positive role of a religious motivation. . . . and the church has come to understand that the scientific tools of Marxism can be used for the liberation of the human person, and are not tied to a certain Marxist vision of the world that the church is unable to accept.[68]

This statement is especially significant for the acceptance and further development of CME in Italy because in the past bishops were usually selected for their opposition to CME.

ITALIAN CME OPENING TOWARD TOMORROW: THE CULTURAL QUESTION

Just as the secular and nonideological nature of the party and the state was gaining acceptance in the Italian CME a new and highly complex problem arose—"the cultural question." Quickly it became the center of new debate. Ossicini had touched upon the issue when he referred to the subjective dimension of political choices. The central question is, How are we to guarantee the possibility and right for different cultures to make contributions on an equal basis to the new society we plan to establish?

Given the complex and varied use of the word "culture" in Italy, a definition is required at this point. In this context, "culture" refers to a nation's or group's values and ethos which sets the parameters within which group and individual actions occur, provides the style in which they take place, and often limits the degree to which new options may be actualized.

A theoretical paper by Carlo Cardia, a non-Christian, Communist theoretician, canon lawyer, and recognized scholar of the "Catholic world" in

Italy, addressed some of the major issues in the "cultural problem." He asked whether "the secular nature" of a party and a state lies simply "in deep respect for each individual's ideal convictions." He suggested that the profound meaning of "secular" lies in the never-ending search for ideas and values within one's own cultural history and the cultural histories of others which can provide "original contributions for the transformation of society and its structures" into a more equitable social order.[69] "If all of this is true," Cardia continued, "then that which is to be asked of a *political party*" is that it "accept and favor cultural exchanges that do not limit themselves to verifying only the convictions (or the counterpositions)" regarding one's ideology or religious faith, "but that it extend this cultural exchange to all the spheres of human, social, and ethical relationships," and find ways to transform this broad exchange into concrete political proposals.[70]

Cardia suggested a functional approach for political parties to follow when they seek to deal with the delicate relationship between culture and politics.

> It is the political party's task and duty to respect the dividing line between a *political program* which is necessarily rigorous, concrete, and coherent, and to which persons of different inspirations contribute, [and *the autonomy of culture and cultural development*] which may have no predetermined and crystallized boundaries but constantly enriches itself through free discussion.[71]

An important recent example of the PCI's intent and effort to increase multiple cultural contributions to the full development of its policies is reflected in a meeting in March 1982 attended by Berlinguer, the moderator of the Waldensian Table Pastor Giorgio Bouchard, and the president of the Methodist Church Pastor Sergio Aquilante.[72] The purpose of this encounter was to discuss the present state of the Intesa (bilateral agreements between non-Catholic religions and the state foreseen in Article 8 of the Constitution) reached in 1978 between the two churches and the Italian republic. The bilateral text was first drafted on 4 February 1978, slightly modified and finally approved on 24 April 1981 by the joint commission of the two churches and the Italian republic. However, it was set aside by subsequent governments due to pressure from the Vatican which wanted its Concordat with the state updated first. In a December 1982 interview devoted exclusively to the PCI's position on religion, Berlinguer referred to this meeting, affirmed the PCI's support in Parliament of the Intesa, and went on to state that his party must

> pay attention to the different cultural and religious traditions which exist in Italy. This is necessary because political-cultural realism is required to build a more egalitarian society. The tutelage of minorities in general and, hence, also of

religious minorities is for us [the PCI] an irrenounceable principle . . . and obligatory function of the democratic state.[73]

This new openness to all religions clearly is a result of the CME in Italy.

CONCLUSIONS

This chapter has described the historical origins and theoretical principles which undergird the development of CME in Italy. Central to this CME was the positive outcome of the obstinate efforts from 1937 to 1945 of the Communist Catholics to move the PCI from a dogmatic to a dynamic reading of Marxist canons regarding religion. It was a revolutionary break with the past and brought religious and philosophical freedom within the PCI. More-over, it is accurate to claim that CME has significantly helped Italy become an open, pluralistic, and democratic state.

Given the impact of this CME on the largest Communist Party in the West (1.2 million registered members and 30 percent of the popular vote) and given the strong religious sentiment of Italians, accurate knowledge about this movement is essential for those who want to understand not only Italian CME but also Italy itself.

In fact, these principles and their development are not only rooted in a Communist Party—already a significant fact—but have deep ramifications within the Catholic community and intertwine with its evolution. Lombardo Radice reinforced this view when he stated, "Due to the radical changes within the Catholic Church resulting from the Second Vatican Council and due to the PCI's growing clarity on the subject [CME], the phenomenon of the double activist is spreading. Today, in fact, Catholics who become registered members of the PCI are very often active in Catholic organiza-tions."[74] He gave as examples ACLI (the Italian Catholic Workers Associa-tion, founded in 1944 and promoted by Monsignor Giovanni Battista Montini, the future Pope Paul VI), Catholic Action, and Christian grassroot communities. Going even further, Father Enrico Chiavacci, president of the Association of Italian Catholic Theologians, stated that the phenomenon of double activists occurred not only in Catholic organizations but in the life of the local parishes. For example, he reported that about half of the signifi-cantly active members of the parishes in the dioceses of Florence are also members of the Italian Communist Party.[75]

Since this CME was born in the Resistance movement against Fascism and Nazism for the purpose of reestablishing democratic government, its fifty-year legacy needs to be made more accessible to men and women in Latin America, Asia, and Africa who confront similar problems. Also, because this

FIRST WORLD ENCOUNTERS

CME developed in an industrialized, democratic country, it has implications for those who are concerned with affirming religious and individual liberties while working democratically for the establishment of a Socialist society. Likewise, since this CME is the patrimony of a Communist party, it has significance for other Communist parties in that it demonstrates that in the transition to socialism a Communist party can be a *party* and work for a *state* which is secular, democratic, and pluralistic.

NOTES

1. *Bolletino della Doxa* 17 (1963): 4–5, 35; 28 (1974): 14, 111–15.

2. This second estimate has been verified by personal conversations with bishops, priests, theologians, and lay persons.

3. The voting percentages have been kept low and are probably an underestimation in that almost no Italian Protestant is a Fascist, few are Christian Democrats (the Catholic party), and many are workers, farm workers, or part of the progressive intellegentsia. This data has been confirmed also by the heads of these respective churches.

4. Lucio Lombardo Radice, "I cattolici comunisti e il Marxismo," *Alle origini del compremesso storico* (Bologna: Edizioni Dehoniane, 1978), 91–92.

5. Ibid., 93.

6. Mario Cocchi and Pio Montesi, *Per una storia della sinistra cristiana* (Rome: Coines, 1975), 14.

7. The word *sinarchico* means "contrary to anarchy" or "without anarchy"; "unifying" is the closest single English word, but it lacks the historical significance of its being against anarchy.

8. CME in Italy takes many different shapes, forms, and paths. The type presented in this chapter was selected for its historical significance, its continuity, and its hegemonic role over the central ideas that have guided CME up to the present.

9. Cocchi and Montesi, *Sinistra cristiana*, 44–45.

10. Ibid., 37–40.

11. "Il manifesto del partito cooperativista sinarchico," in ibid., 45.

12. Ibid., 47.

13. Ibid., 55–57.

14. Carlo Felice Casula, *Cattolici-communisti e sinistra-cristiana* (Bologna: Il Mulino, 1976), 65, 81.

15. Ibid., 84.

16. Ibid., 82–83.

17. Cocchi and Montesi, *Sinistra cristiana*, 100–101, 109.

18. Ibid., 99.

19. "Il Concordat tra il Governo e La Sante Sede," *La Luce* 74:9 (2 March 1984): 3–4.

20. "L'Intesa tra il Governo e La Tavola Valdese," *La Luce* 74:9 (2 March 1984): 2–3.

21. An interview with Giorgio Bouchard, moderator of the Waldensian Table

which will be published in a forthcoming issue of *The Bridge* (Italian Ecumenical News Agency, Via Firenze, 38, I 00184 Rome).

22. "Il Comunismo e i cattolici," in *Sinistra cristiana*, 116–17.

23. Ibid., 117.

24. Franco Rodano, "Il materialismo storico e la libertà dell' uomo," *Voce Operaia* 19 (17 July 1944): 3.

25. Fedele D'amico, "Cattolici e Communisti" (a series of three articles), *Voce Operaia* 16 (14 June 1944): 3; 17 (19 June 1944): 3; and 18 (10 July 1944): 3–4.

26. Casula, *Cattolici-communisti*, 182–84.

27. G. Pirola and G. L. Brena, *Movimenti cristiani di sinistra e marxismo in Italia* (Assisi: Cittadella, 1978), 58.

28. Ibid., 59.

29. "Ecclesiam a Jesu Christo,"149–54; "Mirari Vos," 187–97; "Respecientes Ea Omnia," 298; "Ubi Nos," 300; *Tutte le encicliche dei sommi pontefici* (Milan: Oglio Editore, 1964).

30. Casula, *Cattolici-communisti*, 147.

31. Ibid., 166.

32. Pirola and Brena, *Movimenti cristiani*, 60.

33. Ibid., 62. Ironically, Pope Pius X in *Pieni L'Animo* (28 July 1906) condemned the formation of a similar party which was called Christian Democrats and which likewise advocated the separation of church and state.

34. Cocchi and Montesi, *Sinistra cristiana*, 202.

35. Giovanni Tassani, "I cattolici comunisti negli anni '50'," *Alle origini*, 20.

36. The ordering of the words "Communist Catholic" was a deliberate choice of the leaders. "Catholic" was the substantive and "Communist" was the adjective.

37. *Statuto del Partito Communista Italiano*, V Congresso, reproduced by the Circulation Center of the PCI, photocopy (undated), 4. Cf. *Statuto del Partito Communista Italiani*, VI Congresso, (Rome: Tipografia Seti, 1949), 9.

38. Tassini, "I cattolici comunisti," 20.

39. Antonio Tatò, "Communist Catholic, A Personal Experience, 1937–1945," *NTC News*, 7 August 1980, p. 10.

40. The materials that best illustrate the PCI are the speeches of Palmiro Togliatti given 19 February, 11 and 25 March 1947 before the Constitutional Assembly. See *Discorsi alla Costituente* (Rome: Editori Riuniti, 1973), 148, 9; *Opere Scelte* (Rome: Editori Riuniti, 1977), 492.

41. Decrees of the Holy Office, 1 July 1949, made public 13 July 1949. Robert Adolfs, "Church and Communism," *The Christian-Marxist Dialogue*, ed. Paul Oestreicher (Toronto: MacMillan Co., 1969), 29. The article notes that during the last one hundred years atheistic communism has been officially anathematized twelve times. See Sandro Magister, *La political vaticana e l' Italia, 1943–78* (Rome: Editori Riuniti, 1979), 132–42, for background information on the Vatican and DC actions which preceded and followed the proclamation of this decree.

42. Tatò, "Communist Catholic," 12.

43. Tassani, "I cattolici comunisti," 84.

44. The future pope pronounced this welcoming discourse from the pulpit of the cathedral and put up welcoming posters in Venice for the opening of the Socialist Party Congress.

45. Lombardo Radice, "I cattolici comunisti e il Marxismo," 93.

46. Tatò, "Communist Catholic," 10.

47. *Statutes and Theses of the Tenth Congress of the Italian Communist Party* (Rome: Editori Riuniti, 1962), 48.

48. Nicholas Piediscalzi and Robert C. Thobaben, eds., *From Hope to Liberation: Towards a New Marxist-Christian Dialogue* (Philadelphia: Fortress Press, 1974), 6.

49. *XI Congresso del Partito comunista italiano, atti e resoluzioni* (Rome: Editori Riuniti, 1966), 67.

50. Ibid.

51. Carlo Prandi, "Una rivista tra metafisica e scienza politica," in *Alle origini*, 106.

52. Adriano Ossicini, "La sinistra cristiani e cristiani per il socialismo," *Testimonianza* 18:171–72 (1975): 38.

53. Adriano Ossicini, *Cristiani non democristiani* (Rome: Editori Riuniti, 1980), 180.

54. Ibid., 202–3.

55. Aldo Gecchelin and José Ramos Regidor, *Christiani per il socialismo* (Turin: Modadori Editori, 1977), 224.

56. Tassani, "I cattolici comunisti," 63.

57. The letter of Bishop Luigi Bettazzi was published 6 July 1976 in the diocesan weekly of Ivrea, *Il risveglio popolave*. The reply of the PCI general secretary, the late Enrico Berlinguer, was published 14 October 1977 in the PCI intellectual weekly, *Rinascita*. In future references, only paragraphs will be noted.

58. Bettazzi, pars. 1, 4, 5, 7, and 9.

59. Berlinguer, pars. 3–4.

60. Berlinguer, pars. 6–7.

61. Berlinguer, par. 9.

62. Bettazzi, par. 7.

63. Berlinguer, par. 19.

64. Bettazzi, par. 13.

65. Berlinguer, par. 28.

66. Berlinguer, par. 32.

67. Ossicini, *Cristiani non democristiani*, 213.

68. Ibid., 213–14.

69. Claudio Cardia, "La Laicità del Partito e della Stato," *Idoc Internazionale* 9 (January–February 1978): 10.

70. Ibid., 11.

71. Ibid.

72. The encounter took place 25 March 1982.

73. *Adista* 2525, 2526, 2527 (16, 17, 18 December 1982): 12–13.

74. Lombardo Radice, "I cattolici comunisti e il Marxismo," 94.

75. From the author's personal conversation on 6 March 1982 in the parish rectory in Fiesole (near Florence) with Father Chiavacci who granted him permission to publish the information here.

AUSTRIA and WEST GERMANY

Maurice Boutin

Since 1965, the Paulus-Gesellschaft (the Society of Paul, hereafter referred to as PG) has conducted a series of significant Christian-Marxist dialogues in Europe. PG is an international, nondenominational organization which conducts interdisciplinary seminars, conferences, dialogues, and action projects. All of these efforts are dedicated to building a more humane world by transcending the dehumanizing problems caused by modern technology, industrialization, and nationalism. While PG was founded by Christians, primarily Roman Catholic, it is open to and includes many individuals outside the Christian community. Both its commitment to interdisciplinary dialogues and its openness to non-Christians made it natural for PG to become a pioneering leader in conducting Christian-Marxist dialogues.[1]

PG's programs and action projects are informed by three basic convictions. First, no scientific, religious, socioeconomic, or political institution is capable of solving on its own the basic problems of today's world. Second, each institution, while working in concert with the others, is capable of making a unique contribution toward solving these problems by employing the best elements in its own traditions, experiences, and capacities. Third, by joining in scientific studies and rational dialogues which eschew emotional and ideological responses to current problems and conflicts, and by engaging in mutual constructive criticism, it is possible for these institutions to transcend their differences and establish a foundation for the building of a new and more humane world community.

PG seeks neither political power nor official recognition from scientific, religious, or political groups. It is content to provide a forum for constructive, rational analysis and discourse. At the opening of the first Christian-Marxist dialogue conducted by PG in Salzburg in 1965, PG founder Erich Kellner affirmed his organization's belief in the ability of human beings through rational dialogue to transcend the barriers and conflicts that separate them. This emphasis upon rational analysis (which includes material self-criticism) is one of PG's major contributions to a unique form of Christian-Marxist dialogue. At the same time, it is the source of one of PG's major difficulties with both the Kremlin and the Vatican.

HISTORICAL CONDITIONS AT THE
ORIGIN OF THESE DIALOGUES

In countries like Italy or France where the Communist Party has a profound influence on public life, one cannot escape confrontation with Marxism. Thus, PG certainly was not inaugurating something completely new for these countries. The situation was quite different in the German Federal Republic (GFR) and Austria. The Communist Party (Kommunistische Partei Deutschland) in the GFR was outlawed by the Supreme Court in 1956; there was no change in that decree until the foundation of the Deutsche Kommunistische Partei in 1968. Austria finally gained political independence in 1955, but only on the provision that it remain strictly neutral both politically and economically. In these two countries, the Cold War heavily influenced the way they dealt with specific issues brought forth by Marxists who represented the Socialist countries in Eastern Europe.

Particularly for the GFR and Austria—given their geographical situation in Europe—it was impossible in the long run simply to ignore the great significance of Marxism. Obviously, PG was not trying to solve all the problems of the Cold War, as crucial as this might have been even in the 1960s and as important as this still is today. Their more modest goal was to find, through direct experience, ways to break through the Cold War atmosphere. If the matters to be discussed in a frank dialogue were theoretical most of the time, dialogue itself was never conducted for the sake of dialogue.

This was apparently forgotten by those in the late 1970s who thought of the conferences organized by PG on Marxism as involving just "a bunch of idealists." Certainly, PG was no better informed than anyone else on the intentions of the Soviet Union before troops of the Warsaw Pact marched into Czechoslovakia on 21 August 1968. The simple fact that the third PG dialogue took place in Marianské Lazné (Marienbad) at the end of April 1967 could, of course, be understood in the way Jan G. Vogeler understood it in 1970, in his attempt to justify the ending of the so-called Prague Spring initiated by the Central Committee of the Communist Party of Czechoslovakia in January 1968. After this decision, PG supported this new experiment in what has been called "socialism with a human face." But this does not mean that PG should be held responsible for this experiment (which the Soviet Union saw as a violation of the kind of Marxism espoused by its leadership). PG simply did not have a direct influence on the Central Committee of the Communist Party of Czechoslovakia.

The PG dialogues with Marxists were anything but opportunities for compromise on practical matters because of the differences between the

Christian and Marxist world views and the conviction that Christianity and Marxism are incompatible. PG leaves this approach to political and religious establishments. From the very beginning, PG aimed for dialogue on basic problems and issues common to both Christians and Marxists.

This was also the main reason for the rapidly growing interest in the Christian-Marxist conferences of PG as well as for the growing suspicion about these conferences not only in the Soviet Union but also in the Vatican. It was mainly because of the PG dialogues with Marxists that the Vatican stated, at the end of the 1960s, that whoever engaged in dialogue with Marxists should obtain Vatican approval. This was obviously "after the fact" for the Paulus-Gesellschaft. What the Vatican did expect was that the PG would take as its guideline Pius XI's encyclical *Divini Redemptoris* (19 March 1937) and endorse the Roman Catholic Church's stand on Marxist atheism (even though this was not the main issue at hand or the core of Marxism itself). According to the PG, this kind of approach can only foster an anti-communism that is shortsighted and sterile.

THE DIALOGUES AND THEIR SETTING

PG Christian-Marxist dialogues were instituted at the suggestion of Dr. Oskar Schatz, one of the very first to join the Paulus-Gesellschaft in 1956, and Erich Kellner in 1963. The suggestion was not prompted by Vatican II (1962–65); rather, the idea emerged as a natural outgrowth of the PG's purpose, goals, and activities.

In preparation for the three major conferences on Marxism held by PG in 1965, 1966, and 1967, a meeting took place in Cologne in 1964. The Marxists invited to the meeting—among them Adam Schaff who was at that time a member of the Polish Academy of Sciences and a member of the Central Committee of the Polish United Worker's Party—agreed with the other participants that the relationship between Marxism and religion was characterized by a pervasive hostility that could not be taken for granted any longer. Furthermore, that before a change in attitude could occur in Eastern European countries, a careful examination of the current critique of religion by the Communist parties in the West would be necessary. The Marxists attending the meeting were convinced that it was not enough to repeat the traditional Marxist view on religion. What was needed was a complete reappraisal of religion with appropriate changes in the critique. They viewed this as of paramount importance in the West as well as in the East. This implied an evolution within the Communist parties, within the churches, and within society as well. At that time, the situation seemed more promising in Italy than in the GFR or France.

In 1964, PG also organized two conferences on the topics: "Man: Spirit and Matter" (Munich, April 1964) and "Man and Society" (Cologne, September 1964).[2] While no Marxist was present among the seventy-five participants at the conference in Cologne, the one hundred and six members of the Munich conference discussed three papers presented by the Marxist philosopher Ernst Bloch (1885–1977), the theologian Karl Rahner (1904–84), and the ethnologist Konrad Lorenz (1903–). Though thematically related to the Christian-Marxist dialogues subsequently organized by PG, these two conferences should not be included in the six Christian-Marxist conferences held by PG between 1965 and 1978 because they were not organized for that purpose. The six formal dialogues in chronological order were:

1. 29 April–2 May 1965, Salzburg (Austria): an international conference on "Christianity and Marxism—Today."[3]
2. April 1966, Herrenchiemsee (Bavaria, GFR): an international conference on "Christian Humanity and Marxist Humanism."
3. 28–30 April 1967, Marianské Lazné (Marienbad, Czechoslovakia): an international conference on "Creativity and Freedom in a Humane Society,"[4] cosponsored by PG and the Czechoslovakian Academy of Sciences.
4. 16–19 October 1975, Florence (Italy): an international symposium on "Man: Guide of the Evolutionary Process," cosponsored by the Niels Stensen Institute in Florence, PG, and the Italian Teilhard de Chardin Society.
5. 6–10 September 1977, Salzburg (Austria): European Congress on "A Democratic and Social Europe of Tomorrow."[5]
6. 30 August 1978, Dusseldorf (GFR), meeting during the Sixteenth World Congress of Philosophy: symposium on "Marxist Philosophy and Christian Values Today," cosponsored by the American Society for the Philosophical Study of Marxism and PG.

In the meantime, other Christian-Marxist encounters underwent quite significant changes not only in Europe but also in other parts of the world, particularly in Latin America. This is documented, for instance, in the journal *Internationale Dialog-Zeitschrift* (hereafter *IDZ*) founded by the theologians Karl Rahner and Herbert Vorgrimler, and published by Herder Verlag from 1968 through 1974. *IDZ* was established as a quarterly journal for "the encounter and cooperation of Marxists, Humanists, and Christians." The main focus, however, was on Christian-Marxist dialogue and cooperation by means of the written word.[6] During the first three years, the journal followed the line propounded by PG. (Karl Rahner, who was involved in the activities of PG from its inception, also took an active part in the first set of

PG dialogues. Herbert Vorgrimler participated in the 1966 international conference in Herrenchiemsee.)

The PG dialogues dealt with issues closely related to their historical setting. This generated two major questions: 1) What is the relation between dialogues and action-oriented encounters? 2) Can the PG dialogues be viewed as formal? The former focuses on the understanding of *praxis;* the latter refers to the *institutional dimension* of Christian-Marxist dialogue. (This dimension within the Roman Catholic Church will be analyzed on pp. 52–55, below. Some aspects of this analysis, it should be noted, may be relevant to Marxist political institutions and organizations as well.)[7]

DIALOGUE AND ACTION-ORIENTED ENCOUNTERS

Whether the PG dialogues were action-oriented or not is a difficult question to answer. For Moscow the three international conferences organized by PG in the period from 1965 to 1967 were essentially action-oriented. Thus PG's goal for dialogues had been achieved. The Academy of Social Sciences at the request of the Central Committee of the Communist Party of the Soviet Union asked Jan G. Vogeler, professor of philosophy at the University of Moscow, for a report which he subsequently submitted to the Academy in 1970.[8] According to Vogeler, dialogue was for PG nothing but "a mask."[9] Consequently, the suggestion he put forward in the title of his report was that the conferences were not directed toward authentic dialogue, but "ideological diversion against Czechoslovakia and other socialist countries, as well as against the Communist movement in the capitalist countries . . . tactically hidden behind dialogue."[10] Referring to the publication of the papers given at the three conferences on Marxism and of reports on these conferences, Vogeler remarked that "one would be at a loss to find a characteristic feature of the Paulus-Gesellschaft" in these papers and reports.[11] In fact, from the very first dialogue in 1965, Kellner frequently used these conferences as forums to advocate the "principles of the Paulus-Gesellschaft."[12]

The editor in chief of *IDZ*, Herbert Vorgrimler, evaluated the PG dialogues as negatively as Vogeler and the Soviet Academy of Social Sciences; however, the main reason for his criticism was just the opposite: the problem of the PG conferences was not so much that they were action-oriented, but that they were excessively theoretical and too exclusively interested in analyzing different world views. In the first part of the "Introduction" to *IDZ* 4 (1971), Vorgrimler and Dieter-Olaf Schmalstieg, a member of the *IDZ* editorial committee in Bern since 1970, wrote that "part of, and even the whole dialogue today seems unsatisfying and so little future-oriented that it is better to begin anew and to speak of a new period of dialogue."[13] This "new period" was announced in *IDZ* 3 (1970): "The fourth year of the journal will endeavor to progress from predominantly theoretizing *world view dialogue* to a new period: the period of *practical* and *concrete* dialogue."[14] The "thesis" put forward at the beginning of 1971 was: "The transposition of dialogue on a public and mostly institutional level is very conducive to concretizing dialogue."[15] The motto was: "Concrete dialogue is organized dialogue, better organized than the organized dialogue so far."[16]

How should the PG dialogues be viewed from this new perspective? Vorgrimler explains this in "Dialogue with Communists," an article he published on 7 April 1972 in the bimonthly West German magazine *Publik-Forum*: among the many reasons why the Christian-Marxist dialogue of the mid-1960s could only lead to negative results for Marxists was the fact that it was "giving special preference to certain Marxists from Socialist countries except the Soviet Union."[17] Actually, Vorgrimler was ignoring what he had heard at the conference in Herrenchiemsee (1966). During the conference, Kellner reported that the Paulus-Gesellschaft had invited the Soviet Academy of Sciences to the conference, but that the academy had sent no one. The reason given was that the invitation arrived too late. So, for the next conference in Marienbad (1967), the PG sent an invitation to the Soviet Academy of Sciences well in advance. The academy replied that no one among its members was available to participate since all were very busy preparing for the celebrations planned for the fiftieth anniversary of the October Revolution. At the conference in Marienbad, Kellner expressed the hope that another Christian-Marxist conference could be held in a Socialist country in the near future, this time with the participation of Marxists from the Soviet Union. However, such a conference did not take place because of what Vogeler calls "the events in Czechoslovakia"[18] in August 1968. All six Christian-Marxist conferences organized by PG included, among the participants, Marxists belonging to an organized Communist party. But it was not until 1978 at the symposium in Dusseldorf that Marxists from the Soviet Union participated for the first time.

Although in his article of 7 April 1972 Vorgrimler stated that the results of the PG dialogues were generally negative, he added that "one can speak of a ruptured dialogue only with regard to the private and intellectual dialogue." For although the Roman Catholic hierarchy "does not go for a dialogue of 'left Roman Catholics' with Marxists rebelling against Marxist-Leninist principles," and although "the Vatican's Secretariat for Non-Believers thinks nothing anyway of such partners and nothing of a convergence of world views," Vorgrimler said, "the official and authorized dialogue was by no means limited, quite the contrary."

From 1965, the PG, in order to build the understanding necessary for cooperation, focused neither on the "convergence of world views" nor on an "open conflict of ideological systems that would lead to the physical destruction of the opponents," but on the "open confrontation of all systems and ideologies with the new world of reality."[19] The Paulus-Gesellschaft called this in the mid-1970s "a *limited* convergence,"[20] precisely because of the intrinsic link between world view and action, and despite the differences in motivation for action between Christians and Marxists.

Dialogue is fundamental for Christian-Marxist encounters. To deny it for the sake of action confuses and bewilders action itself. Dialogue *or* action is an erroneous statement of the problem. The correct statement is dialogue for the sake of dialogue, what Vorgrimler once called "l'art-pour-l'art-dialogue,"[21] and dialogue *as* action-oriented. The latter best characterizes the PG encounters in the mid-1960s, and even more so in the mid-1970s as we shall see later. Kellner expressed it clearly in the paper "Dialogue in Freedom and Responsibility," which he delivered at the opening session of the conference in Marienbad (1967). He presented a summary of what he then called the "result" of the previous Paulus-Gesellschaft dialogues.[22]

Of course, disagreement on the nature of authentic dialogue is always possible. One may judge at any time that other participants are not action-oriented enough, and hence that dialogue is more or less a waste of time. However, this judgment would be "imposing pre-conditions" for dialogue according to the West German Marxist Robert Steigerwald at the symposium in Dusseldorf (1978). He insisted on the fact that "dialogue is necessary" even though theoretical agreement between Christians and Marxists is not likely to happen in many cases. In 1974, Steigerwald put it this way in a short note published under the title "For Discussion" at the end of *IDZ* 7: the "necessary cooperation" between Christians and Marxists "has to include the open, sincere dialogue on theoretical issues in general and on *world view* issues in particular."[23]

Quoting Steigerwald here does not mean that his position can be identified with that taken by Kellner in 1967. Whereas Kellner speaks of "moving forward from theory to praxis and not the reverse," Steigerwald insists on cooperation "including" dialogue on theoretical issues. If the alternative—dialogue *or* action and cooperation—is the wrong one, then the question about which one comes first, theory *or* praxis, is also the wrong one. "Inclusion" indicates another approach frequently called for in debates on so-called theories of action. This new approach implies essentially the distinction between action and production, between *praxis* and *poiesis*. Experimenting with this distinction may bring us closer to the core of the concept praxis. In fact, in 1976, Rudiger Bubner argued precisely this point in his study on *Action, Language, and Reason: Fundamental Concepts of Practical Philosophy*, by referring to the various nuances brought forth by analytical philosophy on that issue.[24] One of the best opportunities for such an experiment today is Christian-Marxist cooperation.

The "new period" of Christian-Marxist dialogue for which Vorgrimler and *IDZ* were calling at the end of 1970 and at the beginning of 1971 had been envisaged earlier by the leadership of the Russian Orthodox Church. At the opening session of the conference in Marienbad (1967), Kellner reported that he had been told the year before by representatives of the Russian Orthodox Church that dialogue between Christians and Marxists on theoretical issues was only of minor importance. The stress, they contended, should be on practical cooperation in building a Socialist society. But the situation was different in the West—even if one takes into account the so-called *politique de la main tendue* of the secretary general of the French Communist Party, Maurice Thorez, in 1936,[25] and the close cooperation between Christians and Marxists during World War II in France and Italy.

The call for a "new period" of Christian-Marxist dialogue in the West was made for the first time at the beginning of April 1968, and hence before the "events in Czechoslovakia" (August 1968). The occasion was a press conference given by leaders of the Italian Communist Party on the topic of dialogue with Roman Catholics. During the conference, a Communist member of the Italian Parliament suggested that the Concordat of 1929 between the Vatican and Italy should undergo complete revision as a preliminary step to its abolition. He then added that dialogue between Communists and Roman Catholics should develop on an entirely new basis.

In the mid-1960s, PG often referred to the future as a dimension of which Christians and Marxists were particularly aware. Intensified dialogue and cooperation in confronting the reality of today's new world were the main goal. It almost seemed that the future was at hand as the Italian Communist Party began to talk of *compromisso storico* (historical compromise) particularly since its Fourteenth National Congress (March 1975).

The second period of the PG dialogues with Marxists (1975–78) was conditioned by the trends generated by the notion of "historical compromise," and also by the beginning of a very significant political change in Latin European countries known as "Eurocommunism." An important step in this direction took place in 1972 as the Communist Party and the Socialist Party in France began to work out a "common program." These were all solid indications that a movement toward effective political cooperation with Communists was present between 1972 and 1975 in Western Europe. Under these circumstances PG was ready and willing to support this new trend toward cooperation and to work with others along that line.

At the time of the symposium in Florence, the political situation in Italy was particularly important because for the first time politicians were taking an active part in the PG dialogues. At the symposium, a lively debate on the relevance of dialogue took place: Does not the situation in Italy call for more than mere dialogue? Would it not be more appropriate to make dialogue instrumental and try to realize cooperation between Christians and Marxists? Discussions on these issues sometimes gave the impression that "the dialogue between the PG and the Italian Communists did hardly take place" at the symposium.[26]

For PG, concentrating on the future of humankind, as the symposium in Florence did, does not necessarily imply convergence on a global social level or agreement on all political issues but is associated with Christian-Marxist relations in concrete situations. A cooperation effective for all participants can be achieved only by maintaining open communication whereby disagreements between Christians and Marxists can be clarified. To do otherwise would be to poison the possible agreements or even overshadow them. As Kellner pointed out during the afternoon session of 18 October, dialogue is not dead; quite the contrary, it is alive and well. As such, one can ask for cooperation and confidently expect that a way will be found to implement it. This, however, suggests that cooperation can help develop theory itself by freeing it from self-legitimizing ideologies. Kellner added that as long as Marxists keep on developing their own theory of society through an analysis of practical cooperation they can count on PG. Those who refuse to reduce theory to a mere tactical instrument, according to Kellner, should not be excluded from dialogue and cooperation simply on that account.

The program of the Florence symposium was set up after consultations between the cosponsors and members of the Italian Communist Party. The final version of the program was adopted at a meeting in Rome (10 July 1975). Shortly before the meeting, the program was discussed by leaders of the Italian Communist Party. They suggested that the PG organize a European congress in order to analyze the implications for political and social systems in Europe of the "new politics of Man" to be outlined at the Florence symposium. At that time, both the Italian Communist Party and PG were planning the European congress for 1976, either in Florence, Salzburg, or Strasbourg. At the final session of the Florence symposium the participants adopted the principle of a threefold commission to be set up by PG. Key members of the Italian Communist Party present at the symposium assumed the responsibility for inviting Communist leaders from the other European countries to the congress. PG was to send invitations to other groups in Europe.

The date of the European congress was postponed twice. It was scheduled first for Spring 1977 in Strasbourg, and then for September 1977 in Salzburg. The postponements were necessary because it became evident that those who had agreed to involve themselves in preparations for the congress failed to fulfill their commitment.

Between fall 1975 and fall 1977, the political situation in Europe underwent a complex evolution—a development that cannot be overlooked because it is related to the question of whether the nature of the European congress of Christians and Marxists was dialogical or action-oriented. At first sight, it was neither.

There were but a few Communists present at the European congress, and only the Spanish Communist Party sent a delegation. This is really surprising given the final document the delegations of twenty-nine Communist parties adopted on 30 June 1976 at the Berlin Conference on Peace, Security, Cooperation, and Social Development in Europe—a conference originally scheduled for mid-1975 that required eighteen months of preparation. In addition, the Italian Communist Party withdrew its cosponsorship of the European congress because of the national elections of 20–21 June 1976 in Italy. The main reason given by the Italian Communist Party for not sending delegates to the European congress was that political tensions and the increasing complexity of the situation in Italy from spring 1976 required its full attention. The French Communist Party did not send delegates to Salzburg because of the congress on the "Unity of the Left" in France. Scheduled for September 1977, the conference was held only a few days after the Salzburg congress, and they had yet to decide the future nature of the political relationship between the French Communist Party and the French Socialist Party that had prevailed since 1972. The debate on that issue was already very lively among French Communists in spring 1977, and at the congress the French Communists decided it was not possible at that time to continue to work with the Socialists on a "common program." Thus, only the Spanish Communist Party was represented in Salzburg, and this delegation included one person from the Central Committee along with various members of the Central Committee of the Catalonian Communist Party.

Many of the groups invited by the PG attended. In December 1976, the president of the West German Socialist Party, Willy Brandt, replied positively to the invitation. However, at a later date, the party executive decided not to send an official delegate to Salzburg. Due to various tensions within West German society at that time—particularly the kidnapping of

Hans-Martin Schleyer, the president of the West German Managers Association, on the day before the opening of the European congress—the West German Socialist Party decided that it was unwise to participate in a congress with Communist leaders from the Eastern European countries.

To recall all this is not to downgrade the modest achievements of the European congress which numbered around 150 participants from twelve different countries. It shows, however, not only how difficult practical cooperation is between Marxists and others but also the problems of dialogue at that time.

The symposium in Dusseldorf (30 August 1978) took place during the Sixteenth World Congress of Philosophy. Differences on the relevance of Christian-Marxist dialogue were registered among the participants. For non-Marxist participants, restricting dialogue to practical issues, whatever that is, is an oversimplification. And there were Marxists also who reinforced this position contending that dialogue is necessary even though agreement on theoretical issues can rarely be achieved. One of the basic requirements for Christian-Marxist dialogue, Kellner recalled at the symposium, would be for Marxists to acknowledge that human reality is rooted in ethical categories, and for Christians to take seriously the power of our socioeconomic structures. How and to what extent these two main tasks have been achieved already, Kellner added, cannot be understood by mere theoretical observations.

INFORMAL/FORMAL DIALOGUE

The six PG dialogues between 1965 and 1978 were as formal as conferences, congresses, and symposiums usually are—agendas were prepared, programs discussed, publicity arranged, and invitations mailed. The papers given at the conferences were, in most cases, distributed to the participants in advance in order to encourage thoughtful reactions by participants and to improve the quality of the general discussions. Much attention was given to these conferences by the media, particularly in the first period (1965–67). Yet, despite the fact that the encounters did have a wide impact on public opinion, they were often viewed as being only "private."

As already mentioned, this was Vorgrimler's estimation of the situation at the beginning of the 1970s, shortly after he had been appointed a consultant to the Vatican's Secretariat for Non-Believers (created in 1965) and, some time later, secretary of the West German Secretariat for Non-Believers (created in February 1970). In addition to being editor in chief of *IDZ* since the founding of the journal in 1968, Vorgrimler was at the same time secretary of the German-speaking part of Switzerland for questions pertaining to the relationship between Christian faith and unbelief. In his role as secretary he had to coordinate activities and research in Switzerland as well as in the GFR.[27]

Christian-Marxist dialogue, Vorgrimler argued in 1971, has to date developed in the wrong direction. It was generally "not concrete," and there were clearly obstacles that jeopardized its practicality, not the least of these being the Vatican's Secretariat for Non-Believers which neglected to consider the "organization of dialogue" as a "fundamental problem."[28] Although the *Document on Dialogue with Non-Believers* issued by the Vatican's Secretariat on 28 August 1968 acknowledged that there exist three types of dialogue— dialogue as encounter between persons, dialogue on doctrine, and dialogue as cooperation—the emphasis was so much on doctrinal dialogue (Vorgrimler calls it also "rational dialogue" or "dialogue on theory [worldview]"[29]) that *"personal"* and *"practical"* dialogue could not come to the fore. How could this awkward situation be overcome?

Surprisingly enough, Vorgrimler says, the document itself (the Document on *Dialogue with Non-Believers* [1968]) opens up the possibility for this; not simply when one takes the three phases of dialogue seriously, not just by realizing the practical suggestions to be found in the document, but rather through a certain distinction made by the document. In fact, the document does make the distinction between *private* and *public, non-official* and *official* dialogue. This distinction opens up new roads. It makes it possible to understand and to overcome the wrong orientation taken so far, by adopting an organizational viewpoint. Until 1971 the public character of dialogue was mostly concealed (also in our journal [that is, *IDZ*]), and dialogue was mostly nonofficial. Now, the thesis contrary to that and which comes for the first time to the fore in this issue is the following: the transposition of dialogue on a public and mostly institutional level is very conducive to concretizing dialogue.[30]

The "new direction" toward concrete dialogue and practical cooperation between Christians and Marxists has to be based, according to Vorgrimler, on the distinction between private and public, nonofficial and official dialogue—"colloquium officiale,"as stated in the Vatican's document of 1968. This theoretical distinction allows Vorgrimler to identify public and institutionalized dialogue and to infer its factual equivalency with concrete dialogue and practical cooperation. The more institutionalized the Christian-Marxist dialogue is, the more public and the more concrete it will be.

From this perspective, the PG dialogues have to be viewed as "private," Vorgrimler stated in 1972,[31] and consequently as informal. In fact, there can be very few public, official, and concrete Christian-Marxist dialogues and cooperative actions for even some of the encounters between representatives of the Holy See and of Communist countries cannot be considered as dialogue. "One cannot speak here properly of dialogue, but of a search for a *modus vivendi* on concrete problems [and] on specific issues,"[32] said Bishop Giovanni Benelli, assistant to the Vatican's secretary of state, in a paper on "The Church and Dialogue with the World" given on 4 May 1976 before the Austrian Association for Foreign Policy and International Relations in Vienna.

The "new direction" suggested by Vorgrimler in 1971 gave rise to very critical reactions,[33] and it was understood as a priori criticism of the vast majority of Roman Catholics whose participation in Christian-Marxist encounters would simply not be relevant from Vorgrimler's structural viewpoint. This consequence seemed so crucial that most critiques neglected to analyze the starting point of Vorgrimler's position, namely the distinction between private and public, nonofficial and official dialogue.

If dialogue in general, and Christian-Marxist dialogue specifically, was indeed something new for Roman Catholics after the Second Vatican Council (1962–65), the distinction just mentioned certainly was not. It was already an important issue on the agenda at the council, and it had been discussed in lively fashion before and during the council itself. The issue, however, was quite different from the one pertaining to Christian-Marxist encounters—the distinction did not apply to "the dialogue with the world," or to the Christian-Marxist dialogue, but to "the dialogue with God," that is, prayer and worship.

Canon #1256 of the *Codex Iuris Canonici* (hereafter *CIC*), promulgated in 1917, stipulated that public worship *(cultus publicus)* is the one performed in the name of the church by persons duly mandated to do so, and through actions to be fulfilled according to the regulations established by the church. Every other worship is private. As to *cultus privatus*, the well-known canon lawyer Klaus Morsdorf says: "According to canon #1256, private worship *(cultus privatus)* is not institutional worship, be it performed in the most public and ceremonious way."[34]

The restrictive significance given by *CIC* to private worship had already given rise to critiques in the late 1950s. Vatican II's Constitution on Liturgy (4 December 1963) shows some progress on the issue[35] but without taking a stand clearly different from that of *CIC*. As the liturgist Joseph Pascher recalled in 1962 with regard to "the bishop's authority":

> The present law as codified in *CIC* calls "public" only the prayer in the name of the church. Everything else falls under the designation "private." Since "church" means here the church as a whole, there is a gap in the legislation

which should be filled up. One cannot view the liturgy resting upon the bishop's authority as private, or even simply as *pium exercitium*. For this qualification is not just a factual one; it is rather a valuating one.[36]

In the article on "The Nature of Divine Office" published in 1964, Pascher gets closer to the question of *cultus privatus* with regard to the institutional character of worship:

> It is not the obligation that constitutes liturgical action, but rather the vocation of the church. This can be expatiated in two ways: through obligation or through nonobligation. Accordingly, one is justified in distinguishing between an obligatory and a nonobligatory mandate. . . . The laity can enjoy the dignity and honor of liturgy even when they pray the Divine Office alone or in group without a priest.[37]

Vorgrimler was correct when he said that "private associations, scientific societies, etc. that have conducted dialogues are not authorized to do this in the name of the Roman Catholic Church or to speak for that church, even if the majority of their members are Roman Catholics." And he added: "The system of the Roman Catholic Church implies that only the pope, either alone or together with the bishops gathered with him in council, can speak in the name of the church." For instance, the pope may speak through the Roman Secretariat for Non-Believers on matters pertaining to Christian-Marxist dialogue.[38] Vorgrimler contended in 1971 that the question "Who are those who should be mutually recognized as official partners" in Christian-Marxist encounters? is still pending. He is convinced that "progress in dialogue very closely relies on the answer to that question,"[39] and he remarks that real cooperation between Christians and Marxists has not been registered officially anywhere; "it has begun, however, for the first time through participation of authorized persons in this independent journal"— that is: *IDZ*.[40]

The "new direction" in Christian-Marxist dialogue taken by Vorgrimler and *IDZ* at the beginning of 1971 lasted four years. The journal ceased publication at the end of 1974, apparently because the number of subscribers and sales declined dramatically. Surely this denies the charge that Marxists who wrote articles in *IDZ* were using it for their own "propaganda." More important, however, is the fact that the theoretical basis chosen by Vorgrimler in 1971 in order to "open up new roads" in Christian-Marxist dialogue was indeed an old one. The experiment by *IDZ* from 1971 to 1974 shows that the new wine of Christian-Marxist dialogue and cooperation can obviously not be poured into the old goatskins of the distinction between "private" and "public," "nonofficial" and "official," as used by the Roman

Catholic hierarchy so far. As Giulio Girardi, a former consultant to the Vatican's Secretariat for Non-Believers, put it in 1974:

> The inner contradictions of dialogue are visible particularly when dialogue is conducted by church institutions, especially the Secretariat for Non-Believers. Although one cannot deny that these institutions did represent originally a new openness, it becomes obvious today that this openness is structurally limited by the church's refusal to be basically questioned through political analysis. This is also the reason why institutional dialogue on Marxism did remain a formal and sterile enterprise until now.

Yet, Girardi added that his critique of dialogue "does minimize in no way the decisive role played—and still to be played in the future—by institutional dialogue with regard to Christian consciousness."[41]

On the whole, Vorgrimler adopted what Norbert Strotmann would call a "self-defensive strategy" *(Abwehrstrategie)*, because he argued in 1971 and 1972 that no *real* Christian-Marxist dialogue had taken place so far, either because the Marxists participating in dialogue were not "real" Marxists, or because the Christians involved were not "real" Christians. Commenting on this "self-defensive strategy" Strotmann said in 1974, "We suggest that those who adopt this position appreciate the results [of the analyses made by Strotmann] 'in a new way' from their own perspective, instead of rejecting the problem."[42] Strotmann also recalled something that still might well be a reality in Christian-Marxist encounters:

> When participants in dialogue become aware of the cultural conventions which govern the constructions of their world views, then they must decide anew either to accept uncritically their world views or to adopt self-critical stances toward them.[43]

PG was fully and constantly aware of this distinction as expressed by Strotmann—a distinction that cannot, as such, be set apart from the concrete situation and compressed within a model to await mechanical application. Today, the illumination of this distinction qualifies as a future task for the participants in the Christian-Marxist dialogue.

NOTES

1. The Paulus-Gesellschaft was founded in 1956 by Dr. Erich Kellner, a Roman Catholic priest of the archdiocese of Munich-Freising (Bavaria, German Federal Republic). It became the Paulus-Gesellschaft Internationale in 1969, with national organizations in the GFR, Austria, and Switzerland, and representatives in the following countries: Italy, Holland, France, Spain, England, Poland, Yugoslavia,

India, Japan, Canada, the United States, and, since 1977, Brazil, Colombia, and Argentina. It is a society for the encounter of Christianity, science, and society. In the 1960s and early 1970s, it had six hundred members, the majority of whom were scholars and specialists in natural sciences who took an active part in the Paulus-Gesellschaft dialogues with Marxists.

2. The proceedings of these conferences were published in 1965 in Munich by the Paulus-Gesellschaft: *Der Mensch, Geist und Materie,* Dokumente der Paulus-Gesellschaft, vol. 12; *Mensch und Gesellschaft,* Dokumente der Paulus-Gesellschaft, vol. 11.

3. Erich Kellner, ed., *Christentum und Marxismus—heute* (Vienna: Europa Publishers, 1966). Also published in French (Paris: 1968) and in Portuguese (Rio de Janeiro: 1972).

4. Erich Kellner, ed., *Schöpfertum und Freiheit in einer humanen Gesellschaft: Gespräche der Paulus-Gesellschaft-Marienbader Protokolle* (Vienna: Europa Publishers, 1969).

5. Udo Bermabach's discussion paper delivered at the congress has been published in English under the title: "Socio-political Theses for the Christian-Marxist Dialogue," *Journal of Ecumenical Studies* 15 (1978): 87–99. See also "Salzburg Congress on the Future of Europe" (pp. 207–10 of the same issue), a report by R.G. Thobaben and N. Piediscalzi.

6. Norbert Strotmann, "The Language of Dialogue between Marxists and Christians: Reflections on the Vocabulary and Analysis of the Meaning of Major Concepts Used in Marxist-Christian Dialogue of the Internationale Dialog-Zeitschrift (1968–1971) under Application of Content Analysis as a Sociological Method" (Ph.D. diss., University of Innsbruck, Austria, 1973—in German).

7. A. Touraine's analysis of social movements provides an effective tool for analyzing the PG dialogues. See his *Production de la société* (Paris: Seuil, 1973), particularly 346–431; *La voix et le regard* (Paris: Seuil, 1978), and *La prophétie anti-nucléaire* (Paris: Seuil, 1980).

8. J. G. Vogeler, "Pod znamenem svjatogo Pavla—dialog ili ideologičeskaja diversija? Religija v planach antikommunizma," published under the title: "Dialog oder ideologische Diversion," *IDZ* 4 (1971): 207–14.

9. *IDZ* 4 (1971): 214.

10. Ibid., 211 (also 210, 212, 213).

11. Ibid., 210.

12. Erich Kellner, "Wissenschaft und Ideologie," in *Christentum und Marxismus—heute,* ed. Kellner, 17–24; Erich Kellner, "Dialog in Freiheit und Verantwortung," in *Schöpfertum und Freiheit,* ed. Kellner; and Kellner, "Paulus—Apostel Jesu Christi heute: Von Geist, Sinn und Gestalt der Paulus-Gesellschaft," in *Gott in Welt: Festgabe fur Karl Rahner zum 60. Geburtstag,* 2 vols., ed. J.B. Metz, W. Kern, A. Darlap, and H. Vorgrimler (Freiburg: Herder, 1964), 1:724–55.

13. *IDZ* 4 (1971): 2.

14. *IDZ* 3 (1970): 290.

15. *IDZ* 4 (1971): 3.

16. Ibid., 1.

17. H. Vorgrimler, "Dialog mit den Kommunisten," *Publik-Forum* 1 (April 1972): 3.

18. *IDZ* 4 (1971): 213.

19. Kellner, "Wissenschaft und Ideologie," 22.

20. See as an example Erich Kellner, "Einfuhrung" in *Neue Generation und alte Strukturen der Macht,* ed. Kellner (Vienna: Europa Publishers, 1973), 14; see also Kellner's circular letter (August 1975) inviting participation in the Florence symposium (16–19 October 1975).

21. *IDZ* 3 (1970): 289.

22. Kellner, "Dialog in Freiheit und Verantwortung," 19–20.

23. R. Steigerwald, "Zur Diskussion," *IDZ* 7 (1974): 382.

24. R. Bubner, *Handlung, Sprache und Vernunft: Grundbegriffe praktischer Philosophie* (Frankfurt: Suhrkamp, 1976), 74–100.

25. As an example see Francis J. Murphy, *"La main tendue: Prelude to Christian-Marxist Dialogue in France, 1936–1939," The Catholic Historical Review* 40 (1974): 255–70.

26. Hanspeter Oschwald, "Mit geballter Faust diskutiert sich schlecht: Der Dialog der Paulus-Gesellschaft mit italienischen Kommunisten fand kaum statt," *Publik-Forum* 4 (14 November 1975): 3–4.

27. H. Vorgrimler, "Zur Organisation des 'Atheismus-Sekretariats'," *IDZ* 4 (1971): 214.

28. *IDZ* 4 (1971): 2.

29. Ibid., 24.

30. Ibid., 2–3.

31. H. Vorgrimler, "Dialog mit den Kommunisten," 3.

32. G. Benelli, "L'Eglise et le dialogue avec le monde," *La documentation catholique* 1699 (6 June 1976): 516.

33. See H. Vorgrimler, " 'Christliche Angriffe' gegen die 'Internationale Dialog-Zeitschrift'," *IDZ* 4 (1971): 195–204; see for instance the lively debate in the magazine *Publik-Forum* 1 (25 August 1972): 6–8; (8 September 1972): 7; (3 November 1972): 7; (1 December 1972): 5.

34. K. Morsdorf, *Lehrbuch des Kirchenrechts auf Grund des Codex Iuris Canonici,* 3 vols., 11th ed. (Paderborn: F. Schoningh,1967), 2: 366; see also J. H. Miller, *Fundamentals of the Liturgy* (Notre Dame: Fides, 1960), 24–25.

35. See particularly canons #84, 85, and 100.

36. J. Pascher, "Thesen uber das Gebet im Namen der Kirche: Erganzungen zu dem gleichnamigen Aufsatz von Karl Rahner," *Litugisches Jahrbuch* 12 (1962): 61–62.

37. J. Pascher, "De natura officii divini," *Euphemerides Liturgicae* 78 (1964): 339.

38. *IDZ* 4 (1971): 25.

39. Ibid., 3.

40. Ibid., 24.

41. G. Girardi, "Zur gegenwartigen Konfrontation der Christen mit dem Marxismus," *IDZ* 7 (1974): 269. This article (pp. 255–76) deals with the history and goals of the "Christians for Socialism" in its beginnings in Latin America, Spain, GFR, and Italy.

42. N. Strotmann, "Die Sprache des Dialogs zwischen Marxisten und Christen," *IDZ* 7 (1974): 361–75, especially 374.

43. Ibid., 374.

SUGGESTIONS FOR FURTHER READING

Kellner, Erich, ed. *Christentum und Marxismus-heute*. Vienna/Frankfurt/Zurich: Europa, 1966. Also published in French (Paris: 1968) and in Portuguese (Rio de Janeiro: 1972).

Kellner, Erich, ed. *Schöpfertum und Freiheit in einer humanen Gesellschaft: Gespräche der Paulus-Gesellschaft-Marienbader Protokolle*. Vienna/Frankfurt/ Zurich: Europa, 1969.

Nolte, Ernst. *Deutschland und der Kalte Krieg*. Munich: R. Piper & Co., 1974.

Rolfes, Helmuth, ed. *Marxismus Christentum*, Grunewald-Materialbucher 6. Mainz: Matthias-Grunewald, 1974.

Theunis, Franz, ed. *Glaube und Politik—Religion und Staat: Zur Entmythologisierung und Neubestimmung ihres Verhaltnisses*, Theologische Forschung 63. Hamburg: Herbert Reich, 1979.

UNITED STATES
Arthur F. McGovern

The dialogues discussed in this chapter span roughly a twenty-year period in United States' history, from 1965 to the present. The "historical context" will give some indication of Christian-Marxist interactions prior to this period. The term "Marxist," if it most often suggests Marxist-Leninist thought and movements, also includes views and dialogue participants quite at odds with the more dominant "orthodox" Marxism.

HISTORICAL CONTEXT

The history of the United States has not, for the most part, provided promising conditions for a flourishing Christian-Marxist dialogue. Yet in some past eras (the early 1900s, the 1930s) Protestant theologians did grapple seriously with Marxist theory and Socialist ideals, and in recent years Christian-Marxist dialogues have been surprisingly numerous. We will look briefly then not only at the cultural factors that have tended to work against any strong level of Christian-Marxist encounter but also at the causal factors that have prompted dialogues to occur.

Cultural Context

A great deal has been written about the uniqueness of the American experience and the spirit of America. The United States as "the land of opportunity," as the "home of the free and the brave," and as the "defender of the free world," evokes cultural myths that symbolize this spirit.[1] Americans are strongly individualistic and tend to believe that anyone who works hard can achieve success. The courage and integrity of Abraham Lincoln, the drive and competitiveness of Henry Ford, the inventiveness of Thomas Edison, the upward mobility of Irish, Italian, and Jewish immigrants, these are all expressions of how the people of the United States have historically perceived themselves.

Working against this prevailing ideology, Marxism has struggled to make its ideas heard. It could challenge the dominant myths by pointing to the racism, sexism, and exploitation that run through American history. The Marxist movement did contribute significantly to labor union struggles at the turn of the century and again in the 1930s. Yet Marxism has never made great inroads into the political and cultural life of the country. The Communist Party, even at its strongest point in the 1930s, never matched the strength of the Communist parties in Western Europe and has never mounted any significant threat to the major political parties. More broadly based Socialist movements have not fared much better.

Many and varied explanations have been given for the failure of Marxism and socialism to make greater headway: the relative absence of sharp class distinctions which marked European history; the American dream that every hard-working individual can become a successful owner; labor unions working for concessions rather than for radical change, and so forth.[2] Whatever the reasons, even socialism has remained a relatively weak force in the political and social life of the country. Factional disputes have left Marxist-Leninist groups even more marginal, splintered into competing parties with a few thousand, or only a few hundred, members (for example, the Communist Party/USA, the Socialist Workers Party, the Progressive Labor Party, the Revolutionary Communist Party).

Christianity, for its part, has also had a distinctive history in the United States, one which set it apart from the European experience. Many of the first American settlers came to this country in search of religious freedom. Many thought of America as the "promised land." Separation of church and state not only provided religious freedom but protected churches against much of the strident anticlericalism provoked by church privileges in Europe. If in Europe the official, hierarchical church was identified with the aristocracy (especially in the case of Catholicism), American bishops and church leaders came most often from working-class families.

What was the impact of Marxism and socialism on U.S. Christianity prior to the 1960s? The Roman Catholic response was mostly quite negative. A small Catholic Socialist society did develop in the early 1900s, and the Catholic Worker, with Dorothy Day and Peter Maurin in the 1930s, spurred some Catholic interest in socialism. But apart from such exceptions, the U.S. Catholic Church was opposed to socialism and quite hostile to Marxism. Catholic social thought in the United States followed closely the social encyclicals of the popes. These encyclicals, while critical of capitalism, rejected socialism, and Pope Pius XI condemned communism as "intrinsically evil." U.S. Catholics became even more staunchly anti-Communist after World War II as they read about persecutions of the Catholic Church in Eastern Europe and China. Little distinction was ever made between Marx, Marxism, socialism, and communism.

Protestant thought, even though most often supportive of the U.S. free-enterprise system, has shown a greater openness to socialism. The Social Gospel movement, at the turn of the century, included men like Washington Gladden who challenged the inequities engendered by capitalism, George Herron who argued openly for socialism, and Walter Rauschenbusch who developed a theological basis for the movement.[3] In the 1930s Reinhold Niebuhr made a strong case for the validity of Marxist analysis and even spoke of himself as a "Christian Marxist."[4] He felt that socialism, more or less Marxist, was the political creed of the industrial worker of Western civilization, and that Marxism correctly expressed the workers' feelings of idealism and class loyalty. But in later years Niebuhr grew increasingly critical of Marxist pretensions and solutions, and his criticisms of Marxism have been cited much more often than his earlier defense of Marxist analysis. Through these same years a few Christians, like Henry F. Ward of Union Theological Seminary and the Methodist Federation, actively supported many Communist causes. But such direct support became rare in the years following World War II. Charles West's great study *Communism and the Theologians* (1958) provided an objective view of Marxism at a time when anticommunism was still rampant, and West encouraged divinity students to study Marxism, as did James Luther Adams, John Bennett, and others. But prevailing attitudes, in the country as a whole and in the churches as well, did not suggest the advent of Christian-Marxist dialogue.

Causal Factors of Change

In the years following World War II, a "liberal consensus" prevailed, and it militated against Christian-Marxist dialogue. This liberal consensus, as described by Godfrey Hodgson, was built on a twin conviction that the U.S. economic-political system was the best in the world, capable of dealing with all problems, and that communism, the most serious evil facing the world, must be contained.[5] Yet by the mid-1960s new attitudes were emerging within the church and within the country, attitudes which would lead to the encounters we wish to consider. What caused these new attitudes to develop?

Changes Within the Church. The church, and the Catholic Church in particular, underwent a succession of dramatic changes in the 1960s. The personality of Pope John XXIII contributed greatly to the change. He was warm, outgoing, unpretentious, and more ready to praise and affirm than to condemn. His encyclicals on social justice (*Mater et Magistra*, 1961) and on peace (*Pacem in Terris*, 1963) invited dialogue. The Second Vatican Council continued this spirit. It called for the church to be more involved in the world and to help in transforming the world; it called explicitly for "dialogue with unbelievers."[6] Protestant churches likewise wrestled with the issue of transforming the world. The Geneva Conference on Church and Society (1966), sponsored by the World Council of Churches, dealt with many of the same issues discussed at Vatican II. Papers prepared for the Geneva conference dealt with church involvement in social revolutions, liberation struggles in the Third World, Christian responsibility in affluent countries, the impact of Marxism on Christian thought, and similar topics.[7] A Christian-Marxist dialogue was held at Geneva in conjunction with the conference.

Social Unrest. The country as a whole was traumatized by the social unrest of the 1960s, by the struggle for civil rights, the war on poverty, by anti-Vietnam war demonstrations, and by the emergence of a counterculture that challenged most traditional American values. These social issues divided the church. Churches found themselves under attack from within their own ranks. They were attacked for lack of commitment to social change and, on the other side, for abandoning the true spiritual mission of the church. Marxism began to plan an increasingly significant role. Social activism during the early 1960s led to social radicalism in the late 1960s. "The whole system is sick and has to be overthrown" became an oft-heard cry in the late 1960s. Student radicals began to borrow Marxist revolutionary rhetoric; Herbert Marcuse became a guru for many; new Marxist groups were formed. Student activists themselves showed little interest in Christian-Marxist dialogue; they tended to be highly critical both of the church and of the "Old Left." But the social unrest had made Marxism more relevant, and it spurred interest in dialogue.

Intellectual Interest in Marxism. It was primarily within academic circles, at universities and seminaries, that Christian-Marxist dialogues began to emerge in the United States. The factors already noted, shifts within the churches and social unrest in the country as a whole, played a major role. Christian-Marxist dialogues in Europe played an influential role in stimulating U.S. dialogues, and there arose new scholarly interest in Marx's thought. The United States had lagged far behind Europe in this respect. Controversy over the writings of the "young Marx" had raged in Europe throughout the 1950s. But it was not until the appearance of Erich Fromm's *Marx's Concept of Man* (1961), with its appended translations of Marx's 1844 manuscripts, that the process really began in earnest in the United States. By distinguishing Marx's own humanistic thought from prevailing Communist ideology and practice, Fromm opened the door for a reevaluation of Marx's thought.

Translations of Marx's works and dozens of books about Marx followed. The interest in Marx led to a renewed interest in the whole Marxist heritage, to studies of Lenin, Trotsky, Lukács, Gramsci, Althusser, the Frankfurt School, and others. Spurred in part by Marxism, and in part by C. Wright Mills's *The Power Elite*, radical sociologists intensified their study of controlling interest groups within the state. Radical economists, following work already done by Marxist economists Paul Baran and Paul Sweezy, brought Marxist economic analysis into debates.[8]

Economic and Political Factors. A Marxist writer of this treatment on causal factors might begin with the economic. But it would be difficult to argue that economic factors gave the initial stimulus to the dialogue. Through most of the 1960s the U.S. economy was still flourishing; it was one of the most productive decades of the century. Some might argue that it was the very affluence of the country as a whole that sharpened awareness of social problems: the millions of Americans still below the poverty line, the income gap between whites and blacks, between men and women, and the enormous gaps between rich and poor nations. But economic issues did not prompt the first Christian-Marxist dialogues. Economic issues have, on the other hand, been influential in the 1970s and 1980s. They appear to have influenced Christian-Marxist encounters most on problems that link economic and political power: the growing power of multinational corporations, U.S. interventions in Latin America, and the buildup of nuclear arms. Concern for the poor in Latin America and solidarity with church people involved in "liberation" struggles have drawn many U.S. Christians to examine Marxist analysis more closely. Other Christians, with concerns that focus more on East-West relations, have sought dialogue with Marxists about the threat of nuclear war.

Initiatives Toward Dialogue and Encounter

Though the causal factors just noted help explain why dialogue did develop, they were not so compelling that official church bodies or Marxist parties felt any urgent *need* to dialogue. One could hardly argue that "self-interest" on either side made dialogue imperative. The initiative for dialogue rested with individuals and small groups. Their motives in calling for dialogue were probably quite varied: on the Christian side, a desire to lessen antagonisms in the world and a recognition that the church has not always been committed to needed social changes; on the Marxist side, a recognition of change within the church and an opportunity to gain a better hearing for Marxism.

Efforts to organize Christian-Marxist encounters have nearly always come from the Christian side, and Christians far outweigh Marxists in attendance. But one of the first "calls" for dialogue in the United States did come from a Marxist. Gus Hall, leader of the Communist Party/USA, responded to Pope John XXIII's encyclical on peace (1963) with lengthy "Notes" sent first to Communist Party leaders and then to many Catholic universities and periodicals.[9] The first major encounter (to my knowledge) of Marxists and Christians occurred in July 1965 at a Christian summer camp for World Fellowship in New Hampshire. The initiative came from Dr. Willard Uphaus of World Fellowship, working in cooperation with Herbert Aptheker of the then newly established American Institute of Marxist Studies (A.I.M.S.). It brought together several well-known U.S. Marxists and Christians, including Aptheker and Howard Parsons on the Marxist side, and Fr. Quentin Lauer, S.J., Harvey Cox, and others from a Christian perspective.

Almost all the initiatives for subsequent dialogues have come from academicians at private universities and theological seminaries or from church groups. The most significant of these initiatives will be noted in the next section, but special note should be made at the outset of the efforts of Professor Paul Mojzes of Rosemont College in Pennsylvania who revitalized Christian-Marxist encounters in the late 1970s with the support of Christians Associated for Relationships with Eastern Europe (C.A.R.E.E.) and of Professor Charles West of Princeton whose promotion of dialogue spans several decades.

GENERAL DESCRIPTION OF
THE ENCOUNTERS

Types of Encounter

Most dialogues in the United States resulted from individual initiative. The encounters have not followed any "plan" of development set down by church, government, or party officials. Consequently any attempt to classify them will be somewhat arbitrary and must admit of many exceptions. But the encounters do fall, very roughly, into three types and periods: 1) 1965–72: dialogues about the world views represented in Christianity and Marxism; 2) 1972–77: action-oriented encounters based on opposition to capitalism; 3) 1977–84: dialogues on issues of peace and social justice. The first and third types deal with more formal dialogues in which intellectuals were the main participants. The second type, which really should not be enclosed by any end date, involves Christian and Marxist activists.

1965–72: Dialogues About Christian and Marxist World Views. The New Hampshire dialogue initiated by Dr. Willard Uphaus in June 1965 focused on the Marxist critique of religion,[10] as did many other dialogues in this first period. The University of Notre Dame hosted several internationally prominent Marxists and Marxist scholars (Karl Kosik, Gajo Petrovic, Maximilien Rubel, Herbert Marcuse, Robert Tucker, and so forth) at a symposium in April 1966.[11] Christian-Marxist dialogues in Europe played a very direct role in many of the first U.S. encounters. French Marxist Roger Garaudy came to the United States in December 1966 at the invitation of Herder & Herder, publishers of his *From Anathema to Dialogue*. His dialogues on the East coast and in St. Louis centered on points of convergence or conflict in Christianity and Marxism.[12] The U.S. Committee for the Christian Peace Conference, founded in 1965, brought Milan Machoveč to the United States, and it worked with the Presbyterian mission office COEMAR to arrange dialogues, in 1968, involving Czech Marxists Vítězslav Gardavsky and Julius Tomin.

Numerous other dialogues followed with U.S. Christians and Marxists involved. The University of Santa Clara sponsored a symposium on Marxist humanism in October 1967 with Herbert Aptheker, John Somerville, Hal Draper, Robert Cohen, Louis Dupré, and Michael Novak among the speakers. The Chicago Theological Seminary sponsored lectures by Jürgen Moltmann, Charles West, Sidney Lens, and others (later published in *Openings for Marxist-Christian Dialogues*, ed. Thomas Ogletree). Aptheker felt that the Chicago lectures had often misrepresented Marxist views on religion, and he published his own work, *The Urgency of Marxist-Christian Dialogue* (1970), in response. The Society for the Study of Marxism discussed Christianity and Marxism at several of their annual meetings. Christianity and Marxism all but coalesced at a Temple University conference in April 1969, with participants united in their attacks on institutionalized religion and capitalist ideology.[13] It was still a conference of intellectuals (Herbert Marcuse, Richard Shaull, and others), but it marked a shift toward a stress on action. This shift was suggested also by the title of a new book, *From Hope to Liberation: Toward a New Marxist-Christian Dialogue*, which recorded a dialogue held at Wright State University in 1972, organized by Nicholas Piediscalzi and Robert Thobaben.

1972–77: Action in Opposition to Capitalism. Events in Latin America very much influenced a new type of Christian-Marxist encounter. Many Christians in Latin America, outraged by poverty and oppression in their countries, believed that they had much to learn from Marxism (a conviction expressed by many "liberation theologians"), and some felt they should actively collaborate with Marxists in working for socialism (a position taken by the Christians for Socialism, founded in Chile in 1972). They perceived capitalist imperialism as their enemy, and they argued that Marxist analysis could be used without embracing Marxist atheism and philosophical materialism.

One direct consequence of these events in Latin America was the establishment in 1974 of a Christians for Socialism movement in the United States. The links with Marxism are explicit in CFS. The national executive-secretary Kathleen Schultz described CFS as rooted theologically in the biblical tradition and "ideologically in the Marxist critique both of capitalism and religion."[14] This kind of Christian-Marxist encounter differs, quite obviously, from the dialogues described in the first period. The encounters with Marxism here are not formal dialogues but an ongoing process of internalizing and synthesizing elements of both Christianity and Marxism toward the goal of achieving a democratic Socialist society. Other action-oriented encounters have occurred: in the "Theology in the Americas" movement (begun in the mid-1970s), in the much-older Methodist Federation for Social Action, in the Episcopal Church and Society Network, among some Christian members of the Democratic Socialists of America, and through church groups working in solidarity with liberation struggles in Central America. The degree of encounter with Marxism may vary considerably in such groups. A few (like CFS) may collaborate directly with Marxists. Many other groups may borrow from Marxist analysis in working for social justice but may disagree with many tenets and tactics in Marxism. The action-oriented encounters continue on, but a new series of more formal dialogues was initiated in 1977. These new encounters have more in common with the dialogues of the 1960s, except that they have focused less on world views and more on sociopolitical issues of common concern.

1977–84: Dialogues on Issues of Peace and Justice. Paul Mojzes deserves the major credit for initiating a new series of formal Christian-Marxist dialogues beginning in the late 1970s. Working with two peace institutes in Austria, Mojzes codirected an international symposium on peace in January 1977 at Rosemont College. The symposium drew many participants from the Soviet Union, Eastern and Western Europe, the United States, and Canada. Charles West was the principal Christian speaker; the major Marxist speaker was Yuri Zamoshkin of the Soviet Union. A similar international symposium on peace took place in Detroit in September 1980, arranged by the late Prof. Max Mark of Wayne State University.

Three North American dialogues, sponsored by C.A.R.E.E. (an ecumenical program related to the National Council of Churches), have focused on U.S. socioeconomic problems. The first, again initiated by Paul Mojzes and held at Rosemont College in May 1978, dealt with the U.S. socioeconomic order. Its Marxist speakers (Michael Harrington, Victor Perlo, Dick Roberts) reflected the wide spectrum of political views that exist within Marxism. The second North American dialogue met in Dayton, Ohio, in February 1980, with Nicholas Piediscalzi and Robert Thobaben as principal organizers. The conference theme was "dehumanization" and Christian and Marxist speakers were paired off in effective dialogue (Rosemary Radford Ruether and Bettina Aptheker, Harvey Cox and Bertell Ollman, J. Deotis Roberts and George Novack). At the third conference, again under the leadership of Piediscalzi and Thobaben, in May 1982 in Washington, D.C., Christian and Marxist speakers once more paired off to discuss "work," and James Will, president of C.A.R.E.E., addressed the group on the Catholic Church in Poland.

Numerous other dialogues might be mentioned: for example, "A Day of Dialogue" in Minneapolis in October 1981; a seminar at Valparaiso University in June 1982; a symposium on Christianity and Marxism at Santa Clara in October 1983; a conference on Marx's critique of religion at Marquette University in April 1984. The list could be much longer; Howard Parsons alone engaged in several other encounters, and many additional dialogues occurred during the 1983 centennial of Marx's death.

Ground Rules for the Encounters

Paul Mojzes and Howard Parsons have both written about rules and conditions for dialogue.[15] The rules noted by Mojzes include: both partners must have a need for dialogue; do not stereotype; interpret your partner's view in its best light; be open to constructive criticism and avoid destructive criticism; face issues which cause conflict, but emphasize those things upon which partners agree.

The structure of most of the dialogues, with dialogue "partners" as a frequently used format, has permitted mutual sharing. The dialogues at the Second North American Conference in Dayton (1980) reached an extraordinary level of give-and-take intercourse using this format. Speakers addressing each other (not just the audience) and the greater possibility for informal discussion outside formal talks accounted for this success.

How much "self-criticism" has been involved in these dialogues? Many Christians feel that they are far more open to accept criticism and to engage in self-criticism than are Marxists. Harvey Cox raised this issue, asking "whether Marxism is now ready to examine its own sources with real historical candor and rigorous critical precision." "Is it ready to apply the historical-critical method to its own documents?"[16] One does find Aptheker making reference to the "aberrations, crimes, and failures that have marked the course of the history of socialism," and he affirms that such blows require reexamination.[17] But many Christians would still argue that they have carried self-criticism much farther than their Marxist counterparts.

What we have stated about ground rules applies primarily to the more academic dialogues in 1965–72 and 1977–84. The action groups operate from a different basis. Christians and Marxists may find themselves together, for example, in protests against U.S. military aid in El Salvador or in peace demonstrations. But rarely, if ever, is such collaboration the result of formal agreements. It might be noted, finally, that Christian-Marxist encounters in the United States have been conducted openly and legally without government interference. Religious or private institutions, which have most often hosted encounters, have been relatively free in doing so. Some of the initial dialogues met with vigorous protests from alumni and people in the area, but most of the dialogues occurred without incidents.

ISSUES

To attempt to summarize the many books and hundreds of pages of unpublished talks which have emerged from these dialogues would entail writing a complete volume, and simply to list the many topics considered in the course of these dialogues would serve little purpose. What follows instead is a selective discussion of some of the more critical issues and interesting exchanges.

Religious-Philosophical Issues

A central issue in Christian-Marxist encounters has been the Marxist critique of religion. The young Marx, prior to any commitment to socialism, rejected belief in God as a form of servility. Engels's dialectical materialism stressed atheism as a "scientific" explanation to replace religious superstitions about the creation of the world and human life. But their most distinctive critique centered on religion as "alienation," as a reflection of human misery which also reinforces the misery by pacifying the oppressed and justifying the status quo. From this critique a fundamental question arises: Does the Marxist critique of religion constitute a fundamental obstacle to any real and ultimate reconciliation of Christianity and Marxism? The dialogues suggest differing responses to this question both on the Marxist side and from the Christian side.

Most Marxists have traditionally viewed atheism as an essential tenet of Marxism. Christian and Marxist world views are thus totally incompatible, though this would not preclude practical collaboration. George Novack of the Socialist Workers Party expressed this dominant view quite forcefully at a dialogue in Dayton (1980). "As a materialistic and atheistic doctrine and as a scientific method, dialectical materialism is fundamentally incompatible with and opposed to the mysticism, irrationalism and superstition at the heart of religion."[18] Christianity, he continued, offers an illusory and false picture of reality and human nature, and in practice it diverts people's attention and energies from the tasks required to change the world radically. But having made quite clear "the irreconcilable opposition of the philosophy of Marxism to all forms of religion," Novack did say that Marxists must respect individual religious beliefs and freedom to worship and that Marxists are prepared to collaborate with religious groups on progressive causes, as exemplified in Nicaragua.

Herbert Aptheker represents a very different U.S. Marxist perspective, one that he contends is based on a true understanding of the writings of Marx and Engels. To understand the Marxist critique of religion properly, says Aptheker, one must make a key distinction between the Marxist understanding of religious *feelings* and of religious *institutions*.[19] The source of religious feelings lies in a sense of awe and wonder, of helplessness and misery. The source of religious institutions lies in class divisions and in state power which uses religion for the maintenance of its power. Aptheker believes that the Marxist critique is much more respectful of religious feelings, which have sometimes played a very progressive role in history, than of religious institutions which have consistently served as a bulwark of the status quo.

Religious institutions have justified slavery, denigrated women, and served as apologists for oppressive regimes. Religious feelings, though born out of a sense of helplessness, have at times provided motivation for social protest, and Aptheker cites numerous examples from U.S. history (Thomas Jefferson, John Brown, Nat Turner, A. J. Muste) to illustrate this point. Aptheker therefore rejects the view that religion has been simply "the opium of the people." He argues, moreover, that Marx himself, in the passage from which this famous phrase was drawn, "emphasizes the protest potential of religion; he emphasizes its beauty, and its source of refreshment."[20] Aptheker then offers a solution for reconciliation. Let both Christians and Marxists work together to change the world. With the achievement of a truly human society, either Marxism will prove correct and religion will disappear, or Marxism will prove wrong and religion will continue. Neither will suffer except by being proven wrong.[21]

From the Christian side, differing views can also be cited. Most Christians would agree with Novack that Christianity and Marxism are ultimately incompatible. Quentin Lauer, S.J., presents a very nuanced view of this position. He believes that contemporary Marxists can, if they wish, go beyond Marx's critique and that in the course of history a reconciliation of Christianity and Marxism is possible and certainly desirable. But he does not believe, as Aptheker does, that such a reconciliation can be based on Marx's own critique of religion. Lauer bases his argument on an understanding of "dialectics." A *Hegelian* dialectic could lead to reconciliation because it does not cancel out the poles in the dialectic (in this case Christianity and Marxism). The Hegelian dialectic recognizes a partial truth in each; hence a true synthesis is one which affirms and preserves the partial truth in each. But Lauer sees the *Marxist* dialectic as one that posits total triumph of one element in the dialectic over the other. Just as class struggle will end with the triumph of the proletariat and the abolition of the capitalist class, so the struggle against religion must lead to its disappearance. "There is no conceivable God that would be acceptable" to Marx, says Lauer, for "any being in any way superior to man is simply inconceivable."[22]

Harvey Cox approached the problem differently at a dialogue years later (Dayton). His purpose was not to respond to the question posed at the outset of this section, as to whether an ultimate reconciliation of Christianity and Marxism is possible. Cox sought rather to examine the validity and the limits of the Marxist critique. He recognized that the structures of consciousness in existing religions have been shaped by historical conditions. Religions are, in some measure, social products. They have served to maintain repressive attitudes and regimes. But in Marx's own less-quoted phrases that religion is "the heart of the heartless world" and "the sigh of the oppressed creature," Cox found a very positive role that religion has played in the lives of oppressed peoples. Religion has enabled poor peoples to survive suffering and to celebrate in spite of suffering. In some cases, moreover, their class consciousness may depend on religion. Cox therefore called for a dual critique of religion, exposing its use for domination, but appreciating its use in giving dignity to the poor.

At an earlier symposium at Rosemont (1978), Max Stackhouse carried the issue still further. He challenged Marxists on their failure to see the pervasive and powerful influence of religion in U.S. society, where 92 percent of the populace say they are religious and 64 percent say they belong to some church or religious organization. One can hardly expect any popular movement to take hold in the United States that runs counter to all religion.

From the Christian side, then, would come a call for Marxists to deepen and further the examination of the very nature of religion which Aptheker has begun. Religion may be a social product, but does that prove God is illusory (for Marxism is itself a social product)? Does belief in God make humans inferior and relegate human actions to an inferior status (a God-versus-man dichotomy)? Or can belief in God be a source that enriches and ennobles human creativity, as many Christians believe that it does? And might not the Marxist critique of religion apply now to Communist regimes that use Marxism as an ideology with which to resist social change and to justify the status quo?

Anthropological-Sociological Issues

If Christians and Marxists are critical of each other, they share a common concern for overcoming social evils in the world—unemployment, the dehumanization of work, racial and sexual discrimination, poverty, and so forth. Most of this section will be devoted to dialogues on two of these issues. But we might also briefly note an "anthropological" issue that influences their outlooks on these social issues. Marxists are motivated by a very concrete historical hope—a classless society (communism) toward which socialism marks a first stage. Some Christians share in this Socialist vision; all share in the hope for a more just and human society. But Christians also posit an ultimate religious hope, one which recognizes that no human society will ever be free of alienations, and one which sustains life even in the face of repeated defeats and failures.[23] Inherent in these two views of hope are divergent views of human nature. Marxists tend to stress the perfectibility of humanity and the capacity of social transformations to change individual attitudes and behavior. Christians find an inherent sinfulness in human beings which will remain in spite of social change and which sets limits on what social transformations can achieve. But dialoguing Christians and Marxists agree that certain social changes, whatever their limits, can and should be undertaken. Both recognize sexism and racism as problems.

Sexism. At the 1980 Dayton symposium, Christian theologian Rosemary Radford Ruether and Marxist activist-scholar Bettina Aptheker agreed in judging that Christianity had reinforced or ignored sexism while Marxism had failed to recognize the inadequacy of its analysis in dealing with sexism. Feminist groups in the United States, Ruether acknowledged, have too often focused on problems of women from more privileged classes. Christian women's groups in Latin America, on the other hand, have focused primarily on class antagonisms caused by oppressive economic conditions. But, Ruether responded, women from the lower classes suffer even greater dehumanization because they are subject to both class and sexual discrimination. They are exploited at work, relegated to service, cleaning, and auxiliary jobs with consistently lower wages. They are exploited at home as unpaid "reproducers" of the work force. They take on the burden of bearing, nursing, and nurturing children; they also provide rest and recuperation for their husbands (meals, laundry, and so forth). Christianity, by idealizing this service role of women, has really sacralized women's servitude. Ruether also criticized Socialist countries which, despite gains in employment opportunities for women, still have not reversed the service role of women at home. For most working women this amounts to four extra hours of work.

Bettina Aptheker gave high marks to Socialist countries in terms of equality in work and wages, and she praised their elimination of pornography and of most crimes of violence against women. But she found fault with Marxist social analysis in respect to women. Marx focused on social relations of production; he failed to analyze the social relations of *reproduction*. Man is seen as the worker shaping the world; woman is seen only in relation to man. Social relations of production are challenged by Marx as historically determined and hence transformable; but social relations of reproduction are treated as "natural." Marxism needs to examine, then, the roots of women's special alienation. Aptheker then spelled out in detail the many ways in which women are exploited and subjugated both at work and at home.

Racism. As to the fact of racism in the United States and its dehumanizing effects, Christians and Marxists are in agreement. But convergence beyond this point remains difficult, as the Dayton conference made clear. Marxist George Novack argued that the basic reason for the subjugation and suffering of blacks is, and has been, economic. Hence, while he recognized the special sufferings that racism adds to economic exploitation, he would give priority to the struggle against capitalism. The black Christian theologian J. Deotis Roberts challenged this priority claiming that "race and not class is the root cause" of the group suffering of blacks. Hence the elimination of racism must be the top priority for blacks. They differed even more sharply, however, in their appraisal of the role of black churches. Roberts felt that Marxism was alienated from the popular culture and religion of blacks, and he believed that leadership in the struggle against racism must come from within the black churches. Novack questioned this confidence in black churches, for he saw black church leaders as divided in their commitment to change the economic system. He felt that socialism needed no recourse to religious ideas or motivations.

The dialogue reported above reflects the distance that has long prevailed between Marxism and the black church. Even black liberation theologians maintained this distance until quite recently. But a shift has occurred in the last few years. Cornell West, addressing "Black Theology and Marxist Thought," has noted three important points of convergence between black theology and Marxism: (1) they share a common dialectical methodology which is critical of ideologies; (2) both are committed to liberation; (3) both engage in social criticism of prevailing society. West feels that blacks should follow Marxists in analyzing the links between economic exploitation and racism. But he faults most Marxists for failing to acknowledge the positive, liberating aspects of popular culture and religion.[24]

James H. Cone, the most prominent of the black liberation theologians, has attempted recently to reassess the whole relation of black theology to Marxism and socialism, a relationship which he acknowledges has been marked by a long history of mutual indifference. Cone notes the many reasons why blacks have ignored Marxism: Marxism is atheistic; it was viewed as a "white" movement; Marxists have often ridiculed black preachers as ignorant and superstitious; Marxist socialism so stressed the economic as to make racism only a secondary problem. If Marxists are to dialogue, says Cone, they must recognize the uniqueness of black oppression and they must recognize the distinctive contribution made by the black church to the struggle for a new society. But Cone also calls upon the black church and black theologians to dialogue with Marxists and to learn from socialism. He feels that blacks need to look to new visions of the social order and to consider democratic socialism as an alternative to capitalism.[25]

Economic-Political Issues

Internal differences within Christianity and within Marxism affect all dialogue issues to some extent, but they are especially significant in the discussion of economic issues. At a level of closest agreement between Christians and Marxists one could cite two volumes produced as study/action guides by several pro-Socialist Christian groups. These two volumes, *Must We Choose Sides?* and *Which Side Are We On?* explain Marx's historical materialism, expose the "myths" of capitalism, challenge capitalist ideology, and analyze crises engendered by capitalism.[26] At the other end of the spectrum one finds Christians convinced of the superiority of capitalism. Thus John J. Murphy, a Catholic economist speaking at a Rosemont dialogue in 1978, affirmed: "The economic history of the past two centuries suggests that the free enterprise system is the best model for providing an optimum socioeconomic system." Capitalism, he admitted, has created inequities of income and power, but he feels that these could be overcome through legislative reforms. Robert Benne voiced similar views in a dialogue at

Valparaiso University in June 1982, and in his book *The Ethic of Democratic Capitalism* (1981).[27]

Most Christians who participate in the dialogues probably fall somewhere between the two positions just noted. They are critical of both capitalism and Marxist socialism. Thus John Cort, at a 1982 dialogue in Washington, D.C., argued for a Christian democratic socialism which rejects the state ownership characteristic of Communist regimes but calls for worker cooperatives and for measures to give workers more decision-making power.

Marxist critiques of capitalism were expressed in talks given at Rosemont (1978) and in Washington, D.C. (1982). Victor Perlo pointed to the many signs of crisis in the U.S. system: a slowing down of economic growth, inflation, high unemployment, and so forth. Lee Dlugin attacked the growing power of multinational corporations which she argued now control one-third of the capitalist world's industry, one-half of its trade, and nine-tenths of its foreign investment. Exxon's operations abroad, she noted, make up 81 percent of its operations. U.S. bank assets abroad grew from $12.4 billion in 1967 to $219.4 billion in 1977. Dick Roberts focused on concentration of corporate wealth and income in the United States. In 1975 one percent of U.S. taxpayers received 45 percent of dividend income. He presented a detailed study of the wealth and control still concentrated in a few capitalist families (for example, the Mellons, DuPonts, and Rockefellers) to challenge the myth of wide dispersal of corporate ownership and power.

The major political issue which emerges out of this economic debate concerns state power. Critics of Marxism argue that the very efforts to achieve freedom in Communist countries have led to authoritarian regimes because the issue of state power under socialism was never fully analyzed in Marxist theory and has ended with single-party rule in practice. Marxists, in turn, challenge the supposed separation of the economy from the political. Analyses of state power in the United States, they argue, reveal the dominance of the capitalist class at every level of important decision making: millionaire presidents and cabinet members, a Congress made up almost exclusively of members from the business class or professions, powerful lobbies representing giant corporations.

International Issues

The issue of peace and the avoidance of nuclear war has been the subject of at least two international dialogues in the United States (at Rosemont in 1977 and at Detroit in 1980). Distinguished Marxist scholars from the Soviet Union and other countries and Christian theologians from various nations participated in both dialogues. Both sides consistently stressed the gravity of the nuclear war issue. Both sides spoke of peace as a fundamental value in their respective heritages. From the Christian side, Charles West spoke of God's reign as one characterized by peace and justice (cf. Isa. 2:4). From the Marxist side, Yuri Zamoshkin argued that the Soviet Union's desire for peaceful coexistence was an essential doctrine for Lenin, has been proclaimed by recent Communist Party congresses, and is supported by the Soviet people at every level. Both sides in the dialogue stressed the importance of promoting mutual understanding to lessen the differences which could lead to war, and many detailed proposals were made on how to limit and reduce nuclear armaments.

The issues of Christianity and Marxism in Latin America and of U.S. foreign policies toward Latin America have also done much to stimulate Christian interest in Marxism. U.S. theologians have debated the influence of Marxism on liberation theology. Politically involved Christians have argued about U.S. government interventions based on stopping the spread of Marxism in Central America. But these Latin American issues, though frequently discussed within the church, have not figured as prominently in the more formal dialogues which have been the primary focus of this chapter.

STATUS AND PROSPECTS

Christian-Marxist encounters still constitute a very small ripple on the sea of events in the United States. Marxism does not play the significant role in U.S. society which it does in Europe. The influence of Marxism and Marxists in U.S. universities has grown considerably over the last decade or so, but Marxist intellectuals are far more interested in economics and politics than religion. The few Marxists who have shown a sustained interest in dialogue, people like Herbert Aptheker and Howard Parsons, are now familiar figures.

Even among Christians the number interested in formal dialogue remains small. But the issue of Marxism itself has occasioned considerable "internal" debate within the church. More Christian interest in Marxism has probably resulted from discussions on Latin America and uses of Marxist analysis on social issues than from formal dialogues. But a surprisingly large number of dialogues have occurred over the past twenty years, with many of them drawing hundreds in attendance.

What have the dialogues achieved? Few of the formal dialogues were intended to lead to any collaborative action. They have brought greater understanding of Marxism to many Christians, and may have led some Marxists to a greater appreciation of the continued vitality of Christianity. What kind of future lies ahead for Christian-Marxist encounters? Certainly many Christians will continue to study Marx's thought and to use elements of

Marxist analysis in their work for social justice. More Marxists may be moved to reevaluate the nature and importance of religion. Formal dialogues in the past have resulted from the concrete initiatives of people willing to accept responsibility for organizing them. The future of the dialogues will most likely also depend on such initiatives. Whatever the future may bring, Christian-Marxist dialogues in recent years already constitute an interesting chapter in American history.

NOTES

1. James Oliver Robertson, *American Myth, American Reality* (New York: Hill & Wang, 1980).

2. Michael Harrington, *Socialism* (New York: Bantam Books, 1972), chapter 6, and Jerome Karabel, in *The New York Review of Books,* 8 February 1979, pp. 22–27.

3. Charles H. Hopkins, *The Rise of the Social Gospel in American Protestantism, 1865–1915* (New Haven: Yale University Press, 1940).

4. Gordon Harland, *The Thought of Reinhold Niebuhr* (New York: Oxford University Press, 1960), 236.

5. Godfrey Hodgson, *America in Our Time* (New York: Vintage Press, 1978), chap. 4, especially p. 76.

6. *The Documents of Vatican II,* ed. Walter M. Abbott, S.J. (New York: America Press, 1966), from "The Church Today" *(Gaudium et Spes),* n. 21.

7. *The Church Amid Revolution,* ed. Harvey Cox (New York: Association Press, 1967), contains many of the essays prepared for the Geneva conference.

8. For a recent study of the impact of Marxism on U.S. academic life, see Bertell Ollman and Edward Vernoff, *The Left Academy: Marxist Scholarship on American Campuses* (New York: McGraw-Hill, 1982).

9. Gus Hall, "Catholics and Communists: Elements of a Dialogue," *Political Affairs: Journal of Marxist Thought* (June 1964).

10. The New Hampshire talks were published later in *Marxism and Christianity,* ed. Herbert Aptheker (New York: Humanities Press, 1968).

11. The Notre Dame papers were published in *Marxism and the Western World,* ed. Nicholas Lobkowicz (Notre Dame, Ind.: Notre Dame University Press, 1967).

12. One dialogue resulted in a book: Roger Garaudy and Quentin Lauer, S.J., *A Christian-Communist Dialogue* (Garden City, N.Y.: Doubleday & Co., 1968).

13. Papers from the Temple conference were published in *Marxism and Radical Religion: Essays Toward a Revolutionary Humanism,* ed. John Raines and Thomas Dean (Philadelphia: Temple University Press, 1970).

14. See Kathleen Schultz, IHM, "Christians for Socialism: U.S. History & Perspectives," in *Which Side Are We On?* (Oakland, Calif.: Inter-Religious Task Force for Social Analysis, 1980), 172–74.

15. Paul Mojzes, in *Varieties of Christian-Marxist Dialogue,* ed. Mojzes (Philadelphia: Ecumenical Press, 1978), 10–11. See also Howard Parsons in *Revolutionary World,* vols. 41/42, 1982, Part I on dialogue. The whole double volume is devoted to Parsons's views on "Marxism, Christianity, and Human Values."

16. Harvey Cox, "The Marxist-Christian Dialogue: What Next?" in *Marxism and Christianity*, ed. Aptheker, 24.

17. Herbert Aptheker, *The Urgency of Marxist-Christian Dialogue* (New York: Harper & Row, 1970), 30.

18. The talks from many of the U.S. dialogues reported in this section were not published, so I am not able to cite references though I worked with drafts of the talks.

19. Aptheker, *Urgency of Marxist-Christian Dialogue*, 1.

20. Herbert Aptheker, "Marxism and Religion," in *Marxism and Christianity*, ed. Aptheker, 33.

21. Aptheker, *Urgency of Marxist-Christian Dialogue*, 21.

22. Quentin Lauer, S.J., "The Atheism of Karl Marx," in *Marxism and Christianity*, ed. Aptheker, 48.

23. Thomas W. Ogletree, "What May Man Really Hope For?" in *From Hope to Liberation: Towards a New Christian-Marxist Dialogue*, ed. Nicholas Piediscalzi and Robert B. Thobaben (Philadelphia: Fortress Press, 1974), 42–43.

24. Cornell West, "Black Theology and Marxist Thought," in *Black Theology: A Documentary History, 1966–1979*, ed. Gayraud S. Wilmore and James H. Cone (Maryknoll, N.Y.: Orbis Books, 1979), 552–68.

25. James H. Cone, *The Black Church and Marxism: What Do They Have to Say to Each Other?* An occasional paper published by the Institute for Democratic Socialism (853 Broadway, New York, N.Y.) in April 1980.

26. *Must We Choose Sides?* and *Which Side Are We On?* Study/action guides by the Inter-Religious Task Force for Social Analysis (464 Nineteenth Street, Oakland, Calif. 94612) in 1979–80.

27. Robert Benne, *The Ethic of Democratic Capitalism: A Moral Reassessment* (Philadelphia: Fortress Press, 1981). See also Michael Novak, *The Spirit of Democratic Capitalism* (New York: Simon & Schuster, 1982).

SUGGESTIONS FOR FURTHER READING

Aptheker, Herbert, ed. *Marxism and Christianity*. New York: Humanities Press, 1968.

Garaudy, Roger, and Quentin Laurer, S.J. *A Christian-Communist Dialogue*. Garden City, N.Y.: Doubleday & Co., 1968.

McGovern, Arthur F. *Marxism: An American Christian Perspective*. Maryknoll, N.Y.: Orbis Books, 1980.

Ogletree, Thomas W., ed. *Opening for Marxist-Christian Dialogue*. Nashville: Abingdon Press, 1968.

Piediscalzi, Nicholas, and Robert G. Thobaben, eds. *From Hope to Liberation: Towards a New Marxist-Christian Dialogue*. Philadelphia: Fortress Press, 1974.

SECOND WORLD ENCOUNTERS

POLAND

James E. Will

HISTORICAL SETTING

Only Poland in Eastern Europe has a context for Christian-Marxist encounter defined by the equivalent, yet quite different, strength of the two partners.[1] The Marxists have had unlimited political power through the Polish United Worker's (Communist) Party and the support of the Soviet Union since 1948. The Roman Catholic Church has virtually unlimited sociocultural power because of its millennium-long identification with the Polish nation. No political party can hope to govern Poland, to say nothing of creating a new socioeconomic form for its people, if it does not have at least the tacit cooperation of the church.

It is the peculiar reality of this balance of power between Christians and Marxists in Poland that explains why the first formal Christian-Marxist dialogue to emerge in post–World War II Europe took place there. Paul Mojzes expresses some astonishment over this fact in his comprehensive history *Christian-Marxist Dialogue in Eastern Europe:*

> Poland provides the earliest instance of [formal] Christian-Marxist dialogue in the world! This comes as a surprise because heretofore my conclusion, as well as other researchers, have pointed to Italy, France, Czechoslovakia, and the Paulus Gesellschaft dialogues as the earliest instances, dating back to 1964. It is now obvious that the dialogue started in Poland as early as 1956, but certainly by 1962 reached a developed form.[2]

Though the precedence of the Polish dialogue may have been little noted for several decades, the events of the last several years have brought it to worldwide attention: the election of Karol Cardinal Wojtyla of Kraków as Pope John Paul II on 16 October 1978, his "pilgrimages" to Poland in 1979 and 1983, the emergence of the independent trade union Solidarity in 1980 with the support of the church, and the continued influence of the church even under and beyond martial law.[3]

All of this reflects the institutional strength of the church. Over 90 percent of the thirty-five million Polish people are Catholics, including about 1 percent who are Greek Catholics; 2–3 percent are Orthodox or Protestant; and a small number belong to other sects or religions. Nonbelievers in this Marxist-Leninist state comprise only 5–7 percent of the total population. Public opinion polls taken by sociologists of religion indicate strong personal involvement in the Christian faith. In 1968 there were 86.6 percent deeply involved believers; ten years later the result was almost exactly the same, with the polls showing 86.4 percent.[4]

Sociocultural Context

Catholic religious symbols provide much of the substance of Polish culture. Myths of origin in the Christian creation stories correlate with stories of national origin in the baptism in 966 of the Piast prince who united the Polish tribes. A Christian understanding of redemption underlies the powerful myth of the Virgin of Czestochowa, who for six hundred years has been looked to as the queen and protectress of Poland.

The Communist-led government sought to blunt the church's celebration of the millennium of Polish Christianity in 1966 by declaring a boycott of church-sponsored festivities and staging rival national celebrations. Their conspicuous failure demonstrated the impossibility of separating the church and Christianity from the Polish national tradition and led to a loss of face for the party and Gomulka, its first secretary.[5] The martial law government made no such mistake in the celebration of the six hundredth anniversary of the Madonna of Czestochowa in 1982–83.

The Catholic substance of Polish culture is affected, however, by a critical, intellectual spirit deeply grounded in Enlightenment traditions. The German Protestant theologian Paul Tillich once called this the "Protestant principle." But Cardinal Wojtyla, writing in 1972 on the implementation of Vatican II, quotes the "Decree of Ecumenism" to make this point: "Christ summons the church, as she goes her pilgrim way, to that *continual reformation* of which she always has need, insofar as she is an institution of men here on earth."[6] Though the Polish episcopate maintains a slow tempo of reform, it is not insulated from the cultural dynamics of the Polish people. The new primate, Archbishop Joseph Glemp, said in an interview in the nationwide weekly *Polityka* two months after he assumed his responsibilities:

> The church is a part of the society which it serves and—as I have already said—carries a lot of characteristics of the society. The Polish church does not have to fear democracy, since democracy is the most beautiful gift of the twentieth century. It convinced us that people are equal, that they can speak out, and that the will of the majority needs to be accepted.[7]

The cultural dynamic of Poland, however, is more largely in the hands of its intelligentsia. The characteristic features of the old Polish intelligentsia continue strongly: attachment to ideas of freedom, intellectual tolerance, a romantic concept of honor, and a sense that they constitute a bulwark of Western and Christian culture against "Asiatic forces."[8] The Communist Party has accepted the services of this intelligentsia without being able to absorb them ideologically. The spread of education, with nearly four times as many attending secondary and academic schools in the mid-1970s as prior to 1939, has broadened and augmented their influence. An outburst of artistic creativity—especially in poetry, theater, and cinema—in postwar Poland gained and deserved worldwide attention.

Political satire and social criticism have been important elements in recent Polish literature. No author is better known for this than Leszek Kolakowski, once professor of philosophy at the University of Warsaw and now at Oxford University in England. He began as a convinced Stalinist and by 1958 his *The Priest and the Jester: Toward A Marxist Humanism* criticized all "priests," whether religious, Communist, or capitalist, who dogmatically supported the status quo. Kolakowski favored the "jester," who maintains a skeptical attitude toward any absolute.

Kolakowski's early choice of "priest" to characterize all authoritarian dogmatism indicates his rejection of the church at this point. His judgment about religion has changed, however, until today he recognizes it to be one of the few guarantors for the continuance of human culture and community. Adam Michnik names Kolakowski as the model for the Polish secular left.[9] His development was representative for this small group of Polish intellectuals on the radical left who now see Christians as supporters of the human rights they seek for a democratically Socialist Poland.

A far larger proportion of the Polish intelligentsia are more directly identified with the Roman Catholic Church than they are with the radical left. Because the Communist government has not allowed institutional pluralism, the intelligentsia have had to make a basic choice between the official Marxism of the state and the Christian tradition of the church. The vast majority have chosen the church. Sociologist Professor Wladyslaw Piwowarski of the Catholic University of Lublin has studied this phenomenon as part of the development of what he calls "selective religiosity." Over 30 percent of the Polish people selectively form their attitudes as Catholics (religious individuals who practice more or less frequently but do not adhere unconditionally to the doctrines or guidance of the church).[10] The intelligentsia fall largely in this group. Their understanding of the Polish national cultural tradition includes both the substance of the Catholic faith and a long-valued emphasis on tolerance. They protect Polish national culture while refusing to dogmatize its traditional forms.

Motives like these led fifty-two prominent intellectuals in January 1978 to organize a "Society for Scientific Courses" to offer the "unfalsified" understanding of history necessary for mature citizens to cooperate in a democracy. By May 1978, more than 120 classes had been held with up to one hundred participants in each session. The Polish episcopate supported these "initiatives which seek to present the cultural creativity of the human spirit and the history of the nation in an authentic form."[11]

The official Marxist response was highly ambivalent. The government, on the one hand, sought to severely limit, if not destroy, these alternative "schools." On the other hand, well-placed Marxists in the universities welcomed what they called an authentic "dialectics of culture." The election in 1978 of Cardinal Wojtyla as pope led Professor Kuczynski of the University of Warsaw to write in an essay on the potential of his pontificate:

> The actual cultural power of Christianity as well as the social impact of Marxism can prove to be of benefit to communities and mankind. . . . Thus, the point is to cooperate in full awareness of both the differences and the essential philosophical discrepancies. . . .
> I am therefore all for turning to advantage and developing the actual dialectics of culture: the creative power of socially united people who have adopted ontological orientations that exclude each other.[12]

Professor Kuczynski took the same position in November 1977 in addressing the Third National Meeting of the Society for the Propagation of Lay Culture, an organization of 250 thousand members: "Something great, something of historical importance, occurs in the Christianity of our time. Something great is happening within Polish Catholicism." He invited Christians to full participation and cooperation with Marxists "for the common social good in building a truly humanistic society."[13]

Political-Economic Context

The public form of the political-economic context in Poland is well known. It is largely determined by the political process rooted in decisions made at Yalta and Potsdam following World War II. Poland and other Eastern European nations were given to the Soviet sphere of influence. Given the Soviet fear of Germany, it was inevitable that Poland would be built into a military buffer zone between the U.S.S.R. and Western Europe. It is appropriately called the "Warsaw Pact" because Poland, given its geopolitical position, plays a central role in it. Control of its transportation and communication systems is crucial to the logistics of any military action between the Soviet Union and NATO on the European central front. This front is probably the best equipped battlefield in the world today. As long as this military security system prevails in Europe, the Soviet Union will do everything necessary to maintain Poland as an "ally."

The instrument for maintaining this alliance has been the Polish United Worker's Party, created in 1948 from the union of the Communist and Socialist parties with Soviet support. The Communist Party in Poland has never had sufficient ideological or political authority to govern without the external support of the U.S.S.R. and the direct or tacit support of other, often more powerful, social forces in Poland.[14]

The tacit consent of the church was essential, for without it the Communists would only have been able to govern genocidally. Between 1945 and 1947, the Roman Catholic Church retained greater freedom than churches in other Eastern European countries. The nationalist defection of Tito in Yugoslavia in 1948 brought about the Soviet-led overthrow of Gomulka's nationalist leadership in Poland in September 1948 and the "Stalinization" of Poland from 1949 to 1956, culminating for the church in the house arrest of its primate, Stefan Cardinal Wyszinski, from September 1953 until October 1956.

Even during this dark period, a bridge to the church was maintained through the lay Catholic organization Pax, under the highly ambivalent leadership of Boleslaw Piasecki. With Stalin's personal consent, Pax was given an economic base that guaranteed its existence and the support for a range of Catholic publications unknown in the rest of Eastern Europe. The original quid pro quo by Pax was unquestioning ideological support for the regime, but Pax slowly moved ideologically over three decades from the support of Stalinist policies to a point where it gave unqualified support to Solidarity in 1980–81. This culminated in its president, Ryszard Reif, Piasecki's successor after his death, speaking against the imposition of martial law in the Council of State on 13 December 1981.

With the restoration of Gomulka to power in 1956, two other lay organizations emerged to share Pax's function of mediating between church and state: the Christian Social Association, separated from Pax at that time, and Znak, made up of Clubs of Catholic Intelligentsia. All three have an independent economic base, a range of publications, and representation in the parliament. From 1956 to 1980, Pax remained closest to the government, Znak closer to the Roman Catholic episcopate, while the Christian Social Association sought ecumenically to include non–Roman Catholics in its membership. A dispute in 1976 over the amending of the Polish Constitution led to a division in Znak in 1977 whereby ODISS (Center for Documentation and Research) became the center for the renamed "Polish Clubs of the Catholic Intelligentsia" and was given Znak's entire representation in the parliament. The political functions of ODISS were reorganized and transformed into the Polish Catholic Social Union in March 1981.

The Polish episcopate, however, has needed no one to represent it in articulating the social teaching of the church. While bishop of Lublin, Cardinal Wyszinski, before becoming primate, had taught Catholic social ethics in the University of Lublin. Cardinal Wojtyla remained professor of ethics in the Catholic University of Lublin until his election as pope. Though no publication of Catholic social teaching was possible in Poland until 1967, when John XXIII's *Pacem in terris* was published, ODISS now has published all of the social encyclicals in several volumes and commentary upon them in their journal *Christ in the World*.[15] Cardinal Wyszinski gave a series of nineteen lectures in Warsaw on the meaning of the human rights teaching of *Pacem in terris* shortly after its publication, and on the tenth anniversary of *Pacem in terris* the episcopate held a symposium on the realization of human rights as a necessary condition of both domestic and international peace.

Following Vatican II, the Polish church made much use of *Gaudium et spes*, the "Pastoral Constitution on the Church in the Modern World." Cardinal Wojtyla's publication in 1972 of *U Podstam Odnowy* (translated and published in English in 1980 as *Sources of Renewal: The Implementation of the Second Vatican Council*) played an important role in this process. Thus when the General Council of the Episcopate met at the height of the Solidarity crisis on 26 August 1980, they could base themselves on the universal teaching of the church in calling for acceptance of the right of workers to organize independent unions. Section 68 of *Gaudium et spes* had long since taught, "Among the basic rights of human persons must be counted the right of freely founding labor unions . . . [and] taking part freely in the activity of these unions without fear of reprisal."

Popular attention to the economic crisis in Poland since the strikes of 1980 and the emergence of the independent labor union Solidarity has also made the precarious economic context in Poland well known in its major outline. During the 1970s, the regime led by Eduard Gierek undertook a rapid industrial expansion, largely dependent on Western capital and technology, to create millions of new jobs for Poles born in the post–World War II population boom. The first half of the decade went fairly well, but the inflation of energy costs and the recession in the West in the second half of the decade played havoc with their plans. At the end of the decade some factories begun eight to ten years before were not yet functioning. The sale of goods in the West to repay borrowed capital lagged. A 50 percent deficit in international trade developed. A cutback on essential imports—even medicines and components for medicines—had to be instituted, and a larger proportion of production intended for domestic consumption had to be designated for export.

These difficulties caused great dissatisfaction with the bureaucratic, centralized planning and administrative apparatus of the party and government. The result was the strikes of 1980 with their demand for democratic participation in the planning and administration of the Polish economy. The strikes were not a new phenomenon; Poland's history had been punctuated with similar events in 1956, 1968, 1970, and 1976. Attempts to solve the crisis by negotiation, in which the church played a major mediating role, led only to a stalemate between an increasingly desperate Communist bureaucracy holding onto local and regional power positions and an increasingly radicalized Solidarity now demanding political change. The result was the declaration of martial law on 13 December 1981, the internment of Solidarity's leaders and activists, and the suspension of the union.

Martial law provided no solution to any of Poland's fundamental problems, recognized by even the Communist Party as a political crisis of trust in the system and an economic crisis of the breakdown of labor discipline and productivity. Thus the government and party tried to carry through some of the economic reforms discussed with Solidarity before its suspension.

The parliament adopted an economic reform bill in January 1982 to be implemented during a cycle of changes over the next five to eight years. Amongst its stated aims are "active participation of employees in the process of management" and response to "social needs manifesting themselves in the form of market demand," while "protecting the basic principles of the socialist socioeconomic system."[16] Workers' self-management in state enterprises is envisaged, to complement the self-management already present in cooperatives. Cooperatives, in turn, are to "regain the rank of a fully independent branch of the economy," and the private sector is to be enlarged and strengthened. Workers' Councils elected by secret ballot are to make all decisions of crucial importance for the enterprise, including choosing the director of the enterprise, except in those enterprises of crucial importance such as railways, airlines, and certain large industrial enterprises.[17] Under continuing conditions of worker alienation, however, the phasing in of worker self-management is proceeding very slowly, and it remains to be seen whether this reform program will succeed.

Whatever is accomplished must be seen in part as the result of a long process in which many have contended for the necessity of dialogical participation of all in the society. Immediately after the demonstration in March 1968, for instance, the Znak representatives in parliament called upon the government to cease repressing the demonstrations and to create "the possibility of dialogues with the population."[18] They complemented the position taken by the Polish episcopate on 21 March 1968 that "all the problems that divide persons today must be resolved through deepened dialogue and not force."[19] Such teaching of a genuinely national church sometimes bears fruit even in the most complex and problematical political and economic processes.

THE ACTUAL DIALOGICAL ENCOUNTERS

Three recent essays on the history of Christian-Marxist dialogue in Poland are now available in English—one by a Polish Catholic theologian, a second by a Polish Marxist philosopher, and a third by a North American Methodist historian of religion. The most accessible is by Professor Stanislaw Kowalczyk, professor in the Catholic University of Lublin, who published an essay "On the History of Christian-Marxist Dialogue in Poland" in *Dialectics and Humanism* 5:3 (1975). It was republished by ODISS as the last chapter in a volume on *Z problematyki dialogu chrzescijansko-marksistowskiego* (Problems of Christian-Marxist Dialogue) in 1977 and updated and republished by IDOC (Rome, 1979) in its Europe Dossier No. 7, *Poland: Church Facing Socialism*. It provides the best periodization of the dialogue from the standpoint of the Christians involved:

1. Period of polemical discussions (1944–48);
2. Period of minimal coexistence; absence of dialogue (1949–56);
3. Period of spontaneous and mass dialogue (1956–58);
4. State of constructive dialogue (1959–present [1979]).

Professor Paul Mojzes in his definitive history *Christian-Marxist Dialogue in Eastern Europe* (Minneapolis: Augsburg Publishing House, 1981) adopted this periodization for his own interpretation of the Polish experience.

Professor Janusz Kuczynski, editor of *Dialectics and Humanism*, published his essay on "Marxist-Christian Dialogue" in the spring 1974 (1:2) issue of that journal. It appears again in the collection of essays he published in 1979, *Christian-Marxist Dialogue in Poland*. His Marxist periodization is based on the more progressive attitudes he sees developing in the Roman Catholic Church. He defines the dialogue from a "historical-class" perspective as "a form of adaptation of Christianity to the conditions of contemporary civilization," interpreted as the "complex, long and difficult period of transition from capitalism to socialism."[20] Thus his periodization comprehends only two stages: 1) a period of "political" dialogue during the shaping of a Socialist political community;[21] and 2) the second and higher stage of "humanist" dialogue, aimed at the enrichment of man through "mutual exchange of values."[22] He looks forward to a third and highest stage not yet really begun, a "dialogue of truth" that will go beyond the "pluralism of nonantagonistic values" toward a "synthetic unity."[23]

For Christians in Poland the self-confidence of Professor Kuczynski's Marxist perspective, with its Hegelian hope in a historical-eschatological synthesis, gives an "absolutist" bent to the Marxist posture that makes dialogue difficult, if not dangerous. Therefore, a sociopolitical periodization shapes the historical perspective of the Christians involved, differentiated largely by the degree of democratization achieved within a society under Communist rule, which allows for more pragmatic discussion of social values and policies.

The immediate postwar period of 1945–48 under a coalition government of Marxist and non-Marxist parties was a period of polemical dialogue carried on impersonally through the Catholic and Marxist press. Jan Piwowarczyk and Jerzy Turowicz were the principal Catholic protagonists publishing in the Catholic weekly *Tygodnik Powszechny*. They critiqued Marxist philosophy, sociology, and ethics, while defending the philosophical bases and ecclesial expression of the Christian faith. Adam Schaff was one of the principal Marxist respondents and published in *Kuznica*. Though these early exchanges were formally substantive, there was little attempt to discriminate between elements of the various perspectives that might provide some basis for cooperation. The concern on both sides was to demonstrate the superiority of one system over the other.[24]

The overthrow of Gomulka as first secretary of the Communist Party in September 1948, the unification of the Socialist and Polish Worker's (Communist) Parties in December 1948, the purging during 1949 of one-fourth of the party members who had shared Gomulka's views, the installation of the Soviet Marshal Konstantin Rokossovsky as commander of the Polish armed forces, the arrest of Gomulka in August 1951, and finally the arrest of Cardinal Wyszinski in September 1953 consolidated Soviet control over Poland and made dialogue impossible. Though the Polish episcopacy concluded an unprecedented agreement with the government in 1950 without the Vatican's blessing, it was soon violated in this period of increasing repression.

The death of Stalin in March 1953, followed by the publication in Poland of Khrushchev's dramatic speech to the 20th Party Congress of the U.S.S.R. in February 1956 denouncing Stalin's terrorist rule, set the stage for the worker's uprising that brought Gomulka back to power in October 1956. Spontaneous, massive discussions between Christians and Marxists immediately followed. Students of the philosophy departments of Warsaw University and Lublin's Catholic University organized "debates." Representatives of these universities met in January 1957 to discuss the social function of philosophy and again in April 1957 to debate their understanding of "matter." Discussions also again appeared in the press, but now jointly organized by the editorial boards of *Tygodnik Powszechny* and the Marxist periodical *Po Prostu*, on the meaning of humanism, the role of religion, and the necessity of tolerance and cooperation. Professor Kowalczyk's evaluation of this lively period of 1957–58 is ambivalent:

> After the period of misunderstandings and hostility, the need for mutual contacts and discussions was acknowledged. It should be admitted, however, that the discussions held at that time were excessively chaotic as regards their subject matter. . . . Haste did not add to the profundity of the discussion.[25]

A period of "constructive dialogue" followed, which Professor Kowalczyk sees as beginning in 1960 and continuing for the next two decades. It is not possible to review all of the shifts in the sociopolitical contexts during this period, but it may be noted that the dialogue continued during and after the shift of political power from Gomulka to Gierek in 1970, brought on by the student uprisings of 1968 and the worker's strikes of 1970. The importance and necessity of Christian-Marxist dialogue and cooperation were now firmly established in Poland.

ISSUES ILLUMINED THROUGH CONSTRUCTIVE ENCOUNTERS

A more analytic approach to the Christian-Marxist encounters during this stage of constructive dialogue must be taken. Tadeusz Mazowiecki, leader in the Warsaw Club of Catholic Intellectuals, sometime member of the Polish parliament representing Znak, recently chief editor of the national newspaper of Solidarity until interned, wrote when he was chief editor of *Wiez:*

> There are three components in a dialogue: persons, the means of communication, and values. A conversation can limit itself to information, a discussion to different perspectives on a controversy, and cooperative work may be reduced to purely pragmatic activity. But the dialogue consists of a reciprocal sharing of values.[26]

The courage and creativity of persons like Mazowiecki, despite a continuing history of tragic difficulties, have given the Polish dialogue precisely this creative character of reciprocally shared values. The social strength and religious integrity of the Polish church has allowed this process to be reciprocal, despite the totalitarian character of the Communists' political power. Indeed, a slow erosion and transformation of the totalitarian form of Polish politics has been one of the precarious results of the dialogue.

Political Issues

One of the crucial moments in the political dialogue grew out of the questions that the five Znak deputies in the parliament publicly addressed to Prime Minister Jozef Cyrankiewicz on 16 March 1968 concerning the brutal repression of the students in the University of Warsaw during the demonstrations of a week before. Amongst the five deputies were two who continued to play vital public roles: Mazowiecki in Solidarity and Zablocki in ODISS and the Polish Catholic Social Union. They asked the government what it planned to do to stop the brutality of the militia and to bring those responsible to justice; and what it planned to do to solve the causes of the problems that led to the unrest and to answer the questions of the youth concerning the culture policy of the government as it relates to democratic-civic freedoms.

Though these five Catholic deputies did not directly represent the church, the episcopate entered the public dialogue in a similar way in their statement of 21 March 1968. Responding to the "painful and disturbing events" that occurred in university centers during the previous several weeks, the bishops said:

> Social relations must be so regulated that the fundamental rights of the individual and the society are recognized. These rights are the right to truth, freedom, justice, and love. All problems that divide persons today must be resolved through a deepened dialogue and not with force.[27]

The immediate response was the ridicule of the Znak deputies by the Communist parliamentary elite and the accusation of the church for giving moral support to "anti-Polish" forces. But a much-larger part of the Polish population again took the struggle to the streets in the massive worker uprisings of December 1970. Again, the first response of the government was repression through the security forces and the army, with forty-five killed and 1,165 wounded according to official sources. This time, however, the principle of political dialogue finally won a telling victory. The historian M. K. Dziewanowski describes how top party leaders came to Szezecyn on Sunday, 24 January 1971, to dialogue with the workers:

> The first secretary of the central committee, the prime minister, the minister of the interior, and the commander-in-chief of the armed forces all had to appear before the workers and spend some ten hours, from 4 p.m. to 2 a.m., negotiating with them in a free and most outspoken dialogue.... No other Communist regime had experienced a similar phenomenon.[28]

The historical fact that it was in Poland that a Communist government for the first time resorted to negotiation to resolve outstanding issues may properly be seen as a political result of its dialogue with Catholic forces both in and outside of the government. The fact that the successor Gierek regime was increasingly committed to dialogue with the church and other social forces may be seen as a confirmation of that judgment. Some of what was sought in 1968 was partially achieved: censorship was decreased, the works of certain writers previously suppressed were published, funds allocated to scholarly research were dramatically increased, and scholars were invited to advise the party and government.[29]

Difficult problems remained unresolved during the Gierek era, however, as was dramatically revealed by the worker uprisings of August 1980. Yet it was a victory for the principle of political dialogue that this time there was no violent repression and the result was the emergence and legal constitution of the first independent union in a Communist-governed country. Martial law dealt a grievous blow to this practice of political dialogue, but it remains to be seen whether it can be sustained through and after martial law. The church has continued resolutely to call for it. And General Jaruzelski said to the parliament on 25 January 1982 in its first session under martial law:

> Cooperation between the state and the Catholic Church, and other beliefs, belongs to permanent principles. . . . The dialogue continues. We are sincerely interested in it. . . . I believe that the permanent contacts between the government and the church will enable all misunderstandings that arise to be cleared up.[30]

The sanguine belief that all misunderstandings will be resolved remains unproven. But it remains to be seen whether the genuine progress of political dialogue achieved during the last two decades in Poland may yet continue and perhaps even prevail.

Religious Issues

The Polish church's success in helping to establish the principle of dialogue in Polish politics is in part the result of the Polish Marxists concluding that the classic Marxist view of religion is not generally valid. Christian faith was increasingly recognized as authentically motivating social conduct in a way that must be respected. We have seen that as recently as 1974 Professor Kuczynski could interpret the Christian participation in the Polish dialogue as largely an "adaptation" to the Socialist reality now established. But he published a very different judgment in 1979:

> However, on reading the works of Teilhard de Chardin, Maritain, and others, but above all on reading the documents of the Second Vatican Council, the Marxists find with satisfaction that Marx's statement ["Religion is the opium of the people"] has lost its validity as a generalization.[31]

An encounter that led to important reassessments of the contributions of Christianity to social values on the part of Marxists, and vice versa, was a conference on "Philosophy and Peace" held in January 1972. Mieczyslaw Gogacz, a professor at the Academy of Catholic Theology in Warsaw, contended that a philosophy of peace depends on an adequate anthropology, which he presented in terms of an existentially modified neo-Thomism. Janusz Zablocki argued that the Christian view of peace in John XXIII's *Pacem in terris* and Paul VI's *Populorum progressio* transcends ideology and provides the basis for common work for peace. According to Kowalczyk's report, Marxist Professors Tomaszewski and Dobrosielski of Warsaw University "expressed agreement with many of the statements by Catholic participants in the conference, emphasizing the need for the philosophers' engagement in sociopolitical activity."[32]

The changed religious situation in Poland may also be seen in the number of Christians who joined the Polish United Worker's Party. Sociologists of religion in the Academy of Catholic Theology reported in 1980 that 70 percent of the ruling party's three million members were Catholic believers and 50 percent of them were practicing. What was thought to be characteristic only of the "Eurocommunism" of the Communist Party of Italy is true also for Poland. Both Communist parties dropped any commitment to metaphysical materialism and atheism from their statutes so that many Christians joined. The high percentage of Catholic membership in the Polish party has declined, however, since the events of 1980–81.

The emergence of ODISS in the early 1970s added a clearer doctrinal dimension to the religious discussion. ODISS understands its function to be the interpretation of the Catholic social teaching. Both the hierarchy of the church and the party leaders have given some support to this effort. The government transferred some economic support from the Znak journal *Wiez,* then edited by Mazowiecki, to ODISS. Zablocki had been the deputy editor of *Wiez* before founding ODISS; but he and some leaders in both the church and government saw this journal as compromised by too close an association with the radical lay left. The struggle for freedom and human rights was now given a more doctrinal mode of expression.[33] It was expressed no longer in philosophical principles and values that might unite the church with secular humanists but in the doctrinal/ethical teaching of the Vatican.

The danger seen by some is that this could lead the church to a too-easy compromise with the government for the sake of institutional religious liberty. On the other hand, the integrity and courage of ODISS's commitment to more broadly realized human rights may be seen in that all five of their deputies voted against the declaration of martial law when it was submitted to the parliament on 25 January 1982.

It remains to be seen whether or not the introduction of Catholic doctrine more clearly into the dialogue shall provide a better basis for creative encounter. In any case, it gives an integrity to the Catholic position that protects them from the charge, if not entirely from the danger, of political opportunism.

Philosophical-Anthropological Issues

Christian-Marxist dialogue in Poland inevitably dealt with anthropological issues. At the very beginning this was part of the polemical dialogue. Jan Piwowarczyk argued in *Tygodnik Powszechny* (21 October 1945) against the "anthropological monism" of Marxism, contending that the dependence of psychic processes upon biological-neurological processes does not mean their existential identity.[34] Amongst those who answered him polemically at that time was Adam Schaff. The post-1956 period of de-Stalinization in Poland allowed Schaff to recover the more humanistic writings of the young Marx. He made full use of this recovery to write *Marxismus und das menschliche Individuum,* which became available to Western readers in German translation under this title in 1965. Iring Fetscher, a member of the Marxism Commission of the Evangelical Academies in West Germany, expressed astonishment over its openness and humanism when he reviewed it in 1966:

> Before everything else, the book is noteworthy because of its author. Adam Schaff is the leading ideologist of the Polish United Labor Party and a member of its Central Committee. Until now, however, hardly a leading member of one of the ruling Communist parties has so emphatically defended the matter of individual freedom and the humanism of the young Marx as has Adam Schaff.[35]

Fetscher's surprise is a measure of the relative creativity of the Polish dialogue on anthropological issues. Though conservative members of the Central Committee criticized Schaff for turning away from fundamental principles of Marxism-Leninism, P. K. Raina, a graduate student from India then studying at the University of Warsaw, reported that 90 percent of the faculty and students of the University of Warsaw agreed with a humanistic interpretation of Marxism similar to those of Schaff and Kolakowski.[36]

Tadeus Jaroszewski, another leading Marxist philosopher, took up the anthropological dialogue more directly with Christian thinkers in his 1970 volume, *Osobowosc i Wspolnota* (Personality and Community), finding the anthropology of Emmanuel Mounier and Pierre Teilhard de Chardin especially useful for advancing the dialogue with Marxist thinkers. Stanislaw

Kowalczyk, then a docent at the Catholic University of Lublin, began to make his literary contribution to the dialogue at this point with two essays on "The Social Character of Man as a Basis for Christian-Marxist Dialogue" and "The Marxist and the Christian Concept of Freedom," published in *Collectanea Theologica* in 1971 and 1972, respectively. Though radical ontological differences remain, especially in the understanding of human freedom, Kowalczyk saw developing convergence in understanding the social nature of man, the reality of self-determined action in existential freedom, the existence of objective and subjective limiting conditions of human freedom, and the importance of civic freedom for developing an authentic humanism.[37]

Given this brief insight into the substantive character of the anthropological dialogue during the decade of the 1970s, one can accept the sincerity of Kuczynski's sentiment expressed at the end of the decade after the election of Pope John Paul II:

> Teilhard de Chardin gave the phrase "comrade Marxists," which he frequently used, a sympathetically ironic twist. Should it not be our task to struggle toward a situation in which the Marxists could address their opponents with the phrase "brother Christians" with nobody wincing?[38]

STATUS AND PROSPECTS

The terrible tensions still manifest in Polish society indicate how ambiguous are the prospects of Kuczynski's hope that the encounter in Poland may soon take the form of dialogue between "comrade Marxists" and "brother Christians." The difficulty of Poland's geopolitical position magnified by the differences in Christian-Marxist traditions and the present terrible alienations in the society require realism about the tragic possibilities inherent in the present situation.

Yet the strategy of the leadership of the church is to seek resolution of the alienations through dialogue. Archbishop Glemp expressed this beautifully in a sermon preached in Rome on 7 February 1982:

> We are confident that with God's help, we will be able to explain to ourselves the reasons for our anger, in a dialogue, and not by force. Poland must not become an arena of bloody confrontation. No one must be allowed to manipulate our wrath, because the people want to shed this illness of rage all by itself, and emerge all in one, and be healed.[39]

The identification of the Polish church with the entire Polish nation, including its Communist leadership, is eloquent in this statement. The church intends the Polish people to be "one and healed."

If the church is to contribute to the dialogical resolution of these tragic alienations, it must remain willing to allow the Marxists to contribute to their critical reflection about modern individualism in industrial societies.[40] The teaching of the church's magisterium, now articulated by a Polish pope, has affirmed that individual rights may never take precedence over, but must always serve, the common good. The common good in Poland may only be worked out in dialogue with the Marxist's understanding of social justice.

The foundation for such creative dialogue has been laid during the last two decades. There are grounds for realistic hope that the new social and economic forms precariously emerging from the struggles of 1980–82 may yet shape a geniune *commune bone* for Poland. The converging anthropological perspectives we have noted must now be translated into concrete agreements on political and economic structures and processes that may maximize free participation in a Socialist society while accepting the necessary limitations on human freedom for the common good.

It is no easy task anywhere to achieve a working consensus on where the necessary limits to individual freedoms are. They differ contextually from society to society and age to age. The task is the more difficult in Poland because of the heightened degree of alienation in the society. But the grounds for hope that it may be accomplished lie in the unity of the Polish people, the commitment to reconciliation of the Polish church, the realism and moderation of the Polish United Worker's Party, and the wisdom that has grown in the tradition of Christian-Marxist dialogue in Poland.

NOTES

1. Only Romania approximates the Polish situation, because of the great religious and social strength of the Romanian Orthodox Church which embraces 80 percent of the population. But the Orthodox Church's understanding of its "symphonic" relation with the state does not foster the differentiation requisite for dialogue.

2. Paul Mojzes, *Christian-Marxist Dialogue in Eastern Europe* (Minneapolis: Augsburg Publishing House, 1981), 73. The claim to be "earliest in the world" is somewhat exaggerated. Certainly the work of Christoph Blumhardt, Leonhard Ragaz, Paul Tillich, and other "religious socialists" done prior to World War II must be recognized as earlier forms of Christian-Marxist dialogue. But the Polish dialogue is the earliest in post–World War II Europe.

3. When General Jaruzelski, as prime minister, first secretary of the Communist Party, and chairman of the Military Council, addressed the Parliament on 25 January 1982 for the first time after declaring martial law, he said, "Cooperation between the State and the Catholic Church and other beliefs belongs to permanent principles" (press release from Consulate General of Poland in Chicago).

4. Cf. James Will, *Must Walls Divide?* (New York: Friendship Press, 1981), 16, 72–77.

5. Cf. M. K. Dziewanowski, *Poland in the 20th Century* (New York: Columbia University Press, 1977), 191.

6. *Unitatis redintegratio*, 6, quoted in Wojtyla, *Sources of Renewal*, trans. P. S. Falla (San Francisco: Harper & Row, 1980), 328, emphasis added.

7. *Polityka* 31, (31 July 1981); translated in *Ch SS Information Bulletin* 9 (September 1981): 31.

8. Cf. Dziewanowski, *Poland in the 20th Century*, 250–54.

9. Adam Michnik, *Die Kirche und die polnische Linke: von der Konfrontation zum Dialog* (Munich: Kaiser Verlag, 1980), 172.

10. Cf. the Piwowarski essay in Will, *Must Walls Divide?* 77.

11. Reported by Hans-Hermann Hüeking and Tadeusz Swiecicki in the "Afterword" to Michnik, *Die Kirche*, 230.

12. Included as the first essay in Kuczynski's *Christian-Marxist Dialogue in Poland* (Warsaw: Interpress, 1979), 27.

13. Ibid., 57.

14. Stalin's liquidation of several hundred leading Polish Communists from 1936 to 1938 is well known and greatly weakened the Polish party. Cf. Dziewanowski, *Poland in the 20th Century*, 96–97. The Polish Worker's (Communist) Party had only twenty thousand to thirty thousand members when it began to exercise power in 1945.

15. Cf. Joachim Kondziela, "Chancen und Möglichkeiten katolischsozialen Denkens in der polnischen Gesellschaft," in *Christliche Soziallehre unter verschiedenen Gesellschaftsystemen*, ed. Rauscher (Cologne: J. P. Bachem Verlag, 1980), 38–53.

16. Office of Government Plenipotentiary for the Economic Reform, *The Polish Economic Reform* (Government Press Office, 1982), 5.

17. Ibid., 13–15.

18. Cf. Michnik, *Die Kirche*, 82–83.

19. Ibid., 75, 77.

20. Kuczynski, *Christian-Marxist Dialogue in Poland* (Warsaw: Interpress, 1979), 39, 41.

21. Ibid., 43.

22. Ibid., 44-46.

23. Ibid., 47.

24. Cf. Kowalczyk, *Poland: Church Facing Socialism* (Rome: IDOC International, 1979), 77–80.

25. Ibid., 81.

26. Quoted in Michnik, *Die Kirche*, 165, translation mine.

27. Quoted in ibid., 75, translation mine.

28. Dziewanowski, *Poland in the 20th Century*, 207.

29. Ibid., 211–12.

30. Press release from the Consulate General of Poland in Chicago of excerpts from a speech of General W. Jaruzelski to the Polish Sejm, 25 January 1982. U.S. newspapers did not report this section of the speech.

31. "To Elevate the World: The Potential of John Paul II's Pontificate," in Kuczynski, *Christian-Marxist Dialogue in Poland*, 17.

32. Kowalczyk, *Poland*, 91.

33. Cf. Michnik's very critical interpretation of this development in *Die Kirche*, 157–62.

34. Kowalczyk, *Poland*, 78.

35. Iring Fetscher, in *Literaturblatt* 30 (5 February 1966).

36. *Neues Forum* (März, 1967), 213.

37. Cf. Kowalczyk, *Poland*, 88–90.

38. "To Elevate the World," in Kuczynski, *Christian-Marxist Dialogue in Poland*, 30.

39. Quoted in the *New York Times*, 8 February 1982.

40. Cf. John Longan, "Human Rights in Roman Catholicism," *Journal of Ecumenical Studies* (Summer 1982): 34–35, for articulation of the "church's struggle with modern individualism and liberalism" as a "challenge of the near future" for all Roman Catholic teaching on human rights.

SUGGESTIONS FOR FURTHER READING

Dziewanowski, M. K. *Poland in the 20th Century*. New York: Columbia University Press, 1977.

IDOC International. *Poland: Church Facing Socialism*. Europe Dossier No. 7. Rome, 1979.

Kuczynski, Janusz. *Christian-Marxist Dialogue in Poland*. Warsaw: Interpress, 1979.

Michnik, Adam. *Die Kirche und die polnische Linke: von der Konfrontation zum Dialog*. Munich: Kaiser Verlag, 1980.

Will, James. *Must Walls Divide?* New York: Friendship Press, 1981.

Wojtyla, Karol (Pope John Paul II). *Sources of Renewal: The Implementation of Vatican II*. Translated by P. S. Falla. San Francisco: Harper & Row, 1980.

EAST GERMANY
Stephen P. Hoffman

As both the chief of state and general secretary of the Socialist Unity Party (SED), Erich Honecker is clearly the most powerful person in the German Democratic Republic (GDR). On 13 June 1980 he assumed a new responsibility: chairman of the Martin Luther Committee, a body charged with directing the state's celebration of the five hundredth anniversary of Luther's birth. In his speech inaugurating the committee, Honecker referred to Luther as "one of the greatest sons of the German people" and declared that a "common appreciation of the personality and work of Martin Luther in our state reflects the cooperation of our country's citizens without regard to world view and religion." On the platform with Honecker was Bishop Werner Leich, representing the East German Evangelical Church.[1] He commented in his own speech that it seemed unusual not only for the highest representative of the Socialist state to be honoring Luther but also for a bishop to be speaking at a state-organized event.[2]

In Communist East Germany, as in the other Eastern European states which emerged from World War II under Soviet-dominated regimes, both religion and national tradition were considered threatening to the new order. The early postwar view of Luther was in keeping with this. He was portrayed as the source of everything that destroyed Germany: an early advocate of chauvinism and counterrevolution.[3] Antireligious policy included the establishment in 1954 of the *Jugendweihe* (youth dedication), a pseudo-religious ceremony intended to supplant confirmation. This was part of an effort to promote Marxism-Leninism as a desirable world view and the state as the object of primary loyalty.

While the GDR shared in major developments affecting the other Soviet client-states, its unique geopolitical situation required that it function in a policy environment very different from that of its Communist neighbors. It was forced to compete for legitimacy with a rival state which actively promoted religion and the national cultural heritage of which religion was a part. Moreover, the porous border in Berlin made it relatively easy for dissatisfied East Germans to opt for the alternative. Consolidating the new state and remolding its society was therefore particularly difficult for the SED.

After the death of Stalin, most Eastern European regimes sooner or later instituted reforms aimed at eliciting a greater degree of active support from their respective populations. Such efforts included a reversal of previous patterns of neglect or hostility toward national history and culture, as well as a shift toward a policy of coexistence with the churches. In 1952 East German historians began to identify certain aspects of tradition as "progressive." This turnabout eventually led to a reassessment of Luther, who by the time of the officially sponsored celebration of the four hundred fiftieth anniversary of the Reformation in 1967 had long since ceased to be regarded as a spiritual ancestor of Hitler. Despite the conflict over the *Jugendweihe*, East German churches were never completely cut off from organizational relations with the West. They were able to receive substantial contributions from their counterparts in the Federal Republic, an important source of support that had no equal elsewhere in Eastern Europe.

As the GDR celebrated its twentieth anniversary in late 1969, more and more East Germans were coming to terms with their government. In part this was simply a recognition that the erection of the Berlin wall left them no option. But it was also the result of a growing pride in their economic and social achievements, especially in comparison with both their Communist neighbors and their own recent past. This sense of accomplishment was to some degree enhanced by resentment at being patronized by West Germans. Recognizing the need to accommodate political reality, East German Lutherans in 1969 reorganized themselves into a new body: the "Federation of Evangelical Churches in the German Democratic Republic" (the *Bund*). In so doing, they withdrew from the West German–dominated Evangelical Church of Germany (EKD).

Churches in the GDR have never enjoyed the privileges of those in the West. In the Federal Republic, a "church tax" is levied on most citizens and the funds accumulated are distributed proportionately among the Catholic and Protestant churches. Parochial education and church-based special interest organizations, such as youth groups, carry on their activities without state interference. In the East, the government actively promotes a secular religion in such a way that practicing Christians are often discriminated against in education and employment. Membership in Protestant churches has dropped from nearly fifteen million in 1950 to about six million today, and less than 20 percent of these attend church regularly. The number of baptisms and church weddings has also declined, as has participation in confirmation.

To a large extent this is due to the fact that church involvement is socially and politically disadvantageous in Communist states. But the decline can also be attributed to the secularization that has thinned the ranks of practicing Christians in Western Europe. Nevertheless, the Evangelical Church in the GDR is a conspicuous and active organization. As the East German state has matured, tolerance and even qualified support of the church has become normal.

The state radio carries a weekly Sunday church service, and the church publishes many periodicals and books, including Bibles. The regime spends millions of marks each year in subsidies for theological education at state-controlled universities. A limited form of conscientious objection is possible, a rarity in the Communist world. As in West Germany, the state looks to church welfare institutions to provide significant social services, although its funding of these programs is inadequate.[4] Regional church conferences have attracted as many as fifty thousand participants. In 1972 the state began referring to church members as "Socialist citizens of a Christian persuasion," signifying its concern to integrate them into the political community.

By the early 1970s the Evangelical Church leadership had settled into a pattern of cooperation with the regime within which the church could take advantage of what opportunity there was to minister to its members and to the society as a whole while still maintaining its independent, Christian identity. The church sought to affirm the basic legitimacy of the state and to support its policies whenever they seemed to coincide with the advancement of Christian principles. Bishop Albrecht Schönherr, head of the *Bund,* stated that "the church will oppose all attempts to militate against the state." Congregations were reminded that while God was certainly above the state he ordained even Socialist states to maintain order. A refusal to accept the situation would lead not only to fruitless opposition but also to a kind of self-imposed persecution and individualistic self-pity that prevents Christians from taking advantage of very real opportunities for ministry. In short, God gave Christians the capacity to live even in a Socialist state that was officially atheistic in its ideology.[5]

Speaking to the 1977 synod of the Evangelical Church in Saxony, Bishop Johannes Hempel urged his listeners to recognize that social prominence was not necessary for the church to fulfill its mandate. He acknowledged that many were frustrated by the fact that the church in postwar East Germany no longer enjoyed the social recognition, political support, and wealth in numbers and assets that it once had. But he pointed out that it was inconsistent with biblical teaching to assume that a viable church could exist only when it had the backing of the establishment. Hempel also stated that while Christians in the GDR had difficulties with the state, these difficulties paled in comparison with the desperate plight of the many suffering in certain

Third-World countries. Moreover, he added, improvement in religious conditions was possible in the GDR through frank discussions between church and state.[6]

Church-state dialogue received a major boost four months later when *Neues Deutschland*, the organ of the SED, featured the unprecedented "summit meeting" of Honecker with Schönherr and Bishop Werner Krusche of Magdeburg on its front page. This meeting signified at least a general acceptance by the government of a formula that had already gained general acceptance in church circles to describe the church's relation to the state: neither against socialism nor for socialism, but merely within socialism.[7] The church has taken pains to avoid any appearance of political opposition. For example, it maintains many unofficial contacts with state social workers, promoting cooperation so as not to give the impression that the church is trying to work outside of the system in order to demonstrate that it can solve problems which the state cannot. The dissident folk singer Wolf Biermann had begun meeting with young people in churches before he was forced into exile in 1975. Most church leaders were sympathetic to the letter of protest that a number of well-known East German intellectuals and artists sent to the regime after Biermann's ouster, but none signed. They feared that to do so would be to open the church to charges that it was becoming involved in organized political opposition.[8]

The regime's concept of what the church in socialism ought to be is reflected in the attempt by the East German Christian Democratic Union (CDU) to connect Christianity with socialism as interpreted by the SED. As do minor political parties in other Eastern European states, the CDU functions as an auxiliary of the Communist party. Its purpose is to elicit the active support of a particular constituency, in this case church members. Wolfgang Heyl, chairman of the CDU's parliamentary faction, surely was representing the regime's conception of the ideal Christian when he stated that

> the verdict which a Christian bestows upon a particular society will depend upon the degree to which the basic Christian precepts can be fulfilled in that society. From a social point of view, the most important Christian precepts are without doubt those of peace on earth and love of one's neighbor. Christians in the GDR see that the Socialist state provides the social guarantees enabling civil and Christian duties to converge towards a common aim to ensure peace and solidarity and to work for the well-being of man.[9]

Evangelical church leaders in the GDR do seek opportunities to affirm their support of the government's expressed commitment to such principles as peace and human rights. However, their conception of the church's orientation to the state is very different from that of the CDU. It has been aptly termed "critical solidarity," described as "accepting the responsibility for the proper ordering of society and at the same time retaining [the] right to evaluate the actions of government and individuals in the light of the gospel."[10] Under Honecker the government began increasingly to deal with the church directly rather than through the channel of the CDU. In so doing, the state has accepted in principle the church's position that, while it aims to contribute to the overall health of the society, it must maintain a degree of distance from the state. However, the state interprets this sphere of independence as being delimited by the requirements of SED policy. This suggests Rousseau's concept of the subordination of particular wills to a general will. In the SED's ideal *polis*, public policy in the GDR proceeds according to a unanimously approved direction, arrived at as a result of extensive discussions in which all elements of the community are represented. Once agreement is reached, there can be no opposition to policies pursued in service of such a consensus.

The Marxist-Leninist corollary to Rousseau's proposition is that there is one party to the discussion which is uniquely qualified to determine just how the particular wills are to be combined by virtue of its knowledge of the "laws of history" and its position as representative of the whole people. Thus Heyl asserts:

> the party of the working class [the SED] possesses the scientific social theory through which socialism can be established and further developed. Following logically from the commitment of Christians to socialism is their recognition that the working class and its Marxist Leninist party is the leading political force in shaping the new society. *This is an objective necessity and no matter of opinion.*[11]

The implication for the church is clear. Its independence allows it to preserve religious practice, to avoid political involvement, and even to contribute to the discussion of political questions that are related to those ideals to which it is committed in common with the state. But insofar as the church chooses to be involved in political discussion, it has no right to criticize policy once direction has been established under the SED's "guidance." Heyl drove home the point with a convenient quotation from an East German bishop: "It is not up to the church to proffer advice, let alone give instructions as to what political decisions should be taken and how this should be done."[12] Recent church-state conflict attests to a difference of opinion over what constitutes political interference, or what Gerald Götting, chairman of the CDU, has termed "attempts to misuse Christian belief or church institutions against socialism."[13]

Serious differences arose over the ridicule of Christian beliefs in the schools and over the church's promotion of disarmament and of tolerance for conscientious objection. The church's position has been essentially conservative, appealing either to legal rights or to commonly held principles which the state itself officially acknowledges. The chief problem is that the insistence by the church on maintaining its integrity necessarily implies independent judgment and resistance to state encroachments. Both church and state have been testing the limits of compromise; each in its own way has been defending itself against the intrusion of the other.

In November 1974 Catholic bishops produced a pastoral letter decrying the denigration of religious beliefs in the schools. This was an unusual step, given the fact that the Catholic Church in the GDR has always been less inclined than the Evangelical to speak out on church-state issues. Its issuance suggests that the church was becoming exasperated over a chronic disregard for the freedom of conscience which the state officially guarantees all its citizens. In addition to using "long discredited arguments to falsify or give a one-sided interpretation of church history," teachers stigmatized Christian belief as superstition, bourgeois ideology, or even social deviance on the order of alcoholism and drug addiction, the bishops complained.[14] Indirectly answering stock criticisms, the statement asserted that Christianity did not require isolation from the world, but rather "responsible contribution to the society." Neither was it to function as the ideology of the ruling class. The church's anti-Fascist credentials were recalled, in that the bishops mentioned the names of a number of well-known Catholics who died alongside Communists in Nazi concentration camps. This was a way of stating that it is possible to be a good Catholic as well as a good citizen of the GDR.

Though he is to contribute to East German society, the statement continues, "the young Christian must . . . learn to judge critically where the prospects and limits of his cooperation lie." He may not engage in activities that in effect require separation from congregational life or in which he must represent viewpoints which conflict with his faith or conscience.[15] The state has no right to monopolize education but must defer to the wishes of the parents, who have primary jurisdiction over the moral education of their children. Furthermore, neither the state nor the party may be the arbiter of ethics and morals.

The Catholics were not alone in their protest. A number of Evangelical synods during 1975 took up the problem, generally condemning intolerance and the violation of freedom of conscience. Lutheran adults in Saxony were told to encourage young people to talk back to those who ridiculed the church or Christian belief. The synod of Berlin-Brandenburg advised that pastors make copies of relevant GDR regulations providing for non-discriminatory treatment available for parents to cite when discussing the "problem" with school or civil officials. The tone of the Evangelical comment was more conciliatory than that of the Catholic letter, however. The Berlin-Brandenburg synod declared to be sure that "Christian parents and young people cannot and may not deny that Jesus Christ alone is Lord of their lives" and that conflict with a state actively promoting the development of a "Socialist personality" on the basis of Marxism-Leninism was inevitable. But it hastened to add that such conflicts were at least in part soluble if Christians and Marxists would exhaust all possibilities for compromise on the basis of existing legislation in the area of education. Church leaders also stressed that they were not seeking "bourgeois prerogatives" for the church, but merely fairness for every member of the social order. The Berlin-Brandenburg statement was forwarded to the state secretary for Religious Affairs under cover of a letter expressing the hope that, in apprising him of the "deep unrest" in the churches over the matter, the synod could work with the state to resolve the conflict and prevent a recurrence.[16]

On 18 August 1976 Evangelical pastor Oskar Brüsewitz immolated himself in front of his church in Zeitz. He is said to have been despondent over the state's continuing harassment of young people, including Christian youth. Brüsewitz's suicide affected the churches deeply and placed both civil authorities and church officials supporting dialogue on the defensive. Congregations complained that those engaged in dialogue were opportunistic, lacking in courage, and irresponsible in not keeping parishioners sufficiently informed about the nature and directions of the talks they were having with state officials.[17] Church leaders attempted to insert a letter commenting on *l'affaire Brüsewitz* in the church bulletins *(Sonntagsblätter)*, but state censors prohibited this. Both the SED and the CDU felt it necessary to refute the charges against the government that the suicide implied. True to its role as an apologist for the SED, the CDU publicized the alleged observation of a Christian school teacher that Communist education did not lead to atheism but to the development of a multifaceted personality. The SED was sufficiently concerned about the need to defuse the situation so that it wrote into the new party program a provision that prohibited discrimination among citizens according to world view or religious confession.[18]

This was just a cosmetic measure, however, and the issue has remained essentially unresolved. In 1981, five years after the Brüsewitz suicide, the Evangelical Church was still seeking negotiations over the proper relationship of Communist education to freedom of conscience. In the same year, the Catholic bishops found it necessary to issue a second pastoral letter complaining of anti-religious indoctrination in the classroom. Klaus Gysi, the state secretary for Religious Affairs, rejected the discussions proposed by the Protestants as being incompatible with the separation of church and state. Gysi was clearly expressing the regime's determination to keep the church in its place.[19]

The degree to which the Evangelical Church, especially, was becoming "uppity" is evident in another of its initiatives that Gysi would not consider: a call for the establishment of a true alternative service option for Christian conscientious objectors. By 1980 the Evangelical Church's involvement in peace-related matters had become the chief source of friction in church-state relations. One of the most important justifications for a Christian-Marxist dialogue in postwar Europe was the widely perceived necessity of making a common effort to reduce East-West tensions in order to prevent a third world war. Peace and disarmament, especially nuclear disarmament, became watchwords for both ecumenical Christianity and Marxist humanism. Though varying in its intensity depending upon diplomatic requirements, ostentatious support of the same principles has been an important component of Soviet and East European foreign policies. In the wake of the decision by NATO in 1979 to introduce a new generation of intermediate-range nuclear weapons into Europe barring a Soviet move to reduce its newly deployed SS-20 missile arsenal, the U.S.S.R. found it advantageous to launch a new "peace offensive."

The imminent introduction of yet more nuclear weapons into West Germany and the Reagan administration's hard-line rhetoric on nuclear strategy spawned a relatively broad-based protest movement in the Federal Republic by 1981. While only some elements of the West German Evangelical Church actively participated in the movement, the EKD as a whole promoted the discussion of peace and its moral implications for Bonn's defense policy. The Soviet Union advertised unilateral initiatives that it claimed testified to its genuine interest in reducing the threat of nuclear war while warning that new NATO missiles represented a dangerous escalation of the arms race. In this it hoped to contribute to the development of a public pressure that would be strong enough to compel the West German government to change its policy and refuse to accept the missiles. Since the GDR was on the front lines in the diplomatic offensive, promoting peace received a high priority in East Berlin.

Under these circumstances, the SED could hardly gainsay the desire of the Evangelical Church to promote discussion on peace and disarmament. As we have seen, acknowledgment of ideals common to Christianity and socialism has always been fundamental to the SED's efforts to promote in church members an acceptance of the state and its policies as legitimate. However, the SED also encouraged church interest in peace questions in the hope that this would ultimately contribute to the diplomatic objective it shared with the Soviet Union. It facilitated joint discussions on peace between representatives of Evangelicals from East and West Germany. In this it hoped to strengthen the impression in the EKD that both state and church in the GDR were united in their commitment to disarmament. This would encourage West German church leaders to argue forcefully that deployment of the NATO missiles would fly in the face of public opinion in the East and would also slam shut a door to accommodation which the GDR and its allies were trying to open.

Church interest in peace, however, was a two-edged sword as far as the SED was concerned. A peace manifesto known as the "Berlin Appeal" was released on 25 January 1982. It was initiated by East German pastor Rainer Eppelmann, signed by 150 public figures from West Germany and 200 from East Germany, and forwarded to Soviet President Brezhnev. It called for the establishment of a nuclear-free zone in central Europe; the withdrawal of foreign troops from both East and West Germany; the abolition of military instruction in the schools; an end to all public military demonstrations and "so-called civil defense exercises"; sharp reductions in military spending; and a greater degree of accommodation for conscientious objectors. In keeping with their concern that the church not be seen as the spearhead of a political movement, church officials criticized the appeal as being unnecessarily provocative.[20] Nevertheless, the concerns expressed by the Berlin Appeal were certainly shared by many in the church. A synod in Saxony, for example, complained that it was not enough for the government to applaud the peace demonstrations supported by members of the West German Evangelical Church against the government of the FRG. It called for East bloc countries to shift their military emphasis to defense-oriented systems and also to reduce the number of tanks and medium-range missiles that were deployed in Eastern Europe.[21]

The tone of the synod of Saxony's statement was stronger than most official church pronouncements. Even this relatively bold statement, however, advanced its proposals in the form of suggestions, not demands; and these suggestions were made in the context of a position that placed an equal emphasis on the need for NATO to disarm. Yet the very even-handedness in the language was challenging to a government which does not suffer its policy to be evaluated. A major statement by the *Bund* concluded with the assertion that "we must also regard our own country critically," adding that "we know that nobody can be either solely or completely guilty." This must have rankled authorities as much as the implication in another document that the Soviet occupation of Afghanistan was as much a barrier to disarmament efforts as the NATO decision to install the new generation of missiles.[22]

Government policy on military instruction in the schools and on conscientious objection has accounted for much of the conflict between church and state. On 1 September 1978 the Ministry of Education began to phase in military training as a compulsory subject in the upper-school grades. Adolescents had been receiving paramilitary training since 1952 through an extensive network of clubs under the umbrella of the *Gesellschaft für Sport und Technik*. But now it was to become an integral part of everyone's basic education. This elicited vigorous opposition from the churches. They were particularly disturbed by the fact that the subject was presented from a simplistic "us-versus-them" perspective, which had no place for any reflection on the morality of using force. They labeled such instruction as *Hasspädigogik* (the pedagogy of hate). The regime rejected these protests, arguing that military education, by improving defense preparedness, actually made war less likely.

Since at least 1981 the church has strongly lobbied for the creation of a "social peace service" *(sozialer Friedensdienst)*. This would allow conscientious objectors to perform alternative service in nonmilitary settings. Currently the only option is for service in military "construction units" *(Baueinheiten)*, which does not require the bearing of arms but which is, of course, military service. The church has complained about the discrimination in education and employment suffered by those opting for *Baueinheit* service, as well as about the state's refusal to allow anyone who has served in a regular army unit to join a *Baueinheit* later as a reservist. As in the case of military education in the schools, the state has been unwilling to consider changing its policy.

The church has been acting as a broker between disaffected youth and the authorities. Seeking to help its own young people work through the problem of how to relate to the state on such issues of conscience as military service and academic freedom, the church found itself playing host to growing numbers of youths who wanted to talk and listen to each other. On 7 October 1977 there was a serious riot in East Berlin. Thousands had gathered for a rock concert and were dissatisfied when a popular group was replaced at the last minute for no apparent reason. This sparked a noisy demonstration, and police quickly but brutally broke up the concert, killing at least two people in the process.[23] Although the riot was not politically motivated, it was symptomatic of the tension which had developed between many young people and the government. Tired of the pressure to conform in order to get ahead, frustrated at heavy-handed controls (especially the strict limitation on foreign travel), some fled into private life. For others, the church become increasingly attractive as a haven from the pervasive regimentation of life in the GDR. During the 1970s so-called young congregations emerged. These were essentially church-sponsored gatherings in which discussion could take place outside of the confines of the orthodox Marxist-Leninist categories of the official ideology. Many of those who attended were not active church members. Most were interested in humanistic Marxism—in the tradition of Djilas, Kolakowski, and Carillo.[24] Authors and artists representing such non-sanctioned Marxism appeared frequently in churches. Significantly, Wolf Biermann's first performance after an eleven-year hiatus took place at St. Nicholas's Church in Prenzlau.

The proposal for the Socialist peace service grew out of an initiative by Christian youth in Dresden. As in West Germany, peace has been a major concern of the young. On 13 February 1982 a youthful crowd of some five thousand attended a peace forum in Dresden sponsored by the Evangelical Church of Saxony. The occasion was the thirty-seventh anniversary of the city's devastation by Anglo-American bombers near the end of World War II. In keeping with the church's commitment to political caution and public order, the program was limited to a question-and-answer format and was held indoors. It had been organized in the hope of forestalling unauthorized street demonstrations and a potentially explosive confrontation with police. Although there was no violence, at the conclusion of the meeting several hundred of the participants walked to the ruined Church of Our Lady and reportedly sang, in English, the American civil rights anthem "We Shall Overcome."[25]

The government was grateful for the church's role in keeping the Dresden gathering from getting out of hand. However, it feared the development of a movement over which it had little control. In publishing glowing accounts of the peace demonstrations in the FRG, it undoubtedly encouraged many of its citizens to seek their own ways of expressing solidarity with their Western neighbors in the cause of peace. In 1980 elements of the church began to identify with the slogan that had become the motto of the disarmament campaign in the West: "Frieden schaffen ohne Waffen" ("Make peace without weapons"). The graphic representation of this was a patch based on the swords-into-plowshares memorial, which the Soviet Union had donated to United Nations headquarters in New York. Ironically, it became associated with activities that the Communist government regarded as subversive, and its display was eventually prohibited. The official position has been that independent actions for peace are "unnecessary" (read: undesirable), since the government of the Socialist Unity Party itself constituted a "peace movement."[26]

Banning the patch was only one manifestation of repression. A series of incidents during 1982–83 in Jena involving young peace activists culminated in the death of one person while in police custody and the arrest of seventeen others. Late in 1983 about fifty people were put under house arrest in Berlin because of their involvement in a plan to deliver a peace letter to the American and Soviet embassies, a demonstration which had supposedly been cleared by the authorities.[27] Peter Wensierski is convincing when he states that when it comes to peace-related matters there has been such an abundance *(Vielfalt)* of individual cases "that one can no longer speak of individual cases."[28]

Repression was combined with efforts at co-optation. The Free German Youth (FDJ) was pressed into service to organize mass demonstrations and concerts on behalf of peace. There was to be no more clouding of identities: the friends and foes of peace were to be clearly defined. The FDJ's motto was "Frieden schaffen ohne *NATO* Waffen" (emphasis added). Christians who wanted to join in an FDJ-sponsored "world peace day" in Berlin learned that co-optation is not always easy to separate from repression. They were given permission to participate as an independent unit on the condition that their placards be checked by FDJ representatives prior to the day's events. The Christians dutifully complied, but the friendly negotiation with their Communist counterparts that they had anticipated never took place. Instead, the "inspectors" who met them at the designated time and place were security personnel who simply confiscated all of their signs, presumably to ensure that nothing would be left to chance.[29]

More recently, the government appears to have been trying to put the peace genie back into the bottle. Mass demonstrations and other extraordinary efforts failed to prevent the deployment of the NATO weapons, which began in December 1983. The peace theme has reverted to its accustomed role of being one among a number of perennial goals of "Socialist construction." Real peace, from this standpoint, has nothing to do with pacifism. Luther's call for defense against the Turks was even cited as a way of casting aspersion on pacifist ideas. The FDJ's support of government policy was praised for demonstrating the will of the GDR's youth "to defend the fatherland at any time *with weapon in hand.*"[30]

Furthermore, Christians have been told that they can only hope to be *effective* in promoting peace as part of a common effort. During the spring of 1984 the CDU was busy preparing its charges (East German Christians) for the elections to the People's Chamber, set for 6 May. They were exhorted to recognize that "a strong socialism was the best assurance of a secure peace" and to join all citizens in "further deepening the moral-political unity of the people." Only in this way could Christians be "responsibly engaged."[31] The implication is clear: work under the direction of the SED is the only kind of effort for peace in which Christians can be both relevant and effective.

East German leaders have tolerated a higher degree of criticism than one might expect of those who have so vigorously warned of the dangers of the "Polish disease" associated with Solidarity. As the peace offensive wanes, there seems less reason to keep up appearances of church-state cooperation in the pursuit of peace. It is therefore quite possible that the church's room for maneuver, at least on this issue, will be subject to some constraint.[32] In promoting critical solidarity, church leaders have a difficult course to navigate. The extent to which the Evangelical Church in East Germany is able to maintain this posture depends largely on the extent to which the state finds it expedient to allow anything less than *uncritical* solidarity.

The church has sought to maintain the right to admonish the state, however cautiously, by affirming the need for cooperation with the civil authorities whenever possible for the good of society. Although they support the right of conscientious objection, church officials have stressed that each individual must decide for himself whether or not to seek exemption from combat training or from any participation at all in the military. The SED would consider any generalized encouragement of conscientious objection as bordering dangerously on organized political opposition. The church's fear of being misunderstood is credible. At a recent plenum of the SED Politburo, candidate member Werner Walde reportedly characterized the proposal for alternative service as "inimical to peace, the Constitution, and socialism."[33]

Church leaders have been faulted for being prone to fall into the old Lutheran trap of excessive deference to the state for the sake of both public order and access to the prince's ear, as it were. There is evidence that the kind of intrachurch criticism which assailed them in the wake of the Brüsewitz affair has recurred in connection with the issue of conscientious objection. A youth delegate at the September 1982 synod of the *Bund* in Halle reproached the leadership for "excessive anxiety" (*Überängstlichkeit*) over the possibility of offending the state and for throwing away some real opportunities for obtaining concessions on peace-related matters.[34] Non-church opponents of government policy have themselves seen in the church's effort to steer an intermediate course a dearth of commitment, or even opportunism.[35]

Such critics may be forgetting that the church is more than a focus for the aggregation of political interests. Its failure to favor pacifism unequivocally stems less from political pragmatism than it does from its conviction that doctrinaire pacifism is no more valid than the GDR's dogmatic version of "peace through strength." The church regards itself as having an important pastoral obligation to a diverse body of citizens extending well beyond the group of regular churchgoers. The report of the *Bund's* synod on peace, with its clear statements of principle and concrete suggestions for action, demonstrates that the Evangelical Church continues to speak prophetically (and independently) to its society.[36] It has been able to intercede successfully in some cases in which individuals have run afoul of the authorities. It appears to have influenced the policy makers to a limited extent.[37] However, there is no reason to assume that it can always be successful as an *ombudsman*, let alone that it can hope to influence state policy when the political leadership already holds a position. Church leaders undoubtedly realize that their opportunity for ministry is often dependent upon political circumstances over which they have no control.

The Catholic Church has consistently avoided any emphasis on dialogue, interpreting separation of church and state very strictly. It has tried to minimize criticism of the state on much the same basis that the Evangelical Church has deemed such criticism appropriate: that genuine dialogue must involve the exploration of possibilities for agreement and cooperation as well as the articulation of differences. Criticizing the state could in effect force the Catholic Church into the dialogue it does not want, interfering with its effort to minimize state influence on the religious lives of its communicants. In 1981 the newly appointed head of the Catholic Bishops' Conference paid an official call on Honecker. The Catholic press pointedly avoided drawing an analogy between this meeting and the Evangelical church-state "summit" of 1978.[38]

The long-term political significance of the church in the GDR, both Catholic and Protestant, lies in the fact that it sustains in people the idea that the state has no right to claim unquestioned obedience. Refusing to accept Marxism-Leninism as a general philosophy of life and insisting on the right to teach children an alternative world view are themselves an implicit challenge to the type of state that claims not merely to provide order and sustenance but also to fulfill spiritual needs. Whether defending religious rights or promoting Christian values such as peace, both churches have appealed to their government to act in accordance with legal precepts whose validity it does not question. This leaves open the possibility that the regime's authority could be questioned, not to mention its performance in living up to its own ideals.

Should a grass-roots movement for reform ever emerge in the GDR, it will not be initiated by the institutional church, any more than was the Prague Spring or the longer season of Solidarity in church-oriented Poland. However, it seems likely that individuals influenced by the church would readily support and perhaps even be in the forefront of such a movement. Like the church in the GDR—Evangelical and Catholic alike—Martin Luther was politically conservative. Nevertheless he emphasized that no human authority can control conscience and that rulers—whether individuals or institutions—are not above criticism. These ideas continue to have profound revolutionary implications. At the very least, they provide a set of principles, along with the fundamentals of the Christian faith, to which the church must be willing and able to remain openly committed if genuine dialogue is to be possible. So far, the Evangelical Church in the GDR has been in a position to carry on genuine dialogue.

If it should ever disavow these principles or permit the state to determine how they are to be applied, whether under duress or out of a desire for privilege, then dialogue must necessarily come into conflict with integrity. Under such circumstances, the more distant posture toward the state that continues to characterize the Catholic Church in the GDR would seem to be the only way in which the church could remain true to itself and avoid becoming another emasculated organization like the CDU. In the absence of such a situation, there ought to be a continuing basis for church-state dialogue in East Germany, however that dialogue might ebb and flow.

NOTES

1. This chapter is mainly concerned with the Evangelical (Lutheran) Church, the largest and most politically relevant group of Christians in the GDR. Even though there are actually eight regional churches (*Landeskirchen*), "church" is used here for simplicity's sake. In certain contexts "church" has a broader meaning, since some attention is also given to the smaller, less conspicuous Catholic Church.

2. *Neues Deutschland*, 14–15 June 1980.

3. This view is exemplified by Wolfram von Hanstein, *Von Luther bis Hitler* (Dresden: Vico Verlag, 1947), 22–23, and Alfred Meusel, *Thomas Muntzer und seine Zeit* (Berlin: Aufbau Verlag, 1952), 46, 84.

4. For statistics on Catholic and Protestant establishments, see Hans-Gerhard Koch, *Staat und Kirche in der DDR: zur Entwicklung ihrer Beziehungen 1945–1974* (Stuttgart: Quell Verlag, 1975), 244, 246–47. For church publications, see David Childs, *The GDR: Moscow's German Ally* (London: George Allen & Unwin, 1983), 237–38.

5. Kurt Sontheimer and Wilhelm Bleek, *The Government and Politics of East Germany* (London: Hutchinson, 1975), 124; and Hendrik Bussiek, *Notizen aus der DDR* (Frankfurt: Fischer Verlag, 1979), 208.

SECOND WORLD ENCOUNTERS

6. "Christen im Sozialismus," *Deutschland Archiv* (hereafter *DA*) 10 (December 1977): 1336–40.

7. *Neues Deutschland*, 7 March 1978, and Gisela Helwig, "Zeichen der Hoffnung," *DA* 11 (April 1978): 351–53.

8. Sharon L. Kegerreis, "A Church within Socialism: Religion in the GDR Today," *Radio Free Europe Background Report* (hereafter *RFE/BR*) 240 (8 October 1980): 6; and Gisela Helwig, "Kirche im Sozialismus," *DA* 10 (May 1977): 451.

9. *Christians and Churches in the GDR* (Dresden: Verlag Zeit im Bild, 1980), 10.

10. Jonathan Steele, *Socialism with a German Face* (London: Jonathan Cape, 1977), 161; Robert F. Goeckel, "Zehn Jahre Kirchenpolitik unter Honecker," *DA* 14 (September 1981): 945.

11. Heyl, *Christians and Churches*, 16, emphasis added.

12. Ibid., 35.

13. Steven Kelman, *Behind the Berlin Wall* (Boston: Houghton Mifflin, 1972), 49.

14. "DDR Kirchen fordern Toleranz im Bildungswesen," *DA* 8 (May 1975): 550–51.

15. Ibid., 552.

16. Gisela Helwig, "Christen—Bürger Zweiter Klasse?" *DA* 8 (May 1975): 553–55.

17. Helwig, "Kirche," 449.

18. Gisela Helwig, "Christ sein in der DDR," *DA* 9 (October 1976): 1020–22.

19. Peter Wensierski, *"Bericht* (report) on the fourth synod of the Bund der Evangelischen Kirchen in der DDR," *DA* 15 (March 1982): 230–34.

20. Theo Mechtenberg, "Die Friedensverantwortung der evangelischen Kirchen in der DDR," in *Die evangelischen Kirchen in der DDR*, ed. Reinhard Henkys (Munich: Chr. Kaiser Verlag, 1982), 393. Although organized by Eppelmann, the actual text of the Berlin Appeal was reportedly written by Robert Havemann, a prominent professor who was expelled from the university and from the SED in the 1960s for political reasons and who remains perhaps the best-known East German dissident. The Eppelmann-Havemann combination represented the association of the church with political resistance that church leaders so feared. See the *New York Times*, 10 October 1981.

21. Ronald D. Asmus, "New Peace Initiative in the GDR," *RFE/BR* 39 (15 February 1982): 3, and Asmus, "The Evangelical Church in East Germany," *RFE/BR* 334 (3 December 1981): 5.

22. "Die evangelische Kirche in der DDR zur derzeitigen weltpolitischen Situation," *DA* 13 (April 1980): 443.

23. Bussiek, *Notizen*, 284–85.

24. Ronald D. Asmus, "Youth in the GDR: Not a Threat, but a Challenge," *RFE/BR* 224 (19 September 1980): 6.

25. *New York Times*, 15 February 1982; Mechtenberg, "Friedensverantwortung," 392.

26. Ronald D. Asmus, "Peace Demonstration in the GDR," *RFE/BR* 47 (18 February 1982): 4.

27. On the Jena events, see Klauss Wolschner, "Jena—Vorbote eines neuen Deutschland?" *Die Zeit*, 24 June 1983, and Ronald D. Asmus, "Jena: An Atypical City in the GDR?" *RFE/BR* 76 (8 April 1983). On the Berlin incident, see Mike

Jendrzejczyk and Marti Zimmerman, "Walking a Tightrope: Peacemaking in East German Churches," *Sojourners* (February 1984): 10.

28. Peter Wensierski, "Gratwanderung ohne Ende?" *DA* 15 (November 1982): 1131.

29. Klemens Richter, "Das Friedensengagement der evangelischen Christen in der DDR," *DA* 14 (November 1981): 1125. For accounts of FDJ mass demonstrations, see *Neues Deutschland*, 21–22 and 24 May 1983.

30. Hellmuth Kolbe, "*Bericht* (report) on the Seventh Congress of GDR historians in Berlin on 6–9 December 1982," *Zeitschrift für Geschichtswissenschaft* 31 (July 1983): 645; see also the account of the FDJ unit in the official report on the May Day parade, *Neues Deutschland*, 2 May 1983.

31. *Neues Deutschland*, 1 December 1983 and 4 April 1984.

32. Wensierski, "Gratwanderung," 1131.

33. Asmus, "The Evangelical Church," 10.

34. Asmus, "Peace Demonstration," 4, and Wensierski, "Gratwanderung," 1130.

35. Note Havemann's disappointment with the church for disassociating itself from the Berlin Appeal in Mechtenberg, "Friedensverantwortung," 393. One journalist recounted a young man's suspicion that the church has focused on the peace issue mainly out of a desire to attract more youth to its programs (Peter Mosler, "Reise in den fernen Osten," *Die Zeit*, 3 June 1983).

36. "Kirche und Friedensverantwortung" (excerpts from the report of the *Bund* synod in Halle, 24–28 September 1982), *DA* 15 (November 1982): 1219–27.

37. The church's heavy involvement in the peace issue might have prompted *Neues Deutschland*'s rather unusual step of publishing two letters from church members expressing their concern over any proposed deployment of new Soviet missiles in the GDR (*Neues Deutschland*, 22 October 1983).

38. In March 1982 Aktionskreis Halle, a group of activist clergy and laity, criticized the Catholic Church for not participating in the peace discussion (Richter, "Katholische Kirche in der DDR und Friedensbewegung," *DA* 15 [July 1982]: 685). On 1 January 1983 the Berlin Bishop's Conference did issue a pastoral letter on peace and disarmament, perhaps signifying a shift in the Catholic Church toward greater involvement.

SUGGESTIONS FOR FURTHER READING

Beeson, Trevor. *Discretion and Valour: Religious Conditions in Russia and Eastern Europe*. Rev. ed. Philadelphia: Fortress Press, 1982.

Bentley, James. *Between Marx and Christ: The Dialogue in German Speaking Europe: 1870–1970*. London: Verso Editions and NLB, 1982.

Buscher, Wolfgang, Peter Wensierski, and Klaus Wolschner, eds. *Friedensbewegung in der DDR: Texte 1978–82*. Haltingen: Scandica Verlag, 1982.

Henkys, Reinhard, ed. *Die evangelischen Kirchen in der DDR*. Munich: Chr. Kaiser Verlag, 1982.

Knauft, Wolfgang. *Katholische Kirche in der DDR: Gemeinden in der Bewahrung 1945–1980*. Mainz: Matthias Grünewald Verlag, 1980.

Koch, Hans-Gerhard. *Staat und Kirche in der DDR: Zur Entwicklung ihrer Beziehungen von 1945–1974*. Stuttgart: Quell Verlag, 1975.

YUGOSLAVIA
Paul Mojzes

HISTORICAL SETTING

While diversity provides excitement, it often creates complicated problems. Yugoslavia is a good case study of a nation that is experiencing difficulty uniting a group of diverse peoples who harbor century-old traditions of intolerance and animosity toward each other. Unlike Poland, which enjoys a very strong national, religious, and even ideological cohesion, Yugoslavia suffers from an absence of these positive factors.

Yugoslavia is a multinational country which consists of the major nations of Serbia, Croatia, Slovenia, Macedonia, Montenegro, and the multinational state of Bosna-Herzegovina. In organization it is a federal system of six states which have maintained an uneasy and fluctuating relationship since 1918. Sizable national minorities of Albanians, Hungarians, Gypsies, Turks, Slovaks, Romanians, Ruthenians, and others complicate the picture, with the added unique dimension of a "Muslim" nationality recognized recently (a Slavic ethnic stock converted to Islam nearly five centuries ago).

Religious diversity is no less significant. The number of Jews remaining in Yugoslavia after World War II is negligible. The Protestants, accounting for only about 1 percent of the population, represent quite an assortment of religious denominations and do not maintain any effective united stance. As a result, there is no significant force in the religious life of the country. The Muslims, the largest such population in Europe, who number over two million (10 percent of the population), are found in significant numbers among the Bosnians, Herzegovinians, and Albanians, and the dwindling numbers of Turks in Macedonia. The two largest groups are Roman Catholic and Eastern Orthodox. These two groups are closely identified with particular national groups. Croatians and Slovenes are solidly Roman Catholic and account for about 30 percent of the population.[1] The Serbians, Montenegrins, and Macedonians are Eastern Orthodox accounting for about 40 percent of the population. Recently the Macedonian Orthodox proclaimed themselves an autocephalous church, much to the chagrin of the Serbian Orthodox Church, so that even the Orthodox live in a state of tension. The general rule of interreligious relations in Yugoslavia is animosity and intolerance. Ecumenism is looked upon with suspicion and fear due to its perceived political and national implications and due to past attempts at conversion and forcible reunification of churches.

The Marxists of Yugoslavia are also pluralistic. The League of Communists of Yugoslavia (formerly the Communist Party of Yugoslavia) counts about 10 percent of the population in its membership. By party statute they must be atheists and abandon religious identification.[2] Originally, the Communist Party had a high degree of uniformity, having adopted in the 1930s a Stalinistic, dogmatic type of Marxism. But the Yugoslav Party's break with the Soviet bloc in 1948 gradually led to ideological diversity. The mainstream of the party developed a new form of self-managing socialism which tends to differ markedly from the Soviet model and is moderately liberal but with certain pronounced authoritarian tendencies. There is also a wing of humanistic Marxists, especially among the intellectuals with strong tendencies toward democratization and liberalization as well as pronounced critical components. Their criticism is directed not only toward capitalism and other forms of socialism but also to the Yugoslav model of socialism. The dogmatic wing of the party, with its latent Stalinistic tendencies, is far from being dead. While it does not determine current policies, it exerts pressure in times of crisis, advocating a return to rule by an "iron hand." A constant struggle for ideological and political supremacy characterizes the inner life of the party, leading to frequent oscillations in policies and attitudes and to a constant need on the part of party members to be cautious about statements and actions which might become a liability to their career at a later time.

A number of other factors need to be taken into account. The nationalities that make up Yugoslavia had been under foreign domination for many centuries. This has left a legacy of a love of independence along with a certain ambiguity toward authority, that is, both a docile acceptance of power and an anarchistic streak of noncompliance with government decisions. Yugoslavs tend to be suspicious of all who wield power while those in power have a tendency to disregard the wishes of the population.

From 1945 to 1980 the country was held together by the strong though somewhat benevolent hand of Josip Broz-Tito. No decisions had to be made as to who was going to lead the country. Currently a complex system of collective leadership, both in the government and in the League of Communists has been developed, which, for the time being, works by rotating offices along a strict national quota system. No strong leader has emerged as yet.

Yugoslavia lives isolated from the community of Socialist nations with which it has had very tenuous relationships. In foreign policy, Yugoslavia identifies itself as a nonaligned neutral country that is trying to play a leadership role in the Third World. It rarely can count on the support of other Socialist countries; they treat Yugoslavia as a revisionist or renegade country. Many of them do not recognize Yugoslavia's social system as Socialist at all. Yugoslavs, in return, criticize the practices of Socialist countries and frequently have expressed their conviction that the Soviet Union is an imperialist, state-capitalist country ("hegemonist" in Socialist parlance). Moreover, Yugoslavia has not developed close relationships with Marxist parties of the West. Psychologically, it has given Yugoslavs a sense of uniqueness that encourages them to pioneer and experiment at will. But it also creates a sense of anxiety in difficult times that motivates those in power to crack down on dissent in the name of unity.

Economically Yugoslavia also presents startling differences. The country is developing industrially, having changed from an agricultural to a predominantly industrial, urban society with the massive social and psychological dislocations that such change tends to bring. Its industrial growth has been remarkable. At the same time its isolation from the Socialist bloc moved the economy of Yugoslavia closer to the Western and Third World economies. As a result, it suffers the economic maladies of unbalanced budgets, large foreign debt, shortage of materials, and frequent reversal of economic policies. The structure of the economy is Socialist self-management, a system unique in the Socialist world. Self-management, though not fully implemented, has decentralized the economy, put it on a modified market system and emphasized productivity and efficiency which, in turn, has resulted in massive unemployment (about one million Yugoslavs must seek jobs in developed Western industrial societies). A significant segment of the economy is under private ownership, though it is limited by law to small enterprises. The socialized sector is a system of voluntary compliance with planned government direction. Fairly sizable differences in income exist between Yugoslav citizens, resulting in a class of the new rich and a good deal of social discontent among those outside this group. Even more troubling to the Yugoslavs is that the enormous discrepancy in economic levels between the developed northern and underdeveloped southern regions has remained at practically the same level since 1945 despite massive attempts to remedy this situation. It is the source of significant national and political tension.

DIALOGUE BETWEEN CHRISTIANS AND MARXISTS AND ITS GROUND RULES

Before reaching the stage of the dialogical encounter, which is the emphasis of this chapter, Christian-Marxist relations went through several phases.[3]

Phase   I: From 1945 to 1953—severe conflict
Phase II: From 1953 to 1962—deescalation of the conflict
Phase III: From 1962 to 1967—suspension of hostilities and mutual adaptation
Phase IV: From 1967 to 1972—tolerance and dialogue
Phase   V: From 1972 to present—retrenchment on the part of the Marxists but
        cautious continuation of the dialogue[4]

Phase I: Severe Conflict (1945–53)

The immediate post–World War II period was marked by an all-out conflict between the churches and the Communist Party of Yugoslavia, which under the strong influence of the Soviet Communists attempted to obliterate the churches. There were legal restrictions, expropriation of real estate, monopolization of the media, control of education, regulation of public life, antireligious propaganda, attacks in the press, intimidation, arrests, torture, and murder. The persecution of the churches was all the more intense because many church members had collaborated with the antipartisan forces during World War II. The government sought revenge. Severe pain and setbacks were experienced by most churches and their individual members.

During this period of intense conflict, the churches believed that the Communist regime's staunch atheism and persecution of God's people insured its doom and destruction within a relatively short period of time.

One of the positive results of this period was the legal separation of church and state. For the first time in Yugoslavia's history, the small "free churches" were accorded equal status and legal rights with the mainline religious bodies.

Phase II: Deescalation of the Conflict (1952–62)

After Yugoslavia broke off from the Soviet bloc in 1948 it did not immediately implement the reforms which became the earmarks of the Yugoslav path to socialism at a later time. First, it seemed important to show the Soviets and the Cominform bloc of nations that Yugoslavia followed an orthodox path to communism which was equal to, if not superior to, that of the Soviet Union. Thus there was no immediate relaxation of the conflict. By 1953, when the immediate danger of Soviet invasion had passed, and Yugoslavia had embarked on its nonaligned course, and when self-management, decentralization, and a gradual process of liberalization were introduced, the most overt forms of persecution were moderated. Slowly the Yugoslav Communists made some social space for the drastically curtailed activities of the churches.

Phase III: Suspension of Hostilities
and Mutual Adaptation (1962–67)

The gradual process of relaxation continued as the Yugoslav Communists sought theoretical, legal, and practical approaches to adjust themselves to a different mode of coexistence with the churches, one which had to accept the fact that the churches continued to exert an influence over their membership and would continue to do so. It appeared that the hostile postwar policy of confrontation would not be conducive to the form of socialism envisioned by the party leadership and increasingly accepted by the populace. The churches, while not exactly overjoyed by the stabilization of socialism, nevertheless recognized that the relaxation of conflict was infinitely better than the oppression of the recent past. So they too began to adopt a more conciliatory attitude—increasingly aware that the new course of Yugoslav socialism was preferable to the Soviet approach.

Phase IV: Tolerance and Dialogue (1967–72)

By 1967 the government adopted a more relaxed position—religion ought to be tolerated, though not encouraged. Former attempts to interfere in the internal life of religious institutions were practically abandoned. However, it would severely stretch the concept of religious freedom if one were to say that it was practiced unfettered in Yugoslavia. For many of the churches this meant a return to near normal functioning. Some even openly attempted to exert their influence by emphasizing the historical identity of church and nationality and presented themselves as guardians of national rights and traditions. This greatly disturbed the Communist Party and is one of the reasons why after 1972 a new phase, retrenchment from some of the most liberal positions, was initiated by the worried Marxist elite who feared the loss of revolutionary achievements. It was in this context of liberalization of the Yugoslav society that the dialogue emerged, and it is in this atmosphere of cautious retrenchment that the dialogue continues to take place.

The dialogue was initiated by a group of humanistic Marxist scholars who, in their study of religion, decided to abandon the traditional, dogmatic Marxist descriptions and evaluations of religion. They attempted to deal with their empirical findings about religion in Yugoslavia, employing new, creative approaches. The most notable books were those of Esad Cimić (a sociologist at the University of Sarajevo) who published *Socijalisticko drustvo i religija (Socialist Society and Religion)* in 1966; and of Branko Bosnjak (a philosopher at the University of Zagreb) who published *Filozofija i krsćanstvo (Philosophy and Christianity)* also in 1966 and a compilation of essays by various Marxist authors edited by Bosnjak entitled *Religija i drustvo (Religion and Society)* in 1969.

The only response of the religious communities to these studies came from Roman Catholic theologians. Up to the present time no other religious group has reacted in any significant way or participated in the dialogue. Hence the dialogue is between Marxist scholars and Catholic theologians, the intellectual elite of both groups.

The Second Vatican Council, by opening the Roman Catholic Church to dialogue with Marxists, spurred the dialogue in Yugoslavia. The first public dialogue took place in Zagreb between Branko Bosnjak and the Catholic theologian Mijo Skvorc in March 1967 on the theme of Bosnjak's book *Philosophy and Christianity*. The dialogue between Bosnjak and Skvorc[5] was not only the first but also one of the very few public dialogues to take place in Yugoslavia. It drew an excited crowd of about three thousand people at the student center. While the encounter resembled a debate rather than a dialogue, it was nevertheless a risky and potentially explosive new enterprise which the bureaucrats of both party and church looked upon with some misgivings. Somewhat later Yugoslavian Christians and Marxists who attended the international dialogues of the Paulus-Gesellschaft decided to continue the dialogue at home.

The encounter in Yugoslavia was dialogical rather than action-oriented though some expectation of still more harmonious interactions between the two groups existed. The most pronounced expectation voiced by the Marxists in their dialogues was a call for Christians to embrace and support more enthusiastically the new social order and thereby remove their threatening opposition to the advancement of socialism. This is usually phrased, "How can Christians engage in the processes of self-management and thereby support the path of Yugoslavian socialism?" The Christians' major expectation and goal was the cessation of second-class treatment and the guarantee and enactment of their religious liberty which was constitutionally proclaimed but in fact was severely limited. The much vaguer "interest of the nation" was also lauded as a goal of the dialogue.

Phase V: Retrenchment and Continuation
(1972 to present)

The dialogue is both formal and informal and its status is legal. Being a partially decentralized country with a good deal of room for spontaneous and local action, the dialogue never needed or received official sanctions. As noted above, during the period from 1967 to 1972 it was first tolerated, then encouraged. When in 1971 the degree of liberalization and ethnic sentiment

threatened the leading role of the central organ of the Yugoslavian government, the late President Tito stepped in and sharply restricted the process.
From then on those who engaged in dialogue, especially the Marxists,
experienced both subtle and direct pressures to avoid these encounters.
Thus there is some ambiguity as to the dialogue; while it is not illegal, the
Marxist partners risk their jobs or are harassed if they engage in it. Consequently, since 1972 no public dialogues have occurred. They are carried on
merely through the written word and personal contacts. Unlike the case of
Czechoslovakia, these personal contacts are not discouraged by the government and are not interfered with or deemed dangerous. However, many
expectations which people had during the period of the unrestrained dialogue are today seriously deflated.

While the formal dialogue took place in print and in public, the public
dialogues were generally rare. In addition to the aforementioned dialogue
between Bosnjak and Skvorc, two dialogues took place in Belgrade in 1971 in
a library. It centered on the books by the Marxists Cimić and Vuko Pavicević.
At about the same time a Marxist sociology professor in Split, Srdjan Vrcan,
invited Archbishop Dr. Frane Franić to lecture in his seminar. The archbishop reciprocated by inviting Vrcan to lecture at the Split theological
seminary. In Zagreb, Bosnjak gathered a group of Christian and Marxist
graduate students to study religion and atheism, which promoted more
informal exchanges. Groups of foreign Christians traveling through
Yugoslavia heard lectures by those academics engaged in the dialogue with
them. Yugoslavian professors traveling abroad likewise engaged in formal
and informal dialogue, primarily at the Paulus-Gesellschaft gatherings but
also elsewhere.

Not many of the writings of the participants of the dialogue were translated for foreign consumption.[6] This may well be the reason why the pioneering efforts of the Yugoslavs are not well known outside their country, in
addition to the political factors which make Yugoslavs not well accepted in
the main gatherings of East or West.

ISSUES

The main issues of the dialogue may be treated through a brief summary of
the main work of both Christian and Marxist dialogists. The survey will
include the Marxists Bosnjak, Cimić, Roter, Vrcan, Marko Kersevan, and
Andrija Kresić, who may be regarded as the most significant Marxist protagonists (the others number perhaps twice as many). The Christians are all
Roman Catholic clergy and include Bajsić, Tomislav Sagi-Bunić, Archbishop

Franić, Tomo Veres, and Romić (again about one-third of those who at some time actively participated in the dialogue).

Branko Bosnjak is the only Marxist professor of philosophy of religion in Yugoslavia. He teaches at Zagreb University and was one of the editors of *Praxis*. His earlier works were devoted to arguing for the rationality of philosophy—meaning, of course, the Marxist one—and the irrationality of religion. He was convinced that religion will sharply decline in public life, but that it will never die out since individuals will always conjure up eschatological hopes due to their inability to deal courageously with the threat of death. According to him Marxism developed an oversimplified theory of religion. He held that Marxists should acquaint themselves with it empirically. He argued that neither theism nor atheism is essential to humanism, and that the future will bring a pluralistic anthropocracy. Having orginally doubted the very existence of Jesus, his later contact with Christian scholarship convinced him otherwise, and he moved to an appreciative attitude toward Jesus' contributions to human welfare. If one were to judge Bosnjak merely by his writing one would conclude that he is still fairly inflexible toward religion, but those Christians who maintain contact with him have been impressed by his irenic spirit, his goodwill and cooperativeness, his commitment to democratic socialism, and his integrity. He always has shown willingness to cooperate with Christians.

Esad Cimić is an unusually creative Marxist thinker. He is a sociologist of religion who originally taught at the University of Sarajevo. There he was frequently pressured by the more dogmatic wing of the Bosnian Communists. There were times when he had to keep a low profile in order to survive. He later moved to Zadar and most recently is teaching in Belgrade. He started his empirical research on religion for his doctoral dissertation in Bosnia and Herzegovina. Soon he turned to more theoretical work on how a Socialist society should treat religion. While seeing complex causes for religion, he agrees with Marx that the fundamental causal factor is alienation. As a very perceptive observer of the dynamics of Yugoslavian society, this thesis led him to the conclusion that socialism continues to alienate many people and that it continues to create religious and pseudo-religious phenomena (for example, Stalinism and "red clericalism"). He also stated that anti-theistic propaganda does not create free and humane individuals. On the contrary, it tends to create vacuous persons with no moral and spiritual values who mindlessly pursue hedonistic goals. According to Cimić, Marxists should seek to create a humanistic, de-alienated society with no particular atheistic propaganda. The problem of religion would then take care of itself. The state should be neither protheistic nor antitheistic but truly atheistic, that is, neutral. Cimić recognizes that religious people can be progressive not only despite their religion but even because of their religion.

Zdenko Roter, professor of sociology of religion at University of Ljubljana and former editor of *Teorija in praska*, experienced strong party criticism, like Bosnjak and Cimić, for his dedication to a humanistic and democratic Socialist system and for his eagerness to participate in the dialogues. He recognized the contributions of religion and sought to offset the adverse propaganda directed toward the churches by pointing out the positive contributions of recent Catholic theology and the ferment in the church since Vatican II. He aimed to formulate objective sociological models for a better understanding of the dynamics of church-state relations and of the developments within the church.

The works of his colleague at the university, Marko Kersevan, also a sociologist, never received the same kind of attacks—perhaps because he never formally participated in any dialogues. Many Christian theologians find Kersevan's theoretical postulates the most acceptable and refreshing. One of Kersevan's basic interests is in stating how the Communist Party should relate to religion. The model he espouses calls for the Communist Party to refrain from combating religion to extinction and to recognize that Marxism is primarily a strategy for the working class to seize and hold power. If a particular religion is a hindrance in the class struggle, one should attack it; if, on the other hand, a particular religion is of help to the workers, then one should cooperate with it. The evaluation of each specific religion's role should, according to Kersevan, be ongoing, because religions are dynamic phenomena. In some of his writings Kersevan identifies the source of religion not as the fear of death or social alienation but as a unique encounter with the "Other," somewhat akin to Rudolf Otto's numinous experience. This line of thought still awaits elaboration by Kersevan.

Srdjan Vrcan, a sociologist who teaches at the Law School of Split University, reflects primarily an empirical approach to the study of religion. His first comprehensive project was the study of religiosity among the youth of Split. The second was, in cooperation with Stefica Bahtijarević of Zagreb, to study religiosity in the Zagreb region. His findings were that contrary to the expectation of dogmatic Marxists the children of working-class parents were not the most atheistically inclined but continued under fairly strong religious influences. The degree of atheization was directly related to the degree of education of the parents and of the youth. Therefore, Vrcan advocated an enlightened attitude toward religion to be pursued through the educational system. Vrcan's conclusion about those whom he studied is that Roman Catholics for the most part remain traditionally religious (only a small number in his sample are crusading atheists), and that an increasing minority is becoming religiously indifferent. In his view one ought to study religion scientifically to see what changes are taking place in it, and Marxists should not suppress religion. Vrcan continues to interact with domestic and foreign Christians, though on a more limited scale since 1972.

After having taught Marxist philosophy at the universities of Sarajevo and Belgrade, Andrija Kresić served as a high Communist Party functionary in various government capacities. Toward the end of his career he headed the Institute for the International Workers' Movement in Belgrade. He never participated in any of the formal dialogues but emerged rather quietly and yet decisively as a contributor to the dialogue with a book entitled *Kraljevstvo bozje i komunizam (The Kingdom of God and Communism)*. In it he undertook to study primarily the views of Western Roman Catholic theologians toward Marxism, socialism, and communism. He concluded that in addition to the traditional anti-Communists there were many who appreciated socialism and were progressive in their social views. The entire book is sympathetic to the work of these theologians. He concluded that Christians and Marxists have much in common and should therefore work for the emergence of a more humanitarian society where people, some under the sign of the cross, others under the sign of the hammer and sickle, will harmoniously cooperate together. Here Kresić shares with the other Marxists who favor dialogue a conviction that the future may not produce the obliteration of Christianity. Instead, they envision a pluralistic, humanistic, democratic society where issues of atheism and theism will not separate people.

Vjekoslav Bajsić and Tomislav Sagi-Bunić are both professors of theology at the Roman Catholic Theological Seminary in Zagreb. Theologically they are more liberal than the hierarchy, though in general the theologians do not tend to be at odds with the hierarchy on most issues. Bajsić, Sagi-Bunić, and a third colleague Josip Turcinović constitute the "Zagreb circle" which organized an independent theological society, *Krscanska sadasnjost* (Christian Contemporaneity). In the late 1970s and the 1980s these theologians have found themselves embroiled in controversy within the church because they refuse to capitulate to episcopal pressure to dissolve their theological society and pursue only hierarchically approved theological investigations. While the intricacies of this dispute are marginal to this study, it should be stated that both Bajsić and Sagi-Bunić, as proponents of Vatican II, devoted their primary attention to advocacy of the dialogical approach inside and outside the church. Bajsić stressed the intrinsic value of dialogue as a constitutive part of more wholesome human relations and of personal fulfillment. He emphasized the need for more participation on the local level rather than delegating the responsibility for dialogue only to the party leadership and the church hierarchy. In his writings he sympathetically but critically responded to the writings of his Marxist counterparts. Sagi-Bunić attempted to specify the characteristics of an authentic dialogue.

The archbishop of Split, Dr. Frane Franić, a theologian in his own right, is the only bishop to participate in the dialogues and he reflects on these experiences in his book *Putovi dijaloga (The Paths of Dialogue)*. He is an advocate of the dialogue among Christian groups, between Christians and Muslims and between Christians and Marxists. During the Second Vatican Council he involved himself with a group of progressive Third World bishops and was one of the seventeen authors of an episcopal letter interpreting the encyclical *Populorum Progressio*.[7] He tried to point out possible themes for fruitful dialogue and urged theologians to study Marxism critically. He was hopeful that the dialogue would drastically improve Christian-Marxist relations. But in the 1970s his hopes diminished sharply as he saw the party bureaucracy pull back for fear that the dialogue might dislodge it from its entrenched position. Franić doubts that a qualitative improvement will take place during his own lifetime. He also is the main critic of the "Zagreb circle," envisioning himself as the champion of Roman Catholic unity, which he contends is necessary in order to present a cohesive bloc against those who challenge the church from within and without.

The Dominican friar Tomo Veres, also a theology professor in Zagreb, published a doctoral dissertation entitled *Filozofsko-teoloski dijalog s Marxom (Philosophico-theological Dialogue with Marx)*. This study is an exploration of Marx's own writings with brief treatments of contemporary Marxists and the purpose of dialogue. Veres attempts to take seriously the thought and praxis of Marx with special emphasis on the notion of alienation and its curtailment. At the end of the work, he provides a thoughtful short sketch of the contemporary dialogue and the significance of the issues of theism/atheism and Christian eschatology/Marxist future. Veres's most-recent publications have been book reviews about the current translations and publications of the *Selected Works of Karl Marx*. Veres is regarded as an able scholar within the Roman Catholic Church, one well acquainted with Marx's writings.

Jakov Romić from Dubrovnik, a Franciscan friar of the younger generation, wrote a doctoral dissertation in Rome entitled *De dialogo inter marxistas et christianos (The Dialogue Between Marxists and Christians)*[8] in which he reviewed the work of the Paulus-Gesellschaft and the dialogues which it sponsored. He is also the only Catholic scholar who attempted to deal with some of Lenin's views on religion. Romić asserted that, if there is to be fruitful dialogue in an atmosphere of freedom and coexistence, Marxists must reinterpret some of their most deeply held doctrines (for example, dialectical materialism, religion as solely the ideology of the bourgeoisie or "the opiate of the people," economic determinism, the schematic understanding of history). According to Romić, such reinterpretations will not produce an abandonment of Marxism, but rather a more humanistic Marxism comparable to that of Ernst Bloch and Roger Garaudy.[9] He also believes that many Christians provide barriers to dialogue through adherence to outmoded theological concepts and blind opposition to socialism. Romić feels that progressive theologians and progressive Marxist thinkers may be able to find a common language of dialogue.[10]

If one looks at the themes dealt with by the proponents of the dialogue, one sees both sides advocating the dialogical approach over other ways of encountering one another. In addition to this, Marxists have devoted a great deal of effort to reinterpreting the nature and function of religion, while their Christian counterparts have reassessed their evaluation of Marxism and socialism in order to discover positive values in each system and many areas where each shares some compatibility with Christian principles. However, it should be noted that the Christian dialogists have not accepted socialism uncritically like some of their counterparts in a number of Eastern European countries.

The themes of the dialogue point to its purpose: to bring about an accommodation between the Yugoslavian form of socialism and religious institutions, especially the Roman Catholic Church, which would be more harmonious and less confrontational than it has been in the past. Since church-state relations were not smooth, the dialogue held out the promise of a more humane relationship between Christians and Marxists. The theoretically oriented dialogue also held out the possibility of support for the grass-roots encounters that pervade Yugoslavia but receive no guidance or support from either group. At the grass-roots level, Christians worked alongside Communists in many places and in many ways starting with the war of national liberation, then in rebuilding a country almost totally devastated by war, and in charting an independent and creative Yugoslav path to socialism and working with all its successes and failures. These people worked together, fought against one another, and held ambivalent feelings toward one another. The purpose of the theoretical dialogue was to provide a new approach to human relations that, if adopted and implemented, would produce a more humane society benefiting both Christians and Marxists. Thus the protagonists of the dialogue, as few as they were numerically, had a vision which they felt might inspire a much larger group of people to improve the overall social relationships and thus herald an improved future. It is not surprising that they each saw their own movement surviving into the future; it is encouraging that they stopped denying the possibility of survival to the other group and did not see them as an overwhelming threat to their own aspirations. The dialogue partners foresee change in the future for the other, but also for themselves. Those intellectuals engaging in dialogue are not afraid to criticize their own movement, and this openness to self-criticism is precisely why they were often perceived by the dogmatists in their own group as a threat to each hierarchy's stability and survival.

STATUS AND PROSPECTS

Among the proponents of the dialogue, both Christian and Marxist, there is agreement that dialogue is desirable, indeed necessary. While some dialogue partners have a more limited understanding of the richness and potential benefits of the dialogue than do others, there is no serious discrepancy among them as to what the ground rules of the dialogue should be. They all wish to transcend the inflexibility and hostility which have marked their relations. There is still fear of the power and intransigence of the more entrenched traditionalists who, by and large, still dominate both the ecclesiastical and governmental bureaucracies.

It is interesting to note that, on the whole, the Yugoslavian scene is free from the intimidating accusations heard in other countries which allege that dialogue is a form of ideological subversion and that it will lead to a synthesis unacceptable to both Christians and Marxists. The charges suggest that the dialogists are running the danger of abandoning the central tenets of Marxist ideology and Roman Catholic theology. The criticized dialogists, on the other hand, view their openness to self-criticism and reinterpretation as one of the fundamental dimensions of their respective movements. They claim, therefore, that they are not abandoning their fundamental good, but rather fulfilling it. They hold that they are returning to the heart of Christian theology and Marxist theory. They maintain this position even when they are accused by the government of fostering nationalism (in particular Croatian separatism), liberalism, and of weakening the unity of their own group.

The dialogue thus far has not accomplished any fundamental changes in church-state relations in Yugoslavia. Yet it is not without important consequences. Since the dialogue increases when political and social liberty increase in Yugoslavia, it is not only a barometer of the degree of democratization and liberalization of church and society but a harbinger of a more honest and flexible relationship between these two powerful forces. If church and state officials would not place limitations on the dialogue, it would flourish and have a pervasive impact upon Yugoslavian society. This does not mean that tension would be absent. Self-critical dialogue would create an unprecedented degree of liberty which would allow partners to be less indirect and "diplomatic" and more direct and honest with each other. Since the views of Christians and Marxists on many issues are quite divergent, a more open and pluralistic Yugoslavian society would allow the undercurrents of tension to surface. Then the problem would be to ameliorate these tensions as they emerge so they would not evolve into the murderous hostilities of the past. The question is whether Yugoslav society has matured sufficiently to deal with these differences in a constructive rather than destructive way. The answer to this question rests not only on empirical fore-knowledge but on hope and trust.

When Tito ruled Yugoslavia, he decided whether the dialogue should take place. While he or those close to him did not promote or participate in the dialogue, he allowed it to continue until he felt that nationalistic tensions might lead to the disintegration of the country or the loss of revolutionary accomplishments. Since his death in 1980, the collective and rotating lead-ership of the country has not revealed its policy on dialogue. At the present time they seem to be following Tito's cautious post-1972 posture of neither totally prohibiting the dialogue nor encouraging it. One may surmise on the basis of past experience that the decisive influence will probably be the external considerations that will either inhibit or promote the Christian-Marxist dialogue. Specifically this means how the national questions are handled (Croatian or Albanian separatism, Serbian centralism, Slovenian isolationism, Bulgarian aspirations toward Macedonia); what international political and economic pressures are exerted which could cause internal upheaval; how the leadership question is ultimately resolved; and which ideological orientation prevails within the Communist Party. The churches, for their part, also can influence the dialogue for good or ill by the degree of their politicization of issues, their aggravation of tensions between the na-tionalities, their internal institutional and theological vigor, the degree of their openness to social change, and the degree of their courage to enter experimentally into new social-economic-political structures. Thus far the post-Tito era has not brought any major changes on either side. There is cause to believe that Tito's policy will continue and hope that Christians and Marxists in Yugoslavia will continue to pursue various approaches to con-structive dialogue.

NOTES

1. I will not venture here into the question of practicing versus nominal membership nor the issue of how many people have been atheized on account of government pressure or other factors of secularization. No religious statistics are available. The above figures are widely accepted approximations.

2. A large number, between 10 and 20 percent, may consider themselves atheists.

3. For a more complete treatment of these stages see Paul Mojzes, "Christian-Marxist Encounter in the Context of a Socialist Society," *Journal of Ecumenical Studies* 9:1 (Winter 1972): 1–27. For a completely different treatment with a wealth of details see Stella Alexander, *Church and State in Yugoslavia Since 1945* (Cambridge: Cambridge University Press, 1979).

4. For a comprehensive treatment of the dialogue see Paul Mojzes, *Christian-Marxist Dialogue in Eastern Europe* (Minneapolis: Augsburg Publishing House, 1981), 128–58.

5. Stenographic notes of the dialogue were subsequently published. Branko Bosnjak and Mijo Skvorc, *Marksist i krsćanin* (Zagreb: Praxis, 1969).

6. Those most readily available are Vjekoslav Bajsić (Roman Catholic), "The Significance and Problems of the Dialogue Today," and Zdenko Roter (Marxist), "A Marxist View of Christianity," *Journal of Ecumenical Studies* 9:1 (Winter 1972): 29–39 and 40–50 respectively. Also Jakov Romić (Roman Catholic), "Dialogue between Marxists and Christians as a Presupposition of Coexistence in Freedom," *Journal of Ecumenical Studies* 15:1 (Winter 1978): 114–29. Branko Bosnjak (Marxist), "Reflections on Religion," in *Religion and Atheism in the U.S.S.R. and Eastern Europe*, ed. Bohdan R. Bociurkiw and John W. Strong (Toronto: University of Toronto Press, 1975), 18–36. Some of Bosnjak's works were also published in German.

7. "Beyond Dialogue: A Letter from Seventeen Roman Catholic Bishops of the Third World Interpreting *Populorum Progressio*," in *The Christian Marxist Dialogue*, ed. Paul Oestreicher (New York: Macmillan Co., 1969), 232–46.

8. Jakov Romić, *De dialogo inter marxistas et christianos* (Vicenza, Italy: Liberia Internazionale Edizione Franciscane, 1972).

9. See Romić, "Dialogue between Marxists and Christians."

10. Romić spent several years in the United States and some other Western countries working with immigrant Roman Catholics and participating in Christian-Marxist dialogues outside of Yugoslavia.

SUGGESTIONS FOR FURTHER READING

Alexander, Stella. *Church and State in Yugoslavia Since 1945*. Cambridge: Cambridge University Press, 1979.

Bosnjak Branko. "Reflections on Religion." In *Religion and Atheism in the U.S.S.R. and Eastern Europe*, edited by Bohdan R. Bociurkiw and John W. Strong, 18–36. Toronto: University of Toronto Press, 1975.

Kresić, Andrija. "The Kingdom of God and Communism." In *Varieties of Christian-Marxist Dialogue*, edited by Paul Mojzes, 29–40. Philadelphia: Ecumenical Press, 1978. Also published in *Journal of Ecumenical Studies* 15:1 (Winter 1978): 29–40.

Mojzes, Paul. *Christian-Marxist Dialogue in Eastern Europe*. Minneapolis: Augsburg Publishing House, 1981.

———"Christian-Marxist Encounter in the Context of a Socialist Society." *Journal of Ecumenical Studies* 9:1 (Winter 1972): 1–28.

Romić, Jakov Rafael. "Dialogue Between Marxists and Christians as a Presupposition of Coexistence in Freedom." In *Varieties of Christian-Marxist Dialogue,* edited by Paul Mojzes, 114–29. Also published in *Journal of Ecumenical Studies* 15:1 (Winter 1978): 114–29.

THIRD WORLD ENCOUNTERS

BLACK AFRICA
Norman E. Thomas

Africa is a continent with many diverse countries, peoples, and cultures. This diversity is not a modern phenomenon; in fact, there was probably a greater diversity of political and economic systems in precolonial Africa than exists today in industrialized nations. Amidst the kaleidoscope of peoples, cultures, political systems, and religious groups of modern Africa, two significant patterns of Christian-Marxist encounters have emerged—those related to *African socialism* and those related to *revolutionary Marxism*. In this chapter each shall be related to its historical setting. Focus will be placed both on individual leaders who have initiated the encounter and upon selected countries. Finally, a brief assessment will be made of the road ahead with anticipated points of convergence and divergence.

AFRICAN SOCIALISM

In December 1962 President Léopold Senghor of Senegal invited African political leaders to Dakar for the Colloquium on Policies of Development and African Approaches to Socialism. His goal was to create a shock and to attract attention to the importance of development and the need to choose the most efficient ways and means for it. There was a recognition that participants held very diverse views on economic issues, and no attempt was made to pass resolutions. Nevertheless, the vague contours of what is known as *African socialism* emerged in which "nationalism, Pan-Africanism, and socialism are woven together to create an overall African ideology of modernization."[1]

The seedbed for this fusion of socialism and modernization by Africa's future leaders was not to be found in Moscow, Prague, or Peking, but in Paris and London in the 1930s and 1940s. Léopold Senghor (Senegal), Sekou Touré (Guinea), and Modibo Keita (Mali) all were products of Marxist study groups in Paris (Groupes d'Études Communistes), with branches established in five major cities in French Africa by 1943. Meanwhile British Communists and Fabian Socialists were influencing their counterparts from British colonies. Kwame Nkrumah (Ghana), Jomo Kenyatta (Kenya), Hastings Banda (Malawi), and Nnamdi Azikiwe (Nigeria) all were present at the Fifth Pan-African Congress in 1945 where Socialist viewpoints predominated.

The first level of Christian-Marxist encounters for black Africa's future leaders, therefore, took place on European soil. It involved only future African politicians and European Christians, however, because no African clergy were being educated in Europe at that time. These future political leaders, by and large, were products of mission schools. They had been incubated with the century-old linkage of Christianity, commerce, and civilization. Some would rebel against a Christianity that equated monogamy and capitalism with eternal truth. Others sought for a new religious undergirding for a distinctly African social order. The views of four of these African socialists—Léopold Senghor (Senegal), Kenneth Kaunda (Zambia), Kwame Nkrumah (Ghana), and Julius Nyerere (Tanzania)—merit brief consideration here.

Léopold Senghor

Léopold Senghor in the late-1940s was probably the first to use the term "African socialism." He took Marx's ideas and theories as a starting point, but very selectively. He accepted Marx's humanistic philosophy and dialectical method, but he interpreted Marx's early statement that religion is the opium of the masses as *"a reaction of Christian origin against the historical deviations of Christianity,"* judging it to be not necessary to the "positive part" of Marx's work.[2] Similarly, in assessing economic policy options for the new state of Senegal, the philosopher-president considered Marxist-Leninist solutions to be historically conditioned and too deterministic in approach. Instead he favored an open, democratic, and humanistic socialism in tune with the communitarian values of African society.

As for the future, Senghor rejected Marx's vision of a class struggle and inevitable dictatorship of the proletariat. Instead he affirmed the vision of Teilhard de Chardin, the French Jesuit philosopher. It includes the aspiration of human convergence with God at the end of history, called the Omega point, and the possibility of present transformation if love can be the guide in human socialization.

Senghor found no conflict between the utopian visions of his mentors, quoting with approval a Teilhard statement that the synthesis of the Christian "God" on high and the Marxist "God" of the future is the only God we can henceforth adore in spirit and in truth. And then as the eclectic leader of a predominantly Muslim country he added: "As you know, the Christian God is also the Moslem God."[3] He considered both faiths to be revolutionary because they introduce universal values useful in assimilating the values of socialism to those African cultural values which he termed *Négritude*.

Kenneth Kaunda

African socialism is humanist socialism, President Kenneth Kaunda of Zambia, like Senghor before him, consistently affirmed. Whereas Senghor found his sources in the Christian philosophy of Teilhard and the thought of the young Marx, Kaunda found them in the traditional values of Zambian culture and the teachings of Jesus. He believed that Africa's special gift to world culture would be in the field of human relations. For the traditional African community, he believed, was a mutual-aid society characterized by a primary concern for human need, acceptance, and inclusion of all and by cooperative effort. He believed that society has a spiritual undergirding.

> Man is not just a machine nor is he just a higher animal. Man was created by God in His own image and likeness. So Man has a higher density than just living well. Man pursues that higher density best when he is guided by spiritual values. Humanism can provide that spiritual need in Zambia. [4]

Kaunda rejected all attempts to separate body and spirit, politics and religion. "Religion must continue to play an important part in our national life," he declared. In doing so it follows both the teaching and example of Jesus Christ who worked for a classless society. For him the humanist objective was given in the Lord's Prayer as God's will being done on earth as it is in heaven. The cardinal difference between this humanistic view and the Communistic view he found in the latter's denial of belief in the Super-being and afterlife. [5]

Zambia's president saw no tensions between Christ's teachings and an imperative to move from a capitalist to a Socialist model of economic organization. Addressing in 1974 the All-Africa Conference of Churches' Third Assembly in Lusaka, he declared:

> Church leaders must be in the forefront in guiding the African nations and African leaders to move away from economic and social systems that glorify inequality. Let the Church help put the new nations firmly on the road to prosperity which is based on human equality. [6]

Kaunda described his economic goal as movement from a capitalist to a Socialist, or common ownership, economy. This movement to socialize all the means of production, however, was not to be an end in itself, but rather the means to attain a humanistic society. In the 1970s, Zambia government leaders struggled to implement this Socialist philosophy with village regrouping and government ownership of industry (in whole or in part) as key issues.

Kwame Nkrumah

Kwame Nkrumah of Ghana, a third theorist of African socialism, became a transitional Socialist linking the African socialism of the 1960s to the revolutionary Marxism of the 1970s.

In the London Socialist seedbed, Nkrumah became a close friend of George Padmore, a West Indian who had lived for some time in the Soviet Union. From him Nkrumah received both a knowledge of Marxism-Leninism and his dream of Pan-African unity. He returned in 1947 to his native Ghana (Gold Coast) to lead a ten-year struggle for independence. Ghana became the pacesetter in Africa in the drive to end colonial rule, and Nkrumah became Africa's most messianic figure.

Like Franz Fanon of Martinique and Algeria, Nkrumah believed that achieving political and economic independence from colonialism required the education and mobilization of the masses. Both gave a Marxist-Leninist critique of modern capitalism.[7] But whereas Fanon remained the propagandist of a revolution, Nkrumah headed a nation state wedded economically to international capitalism. Out of that crucible he did not proclaim Fanon's view that genuine liberation from colonial domination could be achieved only by breaking all economic ties with capitalist countries. Although he aimed at establishing a Socialist society, Nkrumah avoided the term Marxism-Leninism. Instead he called Ghana's system *Nkrumahism* and his philosophy *consciencism*. He claimed as its sources both Islamic and Euro-Christian traditions, as well as "the cluster of humanistic principles which underlie the traditional African society."[8]

Toppled from power by a military coup in 1966, Nkrumah fled to Conakry in neighboring Guinea. Freed from Ghana's partnership with international capitalism, he began to expound Marxism-Leninism publicly.

> There are only two ways of development open to an Independent African State. Either it must remain under imperialist domination via capitalism and neo-colonialism; or it must pursue a socialist path by adopting the principles of scientific socialism.[9]

During this period Nkrumah rejected African socialism as meaningless and irrelevant, as well as the assumption that traditional African society was classless. Instead he advocated class struggle. The true Socialist government was to be achieved through revolutionary armed struggle by the peasantry, in alliance with the Communist world against the reactionary bourgeoisie.

In his attitude toward religion Nkrumah became a precursor of those revolutionary Marxists who would condemn Christianity as part of the old order, and church leaders as tools of neocolonialism and Western imperialism. He claimed that the Christian idea of original sin is opposite to traditional African humanism which affirms a person's inward dignity, integrity, and value.

These first theorists of African socialism sought to affirm the basic values of African communalism. From each according to ability to each according to need was understood as a traditional African approach to social security. Holding property in common was the traditional way of land ownership. Finally, both land and people were understood as inextricably linked to the Creator and Sustainer of all life, health, and prosperity.

This was the cultural bedrock upon which Senghor, Kaunda, and Nkrumah built their ideologies. Their ideologies varied, however, according to the degree to which they incorporated either Marxist-Leninist or Western Christian values. On the one hand, each found the Marxist critique of Western capitalism useful as their nations struggled for both political and economic independence. On the other hand, they eschewed frontal attacks using Marxist-Leninist rhetoric which might scare off that Western capital which they needed for national development. They varied widely in their incorporation of Christian values. Kaunda, son of a pioneer African evangelist, acknowledged the affinity of his social ideals with Christ's teachings. Senghor attempted a philosopher's blending of the thought of Marx and Teilhard. Nkrumah, by contrast, developed an explicitly secular ideology with an anti-Christian bias in its final revision prior to his death in 1972.

African socialism, however, was more than a theory, despite the judgment made on Nkrumah's later works that they "are strictly philosophical and theoretical in nature, bearing no actual relationship to either peaceful or violent movements for socialism in Africa."[10] The actual implementation of African socialism in public policy received its clearest development in Tanzania under the leadership of its president, Julius Nyerere.

Tanzania: A Case Study

The United Republic of Tanzania resulted from a 1964 union between the former Tanganyika and the two offshore islands of Zanzibar and Pemba. It has an area of 361,800 square miles, which is a little larger than Nigeria. Only 20,000 square miles, however, is arable—the rest being mostly tsetse fly–infested woodland inimical to cattle raising. Nevertheless, most of Tanzania's more than fourteen million people from 120 diverse tribal backgrounds engage in subsistence agriculture.

Six years after independence, President Julius Nyerere in 1967 electrified African politics with the publication of his *Arusha Declaration*. By it, socialism was to be moved from the status of a slogan (*Ujamaa*, meaning familyhood) to that of a detailed social policy.

> To build and maintain socialism it is essential that all the major means of production and exchange in the nation are controlled and owned by the peasants through the machinery of their Government and their co-operatives. Further, it is essential that the ruling Party should be a Party of peasants and workers.[11]

This shift came neither as a result of revolution nor of electoral victory by a Socialist party. Concerning the new commitment one historian has written:

> The conclusion is unavoidable. There were no policy imperatives . . . providing an influential application of Marxian analysis to Tanzanian affairs. There were no substantial political or class demands for socialist initiatives. Without Nyerere, Tanzanian socialism would have been most unlikely to become a major force in these years.[12]

Nyerere developed four strategies for the transition to socialism: the promotion of greater equality, the maintenance of Tanzanian self-reliance, the creation of a Socialist environment, and the enhancement of democratic participation. He believed that socialism (like democracy) is an attitude of mind. It is akin to the traditional value which gave the security to each individual that comes of belonging to an extended family. Nyerere believed that *Ujamaa* (familyhood) could be the social cement in the wider society of the nation-state. The class struggle, in his view, is irrelevant to Tanzania's situation, yet very relevant on the international scene where the world is still divided between haves and have-nots.

Initially Soviet analysts evaluated positively the Tanzanian experiment seeing it as a possible transitional stage to scientific socialism. Later they became critical both of Nyerere's counterpoising of African socialism against scientific socialism and of his rejection of class struggle as inappropriate in the African cultural context.[13]

Nyerere's dialogue with church leaders following the *Arusha Declaration* helped many move from initial suspicion to growing acceptance of the principles of African socialism (while remaining critical of specific government policies). Nyerere recognized that the churches were by far the most powerful and influential nongovernmental institutions in Tanzania. During the earlier colonial era they had developed most of the country's educational and health facilities, as well as certain roads, bridges, and electrical services in rural areas. He also recognized that church leaders retained close ties with their counterparts in Western Europe. As a result they tended to echo stereotypes of communism and socialism common in Western Europe. For example, as late as 1970, the Tanzanian Catholic bishops reissued a Swahili version of the older (1937) papal letter *Divini Redemptoris* with its denunciation of communism rather than the later and more conciliatory Vatican II documents.

Responding to the apprehensions of church leaders, Nyerere stressed his own faith as a devout and practicing Roman Catholic. But Nyerere did not believe that the state should endorse any one religion. Instead it was to guarantee religious freedom to all. He wrote:

> Certainly in Africa socialism is everywhere accepted as a secular doctrine, and as one which has no comment to make upon metaphysics. All the States which profess socialism in Africa do accept the freedom of religious beliefs, and of all religions.[14]

"I am trying to build a socialist, not an atheist, society," he told the religious superiors of Tanzania (RC) in 1976.[15]

Next, Nyerere challenged the churches to work with the Socialist state in the struggle for justice. In a major speech on "The Church and Society" to the Maryknoll Sisters Conference in 1970, he said:

> Unless we participate actively in the rebellion against those social structures and economic organizations which condemn men to poverty, humiliation and degradation, then the Church will become irrelevant to Man and . . . will become identified with injustice and persecution.[16]

Later he was to summarize this as the two-sided function of the church in the development of people: to develop personal integrity and to participate in the encouragement of development activities. For the president that implied joint sponsorship by church and local government of some development activities at the village or district level. At other times he urged church development organizations to take the initiative in areas where Christians perceive a need but the state is unwilling or unable to give a high priority.[17]

Such church initiatives have taken place. The Team Ministry in Singida, for example, was a cooperative effort by party, government, and the churches in an economically backward area where the Lutheran Church is strong. The team's underlying philosophy was that government and church are "the two hands of God, which have to work together." Many of the civil servants involved are both church-educated and active members of local parishes. The team successfully completed several development projects with the joint approval of the central government and of the church's Central Synod. They learned that the chance of tension between party and church was significantly reduced when they worked together. The party supplied formal political and administrative leadership, and the church financial aid and moral leadership.[18]

In other areas tensions have arisen. The villagization (*Ujamaa*) program of resettlement received a mixed reception. Priests and pastors often became spokespersons for church members reluctant to move.[19]

Evidence that contextual rather than ideological factors may be more significant in the attitudes of church leaders to *Ujamaa* policies comes from an attitudinal survey of seminarians of the Evangelical Lutheran Church in Tanzania (ELCT) conducted in 1978. Of those interviewed, 64 percent looked forward to the day when all citizens live in *Ujamaa* villages with a substantial amount of collective production. The students emphasized their conviction, however, that moves must be voluntary. Students from areas in which people had been moved by force strongly disagreed with this way of implementing *Ujamaa*. As for socialism, 64 percent agreed with the statement that "Socialism, in its essence, should be attractive to believers and in particular to Christians because its fundamental principles are similar to the Gospel." The remainder were unsure or disagreed because they felt that the center of Christianity is Christ, whereas the center of *Ujamaa* is man. The author, reflecting on these results, asks:

> Have they from their middle or upper middle strata social background or from political education really understood what socialism may require of the Church? Is the real danger in the ELCT's relation to the Western churches . . . which prevents the leaders and pastors from becoming really committed socialists?[20]

In contrast to this sanguine view, Father Laurenti Magesa finds a close affinity between the *praxis* (action/reflection) of *Ujamaa* and liberation theology. He believes that the ruling TANU party's policy of *Ujamaa* is the driving force behind all aspects of Tanzanian life—morals, social organization, economic life, education, and symbolism. Rather than feeling threatened by this fact, Magesa is challenged to develop a political theology aimed at human liberation that is sensitive to the dynamics of Tanzanian culture. He believes in the central values of *Ujamaa*—brotherhood, development, economic justice, equality, freedom, and the continual betterment of human beings. "The spirit of the Tidings of the Gospel and that pursued by *Ujamaa* are not antithetical but identical," he reasoned.[21] But agreement in theory does not presume perfection in practice. He concedes that abuses of dishonesty, opportunism, coercion, and so forth do exist in the practice of *Ujamaa*. For Magesa, Christians face dual temptations: to remain neutral and do nothing about these abuses or to reject *Ujamaa* because of some mistakes and injustices in its practice. He appeals to Christians to become involved critically in the struggle for justice in Tanzania's Socialist society.

CAN AFRICAN SOCIALISM BE CALLED MARXIST?

Is African socialism in Tanzania and other countries a form of Marxism? If not, should it be included in a discussion of Christian-Marxist encounters in Africa?

Some scholars would argue that *African socialism* is in essence not true socialism, but instead modernizing nationalism. They say that, although its proponents accept Marxist tools of analysis, they reject basic concepts of the Marxist ideology. They would distinguish the resulting populism from Marxism-Leninism in six key features: 1) the authority of a charismatic leader rather than of the party as the vanguard of the workers; 2) the emphasis on ethical dimensions of leadership and development rather than sociological considerations; 3) the political rather than social mobilization of the masses; 4) the emphasis on unity of the people rather than on class struggle; 5) the stress on racial and cultural rather than on economic aspects of colonialism; and 6) the concentration on national development more than on the international Socialist revolution.[22]

Nevertheless, Marxist categories of analysis have been introduced in the continent by the proponents of African socialism. This enabled Christian leaders to move to a generally positive acceptance of this first wave of socialism—a necessary preparation for the more rigorous encounter with revolutionary Marxism to come.

REVOLUTIONARY MARXISM

If 1957 (Ghana's independence) and 1967 (the *Arusha Declaration*) were the critical years for African socialism, 1975 stands as the seminal year for the second phase of socialism in Africa—that of revolutionary Marxism.

In April 1974 a radical military group seized power in the Portuguese capital of Lisbon, giving new hope to liberation movements in its colonies. Within eighteen months new governments espousing Marxism-Leninism had come to power in the former Portuguese colonies of Angola, Mozambique, and Guinea-Bissau. Meanwhile, in June 1974 a "creeping coup" by military officers began in Ethiopia. Within three years Africa's most feudal systems had been replaced by the continent's most orthodox Marxist systems.[23]

The rapidity and dynamism of these changes took many observers by surprise both in the East and West. Although certain guerrilla leaders had been trained in Moscow and Peking and arms flowed from Communist countries, these changes could not be explained as Russian expansion south of the Sahara. "We do not intend to become another Bulgaria," remarked a top political adviser to President Samora Machel of Mozambique.[24] Having thrown off one form of colonial domination the new nations did not want to replace it with another.

In contrast to African socialism, revolutionary Marxism has a specific ideology based on Marxism-Leninism. Some of its components are: 1) a single-party system with a small vanguard party rather than a mass one; 2) formation of broad national bodies for women and youth, with local branches plus neighborhood "action committees" to incorporate every citizen in the movement; 3) nationalization of major industries, banks, and insurance companies; 4) state control over exports and imports; 5) a preference for state collective farms; and 6) the development of comprehensive economic planning for the nation.

In practice, however, states committed to a Marxist-Leninist ideology in Africa are finding it as necessary to develop mixed economies as have the Soviet Union and the People's Republic of China. In 1980 President Machel of Mozambique announced the denationalization of small grocery stores and restaurants which had been paralyzed by inefficiency under government control.

CHRISTIANS AND THE REVOLUTIONARY STRUGGLE

Before discussing specific Christian-Marxist encounters it is important to understand the shift that took place from alienation to rapprochement between certain church bodies and the liberation movements in southern Africa.

In many African countries political leaders throughout their training retained close links with the churches. Many began as students in mission schools and went on to teach there. Early meetings of political associations and parties often were held on church premises.

In contrast the liberation movements organized outside their home countries. They needed guns and an ideology justifying the armed struggle rather than church halls or schools to meet in. The new ideology not only justified the armed struggle against colonialism but also denounced Christianity as part of the old oppressive order. Certain facts supported this latter charge. Scarcely a wall separated the residences of the Portuguese governor and Catholic archbishop in Lorenço Marques or Luanda, for example. It was more than coincidence that the Anglican cathedral in Salisbury adjoined the Parliament of Ian Smith. To many Marxist revolutionaries the church and colonial state appeared inextricably linked in an unholy alliance. As a result, by the late 1960s an almost complete divorce took place between the liberation movements and the churches. Even such highly committed Christians as Eduardo Mondlane, leader of FRELIMO in Mozambique, had ceased to identify themselves with the church.

During the 1970s, however, a significant shift took place. Church organizations began to make overtures to the liberation movements. New concepts emerged—political theology, the theology of liberation, institutional violence, and "the option for the poor." The World Council of Churches' Programme to Combat Racism, with block grants to liberation movements for humanitarian work, was the most visible symbol of this change of heart.[25]

THE CHALLENGE TO AFRICAN SOCIALISM

Meanwhile the states that have embraced African socialism felt the challenge from those both within and without who favored a more revolutionary Marxism.

In *Tanzania* a vigorous encounter has developed in the past ten years between those affirming African socialism and those espousing Marxist-Leninist principles. It began earlier on the university campus in Dar es Salaam. "Who controls Tanzania's economy?" asked Issa Shivji in an article on "the silent class struggle."[26] International capitalism was his answer, as he unmasked the neocolonial web of multinationals controlling Tanzania's major industries and joint ventures. More recently another critic concluded:

> that the *Ujamaa* experiment . . . did not alter the general mode of production, which remains tied to capitalist forms of production and management . . . Tanzanian socialism . . . remains reformist, hovering between the existing system of exploitation, both internal and external, and a genuine socialist struggle and liberation. Tanzanian socialism remains confused in its attempt to both challenge and preserve the exploitative *status quo*.[27]

For the purpose of this essay what is striking is the total absence of such an economic critique of *Ujamaa* socialism in church statements.

Turning to *Zambia*, in contrast, a lively debate is under way, concerning both the goals and policies of Zambia's Socialist experiment, with church leaders active in the encounter.

Zambia has been caricatured as "the upper class welfare state."[28] Dependent in the mid-1970s on copper exports to provide 95 percent of foreign earnings and 50 percent of government revenue, Zambia was caught concurrently with falling copper and rising oil prices. Although Kaunda's humanistic society was to include an agrarian revolution, the Second Five-Year Plan (1972–76) allocated only 12 percent of capital resources to agriculture. Schemes faltered for rural reconstruction centers, cooperatives, and village productivity committees. The result was a greater gap in 1980 between rich and poor, between the city and the countryside, than had existed at independence in 1964.

Within the ruling party and government a movement grew to replace *humanistic socialism* with *scientific socialism* (or Marxism-Leninism). The means of political reeducation were to include courses for party leaders and "political educators," classes for Young Pioneers (the government-sponsored youth movement), and new lessons in school curricula. Church leaders reacted with a storm of protest that struck the nation like a thunderclap. Since independence the predominant mode of church contacts with government was through the informal network of interpersonal contacts. Public protests were rare. The immediate precipitant was a speech by the vice-president, himself a Roman Catholic, in which he stated that *scientific socialism* should be introduced in Zambian schools.

Church leaders reacted with alarm and with a rare show of ecumenical unity. In August 1979, an open letter was published entitled "Marxism, Humanism and Christianity," which was signed by the nine Catholic bishops and by the Secretaries of the Christian Council of Zambia and the Zambia Evangelical Fellowship on behalf of their organizations. The clerics rejected all forms of capitalism which place profit before persons. Socialism, in contrast, was judged to be in harmony with Christian beliefs "insofar as it means a system which tries, by public ownership of the means of production, to make a nation's wealth serve all its members fairly."[29] Zambian humanism (equated with democratic socialism) was found to be entirely consistent with this criteria. In contrast, however, scientific socialism was condemned totally. An appeal was made to President Kaunda's rejection of the essential atheism of scientific socialism in *Humanism in Zambia, Part II*. They argued that scientific socialism denies God and in doing so denies the sanctity of humanity. They went on to reject the term "Christian Marxist" on the grounds that "the beliefs of Christianity and Marxism are incompatible with regard to religion."[30] Nevertheless, collaboration between Christians and Marxists was accepted in actions to end exploitation and injustice, as well as the use of Marxist analysis for examining social change.

The leaders of the United National Independence Party (UNIP) felt stung by the Open Letter. *Target*, a church newspaper, quotes one UNIP leader as saying that "church leaders should remain within their spiritual domain rather than venture into politics which is a domain for politicians"—an ironic answer since some missionaries had used identical words earlier to justify their lack of involvement in the independence struggle.[31]

The next phase of the encounter began in March 1982 as President Kaunda invited all the religious leaders of the country (Christian, Hindu, and Muslim) to attend a Seminar on Humanism and Development at the government's showplace, Mulungushi Hall, in Lusaka. Kaunda opened the seminar with a lengthy reply to the Open Letter. He sought both to support the ideological positions voiced by the church leaders, and to back the party's decision to introduce the teaching of scientific socialism in schools. He argued that inasmuch as scientific Socialists exist, their ideology should be studied as part of political education. He sought to reassure his listeners that this new subject would not replace religious education.[32]

But the president's explanations did not satisfy the church leaders. After a half-day's reflection they responded with twenty-two theses of rebuttal, reaffirming their 1979 stand. Among their arguments were these:

(8) We wish a society based on the equality of all men, where man is central and free. No decision should be taken to transform Zambia into a Scientific Socialist state, a Marxist-Leninist or a communist state.

(9) Marxism-Leninism is opposed to the idea of God and tries to banish him from life. We totally reject Scientific (atheistic) Socialism.

(10) Because atheism destroys the foundation of true Humanism (belief in God and in men as his children) Scientific Socialism cannot lead to Humanism.

(21) Scientific (atheistic) Socialism cannot be taught side by side with religion, since they are contradictory.[33]

President Kaunda in response avoided every word that rankled the clergy, calling merely for a new approach—socialism leading to humanism. He argued that the nation would develop from a mixed economy to a Socialist one, and finally to what he termed a "humanist" economy.

Although retaining great confidence in their president, the church leaders felt that his closing words seemed to obfuscate rather than clarify the issues. Nor did the encounter end there, as church leaders sought to stimulate discussion on local levels. Archbishop Emmanuel Milingo (RC) focused his Easter message on the issue. The United Church of Zambia discussed it in its April Synod and endorsed the open letter. Some congregations and parishes organized "a day of fast and prayer." Meanwhile, the church leaders' summary of the debate at the President's seminar received wide circulation as a Second Letter from the Leaders of the Church in Zambia.

Revolutionary Marxism in Practice

While the vigorous debate concerning scientific socialism continues in Zambia, a number of countries have opted already for the Marxist model (Angola, Congo Brazzaville, Ethiopia, Mozambique, and Zimbabwe). Each repudiates African socialism as utopian and nationalistic. Of the five, let us consider Zimbabwe as a case study of Christian-Marxist encounter.

In 1980 Robert Mugabe, the committed Marxist leader of the Zimbabwe African National Union (ZANU), was elected to lead a new African government into independence, thereby ending ninety years of white-settler rule. It ended a bitter and costly guerrilla war which had increased in intensity each year following Ian Smith's rebellion (UDI) against Britain in 1965.

Zimbabwe possesses both fertile land sufficient to serve as the granary of east and central Africa and mineral resources of iron ore, coal, and copper needed for industrial development. In its 150,804 square miles of land live more than 6.5 million people, with many still crowded on the least arable lands consigned to them by their former white rulers. Problems are numerous—rivalries between competing parties, reconciliation with remaining white settlers, reallocation of lands, and countering subversion from South Africa.

Prime Minister Mugabe defines the nation's ideology as socialism based on Marxist-Leninist principles and as scientific socialism. Furthermore, he believes that these principles are not at variance with the values and social practices of traditional society.

In his remarkable book *The Theology of Promise*, Zimbabwe's President Canaan Banana, a Methodist minister, develops a liberation theology in harmony with revolutionary Marxism. "Is the revolution a hindrance or a help to Christianity?" he asks. "Can one be a Christian and a revolutionary at the same time?" In his foreword to the volume, Mugabe answers with an emphatic yes to both questions. He calls on the church "to join the state as participant in the process of the social transformation of society."[34]

The prime minister makes a distinction between Christian morality (the tenets of justice, the brotherhood of man, the love of neighbor, equality before God, and so forth) and Christianity. He praises the former but condemns the latter which under colonialism often acquiesced amidst inhumanities to the black population. Since 1965, however, he judges that the church has sufficiently redeemed itself by its outspoken criticism and condemnation of wrongs perpetuated by white-settler rule.

Turning to the present, both Mugabe and Banana call for a revolutionary theology to match revolutionary Marxism. For Banana political action should not be separated from religious motivations:

> A man who is involved in the revolutionary struggle cannot cut himself off from his intimate convictions, neither can he pray to God leaving aside his commitment to other human beings in an effective political action. Religion and politics are two sides of the same coin.[35]

These words have an autobiographical ring for they echo the president's experience during his years of political detention by Ian Smith's regime. As for Christianity and socialism, Banana finds in the New Testament (Acts 2:44–45) a deliberate move toward economic socialism.

Banana advocates a living theology and a living Marxism, each emanating from the people. He would understand the Creator as a God of socialism who is actively at work through all events, including the revolutionary transformation of society taking place in Zimbabwe. Thus he stands the common criticism of Marxism—that it is materialist—on its head. It is the capitalist who is the materialist, Banana argues, because he seeks to divorce religion from economic decision making, relying instead on "market forces." By contrast the Christian Socialist finds evidence of God's promise in the social changes taking place. As for *praxis*, the president begins by cultivating his garden plot at the president's mansion alongside his cook and gardener. He encourages the churches to join with government and party in meeting the massive needs for more schools and clinics. His goal is an active partnership of revolutionary Christianity with revolutionary Marxism.

STATUS AND PROSPECTS

In 1969 Thomas Blakeley, in an essay entitled "Christian-Marxist Dialogue and the Otherworld," claimed that peoples of the Third World were the silent partners in the dialogue movement. He argued that previous Christian-Marxist dialogues had been based on Western assumptions concerning the nature of moral discourse—assumptions quite different from those in African thought and cultural experience.[36]

In this essay we have seen that Africans are no longer the silent partners in the Christian-Marxist encounter, and that the African social context gives a special character to that encounter. Africans replace the political philosopher's argumentation over opposing theories with *praxis*—action for creative social change and reflection upon it.

Points of Convergence and Divergence

Despite the immense diversity of cultures and political experiences in the forty-five nations of black Africa, points of consensus have emerged in the Christian-Marxist dialogue. Out of a common colonial heritage, church leaders have come to accept the value of the Marxist critique of colonialism, of Western capitalism, and of neocolonialism on the continent. Second, traditional African values have been affirmed and found relevant for the contextualization both of Christian theology and of Marxism on the continent. From the basic affirmation of the unity of body and spirit is derived the conviction that politics and religion are inextricably bound to each other.

Major points of divergence occur most frequently among ideological fundamentalists, whether of the Christian or Marxist variety. The sharpest confrontation between Christian leaders and Marxist politicians has occurred when either one side or the other (or both) rests its authority on dogma formulated in Europe, without openness to African contextualization. On the one hand, confrontation intensifies whenever Marxists claim that Marx's condemnation of Christianity as he experienced it in Europe during his youth is normative for all Marxists. It also occurs whenever the concept of class struggle, developed as Europe moved from feudalism to industrialization, is elevated to the status of a universal norm. On the other hand, Christian leaders intensify the confrontation wherever they apply the European judgment that scientific socialism is atheistic to its African formulations.

Consequences of the Encounter

These reflections lead to fundamental questions of epistemology. President Banana of Zimbabwe, for example, identifies two different approaches in the encounter of Christianity and Marxism. One uses an analytical method starting with abstract premises. Concerning it, he writes: "The analytical method is not a discovery because the answers are all contained in the books. Once you accept the premises the conclusions will follow."[37] Using such a method Christians and Marxists often are at loggerheads—the Christians arguing from their holy book that there is a God and the Marxists from their "book" denying it. The other approach Banana calls revolutionary theology. A person using it seeks to listen to the Word of God in historical events. Banana believes that Christians and Marxists (and Christian Marxists!) can achieve a unity of method amidst the struggle. All can be committed together to the struggle for justice in history, and can be open to change through action and reflection upon that action. He relates this to what José Míguez Bonino, the Latin American liberation theologian, calls "a concrete engagement, an active relationship with reality."[38]

Toward the Future

What will African Marxism look like in the year 2000? Per Frostin asks.[39] Our evidence supports his conclusions that 1) there will be great diversity according to the historical situation in each country, and 2) the tendency to define African Marxism as scientific socialism will continue.

Will the church develop a revolutionary Christianity to place alongside the revolutionary Marxism of the state? President Banana sees that development as the only viable option for the church in Zimbabwe. He writes:

> It is apparent that only a genuine form of Christianity which springs from the people's experience would find room in Zimbabwe. . . . For Christianity to rediscover itself in the revolutionary process it would need to abandon the unnecessary baggage that it has gathered through centuries of alliance with western civilization.[40]

Will Marxism in Africa develop its own indigenous character to place alongside the vigorous Christianity of much of the continent? To do otherwise would be to become like dinosaurs—armor-plated with ideology but unable to adapt to a changing climate.

Freed from the legacies of European ideological conflicts, institutions, and political systems, Africa possesses the potential for an ever-new and dynamic encounter between Christianity and Marxism. Truly, no other continent has the same possibilities as Africa to create a new and vigorous Christian-Marxist encounter. At times it will be an external encounter—a debate or struggle between persons and institutions. Sometimes it will be more of an internal encounter in which the Christian Marxist seeks for holism and integrity.

NOTES

1. Aristide R. Zolberg, "The Dakar Colloquium: The Search for a Doctrine," in *African Socialism*, ed. William H. Friedland and Carl Rosberg, Jr. (Stanford, Calif.: Stanford University Press, 1964), 127.

2. Léopold Senghor, *On African Socialism* (New York: Praeger Publishers, 1964), 38.

3. Ibid., 45.

4. Kenneth Kaunda, *Humanism in Zambia and a Guide to Its Implementation, Part II* (Lusaka, Zambia: Division of National Guidance, 1974), 125.

5. Ibid., 8.

6. "The Challenge of Our Stewardship in Africa," in *Third World Theologies*, ed. G. H. Anderson and T. F. Stransky (New York: Paulist Press, 1976), 173.

7. Franz Fanon, *The Wretched of the Earth* (New York: Grove Press, 1966), and *A Dying Colonialism* (New York: Grove Press, 1967); Kwame Nkrumah, *Ghana: The Autobiography of Kwame Nkrumah* (London: Thomas Nelson, 1957).

8. Kwame Nkrumah, *Consciencism* (New York: Monthly Review Press, 1964), 79.

9. Kwame Nkrumah, *Class Struggle in Africa* (New York: International Publishers, 1970), 84.

10. Christian Potholm, *The Theory and Practice of African Politics* (Englewood Cliffs, N.J.: Prentice-Hall, 1979), 65.

11. Julius Nyerere, *Ujamaa: Essays on Socialism* (Dar es Salaam: Oxford University Press, 1968), 16.

12. Cranford Pratt, *The Critical Phase in Tanzania 1945–1968: Nyerere and the Emergence of a Socialist Strategy* (Cambridge: Cambridge University Press, 1976), 228. See also Ahmed Mohiddin, *African Socialism in Two Countries* (London: Croom Helm, 1981), and *Socialism in Tanzania*, ed. Lionel Cliffe and John S. Saul, 2 vols. (Dar es Salaam: East African Publishing House, 1972).

13. See I. I. Potkhin, "On African Socialism: A Soviet View," in *African Socialism*, ed. Friedland and Rosberg, 97–112.

14. J. K. Nyerere, "The Church and Socio-Economic Development in the Context of African Socialism," *African Ecclesiastical Review* (hereafter *AFER*) 23 (1981): 228.

15. "Interview with Religious Superiors of Tanzania," *AFER* 20 (1978): 205.

16. Julius Nyerere, *Man and Development* (Dar es Salaam: Oxford University Press, 1974), 85.

17. Nyerere, "The Church and Socio-Economic Development," *AFER* (1981): 225–30.

18. Jan P. van Bergen, *Development and Religion in Tanzania* (Madras: Christian Literature Society, 1981), 265.

19. Ibid., 242–48. See also J. Heijke, "Socialism and the Church in Africa," *Exchange* 10:30 (December 1981): 20–30.

20. Hans Iversen, "ELCT and its ministry as seen through twenty-two Makumira students," *Africa Theological Journal* 7:1 (1978): 116.

21. Laurenti Magesa, "Towards a theology of liberation for Tanzania," in *Christianity in Independent Africa*, ed. E. Fashole-Luke et al. (Bloomington, Ind.: Indiana University Press, 1978), 510. See also Michael Traber, "African Church and African Socialism: The Tanzanian Model," in *Christianity and Socialism*, ed. J. Metz and J.-P. Jossua (New York: Seabury Press, 1977), 88–98; John R. Civille, "Ujamaa Socialism: An Analysis of the Socialism of Julius K. Nyerere in the Light of Catholic Church Teaching," in *Tanzania and Nyerere: A Study of Ujamaa and Nationhood*, ed. W. R. Duggan and J. R. Civille (Maryknoll, N.Y.: Orbis Books, 1976), 169–268; and David Westerlund, "Christianity and Socialism in Tanzania 1967–1977," *Journal of Religion in Africa* 11 (1980): 30–55.

22. Theo Kneifel, "Marxism, a Rival of the Gospel in Africa," *Missionalia* 8 (1980): 54–66.

23. David Ottaway and Marina Ottaway, *Afrocommunism* (New York and London: Africana Publishing Co., 1981), 6–7.

24. Quoted in Ottaway and Ottaway, *Afrocommunism*, 9.

25. Adrian Hastings, "The Christian Churches and Liberation Movements in Southern Africa," *African Affairs* 80 (1981): 345–54.

26. "Tanzania—The Silent Class Struggle," in *Socialism in Tanzania*, ed. Cliffe and Saul, vol. 2, 305.

27. Sevin Hirschbein, "Tanzania: The Non-Marxist Path to Socialism?" *Monthly Review* 32:8 (January 1981): 24–42.

28. Ottaway and Ottaway, *Afrocommunism*, 37.

29. "Marxism, Humanism & Christianity," *AFER* 22 (1980): 113–14. Also published in *Exchange* 8:34 (December 1979): 56–71.

30. Ibid., 123.

31. Quoted in Gerdien Verstraelen-Gilhuis, "Marxism, Humanism and Christianity: A Provisional Interpretation and Comment," *Exchange* 8:24 (December 1979): 70.

32. "Christianity and Scientific Socialism: The Zambian Debate," *AFER* 24 (1982): 241–52.

33. G. Verstraelen-Gilhuis, "New Debate on Scientific Socialism in Zambia," *Exchange* 12:34 (April 1983): 69–71.

34. In Canaan Banana, *The Theology of Promise* (Harare, Zimbabwe: College Press, 1982), 9.

35. Ibid., 21.

36. Thomas J. Blakeley, "Christian-Marxist Dialogue and the Otherworld," in

Demythologizing Marxism, ed. F. J. Adelmann (Chestnut Hill, Mass.: Boston College, 1969), 184.

37. Banana, *Theology of Promise,* 123.
38. *Christians and Marxists* (London: Hodder & Stoughton, 1976), 118.
39. "The Marxist Criticism of Religion," *Africa Theological Journal* 8:2 (1979): 63.
40. Banana, *Theology of Promise,* 109.

SUGGESTIONS FOR FURTHER READING

Banana, Canaan. *The Theology of Promise.* Harare, Zimbabwe: College Press, 1982.

Duggan, W. R., and J. R. Curlle, eds. *Tanzania and Nyerere: A Study of Ujamaa and Nationhood.* Maryknoll, N.Y.: Orbis Books, 1976.

Hastings, Adrian. *A History of African Christianity 1950–1975.* Cambridge: Cambridge University Press, 1979.

Metz, J., and J. P. Jossua, eds. *Christianity and Socialism.* New York: Seabury Press, 1977.

Ottaway, David, and Marina Ottaway. *Afrocommunism.* New York and London: Africana Publishing Co., 1981.

INDIA

George Mathew

MARX'S ARRIVAL IN INDIA

Marx first "came" to India through the writings of Hardayal and Swadesabhimani Ramakrishna Pillai.[1] Hardayal's article "Karl Marx: A Modern Rishi" appeared in the *Modern Review* (Calcutta) of March 1912. In August of the same year, Ramakrishna Pillai published a biography of Karl Marx in Malayalam—the first book on Marx in an Indian language.[2] In 1871, some radicals in Calcutta contacted Karl Marx about establishing connections with the International Workingmen's Association. Although British rulers wanted to prevent revolutionary ideas from reaching India, several factors contributed to Marxism becoming a significant part of the socioeconomic thought in India: the First World War and its repercussions, the first Socialist Revolution in Russia in 1917, the new awakening among the Indian working class, and the founding of the Third International by Lenin. By the end of the nineteenth century, India was reeling under insufferable poverty resulting from British exploitation. This situation contributed not a little to strengthening the appeal of Marxist ideas to workers living in want. In October 1916, Ambalal Patel wrote approvingly in *Navajivan and Satya* (Gujarati) about Marx's clarion call to workers of the world to unite and free themselves from the chains that enslave them. Another selection from an article by Marx published in the *New York Daily Tribune* in July of 1853, on "British Rule in India," followed. It stated: "Attempts of erstwhile philosophers to justify or explain away the exploitation of poor people are no more effective since the declaration of the Communist Manifesto in the year 1848. The workers of the world can shed the chains of their slavery by their own power."

Thus, while Marxist ideas were gaining currency in the context of the increasing misery of the people in general and of the growing working class in particular, the founding of the Communist Party in India was a logical conclusion. The pioneer of the Indian Communist movement, M. N. Roy, agreed with J. P. Bagerhatta that, by propagating Marxist ideas through the Indian language press and by starting night schools to educate laborers and their children, the names of Marx and Lenin would at once become house-hold names in India. Both were of the opinion that only Communism could free India from bondage and human slavery and that the poor would soon recognize this and embrace communism.[3] The first Indian Communist Conference took place in Kanpur (26–28 December 1925) and the Communist Party of India was formed there.[4] The central office of the party was based in the industrial city of Bombay.

It is interesting to note that Marxism planted its deepest roots in the south of India, especially in the state of Kerala where Christianity is a significant force. The Malabar region in the northern part of present-day Kerala was in particular a fertile ground for Marxism because of the poverty, the density of population, and the exploitation of tenants by landlords. Malabar witnessed the first peasant upsurge in Kerala. The Congress Socialist Party, the left wing of the Indian National Congress, was an ideal political forum for the spread of Marxist ideas. In a meeting during December 1939 in the village of Pinarai in Tellichery, the Congress Socialist Party converted itself into a Communist party.[5] In Travancore, where the Christian population was more influential than Malabar, the seeds of the Communist Party were sown in the commercial port of Alleppey. In that town, the industrial workers were going through untold misery during the opening decades of this century. As a result, the Alleppey Labour Association was founded and a militant trade union came into being in 1928 with the railway strike. Thus, while in the north of Kerala (Malabar) Marxist ideas spread through peasant movements, in the south (Travancore) exploited industrial workers took pains to understand Marxism and organize themselves under the Marxist banner.

CHRISTIANITY IN INDIA

Christianity reached the shores of India through the apostle St. Thomas according to widely held legend. The saint came to the Malabar coast, and it is believed that he converted upper-caste Hindus to Christianity. Kerala's ancient trade connections with the Arab world make the legend historically credible. These early Christians came to be known in later years as Syrian Christians because their liturgy was in Syriac. Their church had strong ecclesiastical links with the church in Persia of that time, also believed to have been founded by St. Thomas. Today the descendants of these early Christians of Kerala are found in many Christian denominations ranging from the Orthodox through the Roman Catholic to the Reformed; together they constitute some 22 percent of the total population of Kerala. This church preserved a castelike social structure and enjoyed a higher social ranking. They did not attempt conversions from other religions. They were agriculturists and traders. Since they were identified as an upper caste, their attitude toward lower castes was one of neglect. When new economic possibilities opened up in the beginning of this century, the Syrian Christians were among the first to use them to their advantage. This resulted in renewed and more systematic exploitation of the lower castes who constituted the bulk of the agricultural labor force. The ancient Christian churches were centers of wealth and local authority; consequently, the poor were alienated from the churches.

Vasco da Gama's arrival in 1498 in Calicut on the Malabar coast marked the beginning of a wave of conversions from among the Hindus and to an extent from among the early Christians to the Roman Catholic Church. Those who embraced Christianity in this phase came mostly from the lower castes— fishermen and tribals. With the arrival of the British at the end of the eighteenth century, the Protestant missions from Western Europe and North America intensified their activity in India in much the same way, and with similar results, as the Roman Catholics from southern Europe. By the time the British left in 1947, the Christian community in undivided India (India, Pakistan, and Bangladesh together) constituted only 1.63 percent of the total population. Although Christianity came to India early in its history, the churches were viewed in the popular mind as an appendage to European colonialism. They did very little to change that image during the national movement for freedom.

As a result of politically aided proselytization over four centuries, the oppressed castes like the Nadars in Tamil Nadu, the Paraiyans (Sambavars) of the south, the Chuhra caste (leather workers, sweepers, agricultural laborers) of Punjab, the Malas and Madigas of Andhra Pradesh, the Dhysiya Chanars of Bihar and Uttar Pradesh, the Doms of Banaras, the Mangs and Mahars in the hinterland of Bombay, and the various Panchma castes in Karnataka swelled the churches in India. The tribals of northeast India, the Oraons and Mundas of Chota Nagpur, and the Santals of Bihar were also attracted to Christianity in large numbers. This does not mean that all those who became Christians were from the lower castes. There was a sprinkling of high-caste conversions too. But the conversions were perceived by the oppressed as an instrument to escape the oppression and exploitation they were subjected to by Hindu society. In this perspective, Christianity was a liberating idea for the oppressed sections.

ANTAGONISMS AND ATTRACTIONS

When Marxism came to India as a liberating force, Christianity became its antagonist. Except in Kerala where the traditional Christian community was a social force, the Christian groups in other parts of India were unconcerned with Marxism. The concern which did develop was one of uncritical hostility. There were several reasons for this attitude:

a. the lowly origins by and large of the Christian community and its minority character made it inward-looking without much concern for society or politics in the large context;

b. the pietistic origin of Western missions and the emphasis on spirituality made it necessary for the missionaries to keep their flock away from the "atheistic" ideology of Marxism; and

c. the large institutions and properties held by the churches became vested interests which caused the churches to opt for the status quo rather than advocate and support social change.

Thus Christianity, which laid a strong emphasis on the improvement of the material conditions of humankind and which in the colonial missionary phase did a great deal to bring justice to the oppressed who were converted to Christianity, clashed with a materialistic ideology (Marxism) on ostensibly spiritual grounds. No desire to understand each other was present.

The strong interaction of the Christian and Marxist movements in Kerala calls for a detailed analysis of their interaction. In this region the Christian-Marxist encounter has passed through four stages. First, the attitude of the official church was negative—anything Marxist or Communist must be opposed. Among Christians there was a powerful group of plantation, factory, and business owners in quest of greater profits. Therefore, they had little or no sympathy for the ascendancy of the working class to significant power, especially under the banner of Marxism. The wealthy Christian entrepreneurs' hostility to Communists was without limit.

By the late 1940s, the All Kerala Catholic Congress (AKCC), the front organization of the powerful Roman Catholic Church in Kerala, had identified communism as its main enemy and started mobilizing an "anti-Communist fund." Recognizing that most of the workers' unions are controlled by Communists, AKCC wanted to found independent labor organizations under the auspices of the church.[6] In Alleppey, Catholic priests made attempts to organize their fiber workers with the hope that the workers would compromise their demands and cooperate with the factory owners. At a meeting held on 9 February 1936, the leftist "Christian" labor leaders realized that this move by the priests would only dampen the spirits of the workers in the fight for their rights.[7] Needless to say, the rich were the policy makers of the churches in Kerala. Thus Christianity and the churches became the major enemies of anyone or anything associated with Marxist thought. When India attained political independence and the Communists began to participate in the elections, bishops issued pastoral letters exhorting the faithful to defeat the Communist candidates. They were read to the congregations and priests delivered sermons attacking Marxist ideology.

Second, at the individual level, several members of the Christian community staunchly believed in Marxist ideology. Some of those who became active workers in the Communist Party during its early days were George Chadayammury, K. V. Patrose, T. V. Thomas, C. O. Mathew, P. T. Punnoose, P. A. Solomon, A. K. Thampy, M. A. George, C. T. Xavier, K. C. George, and Joseph Mundassery. A. K. Thampy, who worked in the underground for the party when it was banned by the government, later resigned from the party saying, "As I am unable to accept the full implications of the Marxist attitude to religion I resign my membership in the Communist Party."[8] However, all others remained and occupied important positions in the party and government when the Communist Party came to power in Kerala in 1957. In the churches there were evangelists like George Kakkanadan who believed that since both Christianity and Marxism advocated the liberation of the oppressed there was no contradiction but only congruence between the two. He helped the Communist workers in their difficult days (1948–51) by giving them shelter. His preaching also leaned toward the left. His church (the Mar Thoma Church) reprimanded him for reconciling evangelism and communism in his church work.

The church in Kerala produced priests like Father Joseph Vadakkan (Roman Catholic) who were supporters of the Communist Party and Marxism. Although he was an anti-Communist in the 1950s, Father Vadakkan's desire to achieve justice for the poor and the oppressed in Kerala and the church's neglect of these deprived groups attracted him to the Communist Party. He says: "I who was an anti-Communist evolved the thesis that there was nothing wrong in cooperating with the Communists in doing good."[9] His own political party, the Agricultural Labourer's Party, was a partner in the second Marxist ministry which came to power in 1967. He cooperated with the Marxists in the struggles of the landless poor. He came to accept the Marxist theories of economics, class war, revolution, and the dictatorship of the proletariat, but he rejected the Marxist views on spirituality and atheism. Father Vadakkan's involvement with Marxism and the Communist Party provided a role model for Christian social action groups in the 1970s. Like him, they studied Marxism closely and took Marxist social analysis seriously.

The third level of interaction between Christians and Marxists was on the intellectual plane. The Youth Christian Council of Action (YCCA) from 1938 until 1954 was a forum of young Christians who sought to understand the theological and ideological bases of social action. From the very beginning

(1939), a group in the YCCA wanted to know the meaning of Marxism. Like Reinhold Niebuhr, they accepted "the Marxist doctrine of class struggle as the only path to justice while repudiating the utopian elements in Marxism itself."[10] The trend was to "combine the Christian Realism of Neo-orthodoxy with Gandhism and Marxism social insights."[11] As a result of the ideological polarization of the YCCA, a section joined the Communist Party of India; another became pacifist and Gandhian. The third tried to synthesize Marxist social insights, Gandhian values, and their own Christian faith. In its declaration, the National Christian Youth Council (NCYC), an offshoot of YCCA under the leadership of M. M. Thomas, accepted the Catholic Christian faith and Marxist scientific socialism. This statement "expressed a certain stage in the dialogue between Christian faith and the ideology of Marxism and indicated how united action with Communists in revolutionary situations may be combined with evangelistic dialogue with them."[12] Because the Communist Party was attractive to intellectuals in those days, such cooperation was possible in Kerala in addition to dialogue with Christian youth. Eventually, the NCYC, the Communist Students Wing, and the Students Federation organized study conferences together. This marked the beginning of the Christian-Marxist dialogue in India in the true sense of the term.

A fourth area of confrontation emerged in Kerala as a result of the "upper-caste" and the "lower-caste" duality of the Christians. When the Church Missionary Society and the London Missionary Society started working in Kerala toward the beginning of the nineteenth century, as it happened elsewhere in India, the lower-caste people were attracted in large numbers to Christianity. But since the new converts came from among the "untouchables" and were economically poor and socially backward the Syrian Christians drawn from the upper castes did not accept them in full communion. In many places separate churches were built for these new Christians. Even separate cemeteries were established. There was no interdining or intermarriage. In this situation, Christianity became an oppressive force. However, the efforts of the missionaries made it possible for the new converts to gain a general acceptance within the wider society, for example, access to schools, government employment, and the like. This social revolution took place in Kerala because of the activity of Christian missionaries. On the other hand, the ancient churches' reluctance to accept them and continue the liberating acts of the missionaries led the new Christian converts to other liberating agencies. Many of them found Marxism a convenient instrument to sustain the democratic values and human dignity shown to them by the missionaries. Those who came to leadership positions in the parties of the left, especially on the agricultural front, were the newly converted Christians.

For the educated people among them, the indifference and injustice shown by the church was intolerable. For the economically deprived class of Christians, as T. K. Oommen observes, "the Communist Party became the new Church and the CPI workers the new Priests."[13]

As noted earlier, the widening gulf between the rich and the poor, the growing working class (both industrial and agricultural laborers), the poverty of the lower classes, and the disenchantment with the political parties which came to power with independence all contributed to the expanding influence of the Communist Party in Kerala. In 1957, they came to power in Kerala through democratic elections. The Communists were antichurch because the Kerala church owned major educational institutions, immense wealth, and vast areas of land.[14] In addition, individual members of the church were landlords and owners of plantations, banks, and schools. On the whole, the churches supported oppressive economic practices and did not hold high standards for their schools or teachers. Moreover, the teachers' pay scale was quite low.

Christians and Christian churches stood to lose much wealth and power when the Communist government brought forward legislation affecting ownership and control of educational institutions and land reforms which limited the area an individual or family might own. Many of the educational reforms were progressive. For example, they would have required the church schools to adopt the same standards used by the "public schools" to evaluate students and to hire and compensate teachers.

The church came to the vanguard mobilizing its members for what they called a "Liberation Struggle" from Communist rule. Other aggrieved communities like the Nairs also joined the struggle. Eventually, the Communist government in Kerala was dismissed by the central government in 1959. The churches and Christians were instrumental in this downfall of the Communist government. Priests joined politicians, planters, bankers, and landlords in direct action against Communists.[15]

All church members, however, were not anti-Communist. A small but influential group of Christian intellectuals believed that the indifference and resistance of upper-class groups, such as the ancient churches, to dynamic social change were major causes of the Communists election to power in 1957. "The Communist government deserves discerning support" because it has the potential "for effecting necessary social change," the group declared.[16] "When the Communist government took charge, a large section of the underprivileged people of Kerala felt a sense of greater dignity and importance than before. This awakening of some of the hitherto suppressed sections of the people was a positive factor working for the strengthening of democracy," they continued.[17] However, they were critical of the introduction of class conflict by Communists which led to violent clashes in the state. They viewed this as a serious threat to parliamentary democracy.

In the colonial countries during the post–World War II period, communism became very appealing to intellectuals. At the same time, Marxist ideology came into conflict with the institutional Christianity which was in most cases nurtured by the colonial masters and befriended by the capitalist system. Against the onrush of Marxism and the intellectuals' romantic view of it and its ideological warfare, Christianity assumed a defensive posture.

Two books which appeared in India during this period deserve mention. The first was *Communism and Christianity*, a popular study-text of the Student Christian Movement of India. The authors stated that a Christian "ought to look at the outcome of any conflict between his faith and Communist ideology with a confidence and expectation that history will be fulfilled in Jesus Christ, a consummation that is beyond tragedy. . . . Even if Communism should be historically inevitable, yet the triumph of Christ is the final consummation of history."[18] The second book was *Communism and the Social Revolution in India: A Christian Interpretation*. The contributors contended that communism "represents both a challenge and a threat to the country as a whole."[19] They provided a perceptive analysis of the roles played by Christianity and Marxism in the process of nation building that still remains valid.

In 1964, the Communist Party of India split into two: a rightist group—the Communist Party of India (CPI)—and a leftist—the Communist Party (Marxist) (CPI-M). The Communists returned to power in Kerala in 1967, with the CPI-M as the major partner of the "United Front" of leftist parties. The decade since 1957 produced considerable changes in Kerala politics. The Congress Party whose mainstay was Christians began to come closer to CPI in the mid-1960s. The Christians voted for the CPI candidates (on the once-hated CPI's sickle and corn symbol) because of the electoral alliances CPI had with the Congress Party. In the power struggle between CPI and CPI-M, the church in Kerala sided with the former. K. V. Verghise in a study of the period observed:

> The Communists who had been characterized by the priests as the agent of the Devil became good citizens overnight. The way in which the CPI ministers were applauded by the Christian Press was a manifestation of the changing mood of the Christian hierarchy. . . . The new trend was indeed a breakthrough in the relation between the Christians and the Communists.[20]

There were occasions when the Communist ministers addressed spiritual gatherings of Christians in Kerala. The experience of practical electoral politics has made the church and CPI strange bedfellows in Kerala since

1967. At the same time, it must be pointed out that CPI-M and the extremist Marxist-Leninists (popularly known as Naxalites) remained anathema to powerful sections of Christians in Kerala.

Because of the anti-Marxist stand of the organized church and the growing disenchantment with democracy and its inability to remove the poverty and misery of the people, a number of Christians were attracted as individuals to Marxist ideas in the 1960s and 1970s. Among them were lay leaders, priests, and bishops belonging to the Protestant, Roman Catholic, and Orthodox churches. This seems to suggest that a creative exchange of experiences and ideas and cooperation among these individuals might begin. On the contrary, there have been marked differences in their perceptions about translating their political convictions into practice. This is due in part to the conceptual/philosophical nuances of their respective Christian denominations.

The YCCA Christian-Marxist tradition crystallized in the founding of the Christian Institute for the Study of Religion and Society (CISRS) in Bangalore in 1957. This institute through its meetings, research projects, and publications brought together Christians and Marxists for the scholarly study of religion and society. The institute completed some commendable study, research, and publication projects in the first half of the 1970s under the Indian Marxism Study Project on Indian Marxism, Marxism and Humanism, and Alienation in Modern Capitalism.[21]

The most significant political development since independence that drew progressive Christian groups and Marxists closer together was "the political emergency of 1975." The "emergency" was the logical culmination of the people's growing disenchantment with the political process that had failed to end their misery or the corruption in public life. The veteran freedom fighter Jayaprakash Narayan gave vent to the people's feelings through his leadership of the Gujarat and Bihar agitations. Prime Minister Indira Gandhi's unseating from the parliament by the Allahabad High Court through an election petition filed by her rival candidate, Raj Narain, coincided with the peak of these popular movements. Indira Gandhi did not accept the court's verdict; instead, she proclaimed the Emergency Act of 25 June 1975 which remained in effect for nineteen months. She assumed dictatorial powers. Civil liberties and human rights were suppressed, the rule of law was abrogated, press censorship was imposed, and political opponents were put into prison. The CPI supported Indira Gandhi's action but the CPI-M and the Naxalites opposed her autocratic rule along with the democratic-Socialist parties. The official policy of the established churches was conformist. However, a small but articulate section of progressive Christians declared their stand against

Indira Gandhi's authoritarian policies and found themselves in the company of Marxists. Some of the Christians organized a distress relief fund for the families of those detained without trial. The beneficiaries of this program were primarily Marxists. During this period, M. M. Thomas chaired the Kerala Civil Rights movement organized at the initiative of the CPI-M leader and former chief minister of Kerala, E. M. S. Namboodiripad. Until the newly formed Janata Party came to power by defeating the ruling Congress Party in the March 1977 elections, the progressive Christian groups and Marxists established closer relationships by fighting authoritarianism and defending civil liberties together.[22]

FORMAL DIALOGUES

As described in an editorial in *Religion and Society,* the Christian scene in India presented an interesting picture.[23] Grass-roots Christianity's attitude to Marxism was marked by suspicion and hatred. Yet, on another plane, individuals and groups within the church accepted the presence of Marxism, believing that an unreflective coexistence was possible. In addition, there were some who were aware of the need for a dialogue between Christianity and Marxism because they saw Christianity and Marxism not as rival faiths but as potential partners in supporting the people in their struggle for liberation from oppression. They were interested in the commitment of Christianity and Marxism to build a more just and humane social order. Realizing that neither group was making an effort to listen to the other, this group, which indeed was very small, met with a few Marxist intellectuals at a convention of "Social Action Groups" held in Delhi in March 1978 under the auspices of the "Forum for Christian Concern for People's Struggle." They established "Forum for Marxist-Christian Dialogue" to discuss social as well as theoretical issues from Christian and Marxist perspectives.

The first dialogue under the auspices of the Forum took place in Madras in July 1978 on the theme of "Freedom." Four papers were presented, two from the Marxist side and two from the Christian. The papers were on 1) Freedom and Economic Life, a Christian Perspective; 2) Marxist Understanding of Freedom; 3) The Abolition of Power: a Biblical Perspective; and 4) Freedom and Political Power According to Marx. *Religion and Society* published the proceedings and papers. One of the participants noted that there was an "intense experience of intellectual sharing. Both Christians as well as Marxists were free from rigid dogmatism in their interpretation of their respective faiths. . . . There was an honest effort to reinterpret the original message of Marx and Jesus in a way relevant to the contemporary situation."[24] In this dialogue, however, Christians were unable to express some of their basic convictions in a "language" that was intelligible to Marxists.

Encouraged by the overall success of this dialogue, a second was convened at Kottayam in February 1979 on the theme "An Appraisal of the Communist Movement in India." The invitation stipulated, "Lest the session take the form of a discussion exclusively on Communism, it is suggested that the papers from the Christian side state clearly the beliefs and values in the light of which they evaluate Indian Communism."[25] Papers were presented on "Christian Faith and Marxism in the Dialectic of Emancipation and Domestication," "Christian Attitudes to Marxism," and "Some Remarks on the Communist Movement in India." Unfortunately, this dialogue was not as successful as the first. The group broke up over a hairsplitting argument sparked by Father S. Kappen, S.J., who insisted that theoretical consensus was necessary for the dialogue to proceed. Ajit Roy, editor of the *Marxist Review* countered that the dialogue could continue without making theoretical consensus a precondition.[26] Another attempt was made to convene a third dialogue in Bangalore in January 1980 on the theme "Problems of Socialist Transformation," but it was cancelled because of the elections taking place in Kerala.

Even though the Forum for Christian-Marxist dialogue only had a brief life span, it created a good degree of interest in intellectual circles on Christian-Marxist interaction and resulted in the publication of some valuable papers. It must be noted here that these dialogues had no official support from either the Marxist Communist Party or the churches. The participants were Marxist and Christian intellectuals and activists coming together as individuals.

Mention may be made of another dialogue organized outside the "Forum." It was held 2–3 June 1979 on "The Concept of Man" and "Religion and Social Change" at Ernakulam, Kerala, convened by Father J. Kottukapally, S.J., of the Roman Catholic Lumen Institute, Cochin, in collaboration with the Dialogue Commission of the Catholic Bishops Conference of India. The invitation stressed that, although there is collaboration between Christians and Marxists in many parts of the world, "no one can ignore the fundamental differences, even contradictions, that exist between Marxism and the Christian Faith, both of which at the same time, claim the whole man." Therefore it is urgent for both to get to know each other's convictions in depth for mutual enrichment.[27] The papers from this dialogue were published under the title, *Search for Man: An Ongoing Project*.[28] Father Kottukapally continues his interest in and support of dialogue. To this end he recently published *The Hope We Share: A New Christian Approach to Marxism*. He concludes the volume by stating that Christian and Marxist

> ideologies, however intimately and inseparably united to the ideal . . . always and necessarily need reform and renewal, development and change, even qualitative or revolutionary change. And this must be brought about in terms of the imperative of the pole star of the ideal on the one hand, and, on the other, of the ever changing concrete situation through all-round exchanges and cross-fertilization.[29]

Despite all of these efforts, formal, organized dialogues between Christians and Marxists are not conducted regularly in India today.

MARXISM AND CHRISTIAN
SOCIAL ACTION GROUPS

Another development has strained the relationship between Christians and Marxists. The success of Christian action groups has turned the Communist parties against them. These groups had their origin in the Urban Industrial Rural Mission (UIRM) phase of the church's understanding of social problems. These groups began to realize that only a radical change in the political system and the socioeconomic structures will bring about social justice for the oppressed. For this change to happen, the rising of the "have-nots" became an imperative. When these groups began to understand the larger social reality and to take up the cause of the working class, they were helped by Marxist tools of social analysis and ideological understanding. A convention of the action groups which met at Charalkunnu (Kerala) in October 1979 declared, "The people's struggles based on a left ideology can free them from oppression and exploitation. The left, as we understand it, stands for the radical transformation of society based on class struggle. It leads to the political option in favour of the working class."[30] At another meeting of the action groups held in New Delhi in July 1981, the participants said that they now realize the class character of Indian society: "Strengthening of the oppressed sections of the society and working towards the resolution of class contradictions ensuring the emergence of a truly socialist society is the historical role the action groups are called upon to play." To achieve this, "the groups must discern and identify class struggles from the local to the national." This means "raising the level of political consciousness of the masses [and] ensuring the emergence of people's power for waging militant struggles for revolutionary change."[31] Therefore, an important area of concern for the groups was a critical understanding of Marxism in the Indian context to be explored in cooperation with Marxist thinkers. No doubt, the underlying tone of the action groups' deliberations was "critical collaboration" with leftist political parties. In their struggle for justice, just as they were critical of the established church, their understanding of Marxism led them to be critical of Marxist parties as well. Independent Marxist thinkers welcomed the growth and spread of action groups because their philosophy was radical, they aimed at raising the sociopolitical consciousness of the suffering masses, and they extended practical concern to the oppressed and exploited masses.[32]

Unfortunately, the Christian Social Action Groups threatened the Communist parties and provoked a repudiation by them. The attack on the action groups was led by the CPI-M. In their Central Committee meeting in Calcutta in June 1981, the party charged that "a systematic offensive from the 'Left' is being opened by some church agencies against CPI-M. They organize seminars, call Marxist party members and leaders to participate in them, the aim being to get a Left image." The committee warned CPI-M members not to be misled by the radical phrases and urged them not to participate in these groups.[33] In January 1982 when the Eleventh Congress of the CPI-M met at Vijayawada, they reiterated the Central Committee's stand on Christian action groups. The CPI-M saw in the gatherings of "these groups" a move to disrupt the unity of leftist forces and to hamper the growing strength of the CPI-M.[34] The CPI at its Varanasi Congress held in March 1982 alleged that Christian missionaries "have set up organizations amongst the agricultural workers, peasants, workers, unemployed youth" and "raise radical slogans." For the CPI, their activities were dubious and divisive and needed to be vigilantly watched and combated.[35]

Not only through statements and writings in general but also in specific life situations serious confrontations took place between Christians and Marxists. According to reports, the CPI-M embarked on a campaign to malign the *Sanghatna* (a group of Christian activists in Thane) when it discovered that its influence over the people of Worli was declining as a result of the work of the *Sanghatna*. The CPI-M Central Committee meeting in Calcutta stated, "Now the Church missionaries call themselves *Kashtakari Sanghatana* and declare that it is a progressive left democratic organization and simultaneously a non-party organization." The committee accused the *Sanghatana* of being an instrument of imperialist agencies for exploiting the tribal problem.[36] The report claims that on the morning of 18 October 1980 clashes took place between the members of the *Kashtakari Sanghatana* and *Kisan Sabha* led by the Marxists in the Thane district. Intellectuals and independent Marxist thinkers were highly critical of the Marxist action. *The Marxist Review* asked the CPI-M to investigate the allegations and to offer facts to refute it or discipline the party workers so that such incidents would not be repeated.[37] A. B. Shah, a rationalist scholar, reflecting on this incident commented

> Normally our sympathies should be with the Marxists rather than Christians if they were to join issue on the basis of the philosophy that each group professes. However, over the years, and especially since the beginning of the Sixties, there seems to be going on a steady secularisation of the Christians' concern for the poor and the oppressed and an equally steady *embourgeoisment* of the Marxists all over the world. Thus the Christians in India, except the few engaged in the business of saving other people's souls, have been attaching greater and greater importance to the material welfare of the poor and the restoration to them of their human dignity. The Marxists, on the other hand, have been treating the poor as their exclusive preserve, on which no one else would be allowed to encroach.[38]

Another writer wondered whether the Marxist party was perturbed over the leftist image of the church agencies.[39] A Christian intellectual who also is a Marxist scholar compared the Communist Party's actions against the Christian Social Action Groups to Stalin's habit of disqualifying any critical question, any dissenting voice, and any quotation from Marx which did not suit the political needs of the hour and had not been authorized by him.[40] In reality, CPI-M's attitude toward Christian action groups differs from region to region. Commenting on the 1982 election in Kerala, the CPI-M general secretary E. M. S. Namboodiripad stated, "Secular forces have emerged among the Christians [and] this, too, helps the future work of the left and democratic forces among the Christian masses."[41]

CONCLUSION

This paper surveyed the history of two important ideologies in India, one religious and the other materialistic. Both have made considerable impact on the social development of this country. Both possess a liberating message for the oppressed but they very seldom cooperate in the emancipation process. The "establishments" of these two ideologies—the church and the party—do not see eye to eye. But there have been individuals and groups among both Christians and Marxists who have tried to set aside their own dogma and to study and understand each other's position. However, the impact of the cooperation of these individuals on Christianity and Marxism has been minimal. Our survey shows that, while many Christian intellectuals have tried to study and understand Marxism in India, very few Marxists have taken the pains to understand Christianity on its "founder's level" because they are misled by the exploitative power structures of the churches.

In India, the opportunities for formal Christian-Marxist dialogue as it happens in the West, are, at this time, limited. Unless some institutes or a group of intellectuals from both sides takes the initiative, the foundation for formal dialogues on theoretical questions will not be established in India in the near future. At "crisis" points, radical Christians may find themselves in the company of Marxists. But the crucial question remains: During "normal" times will Christians and Marxists come together to discuss the issues facing the people in perpetual crisis? The critical issues around which Christians and Marxists can join ranks are: a) how to change the degrading human conditions arising from poverty; and b) how to meet a growing authoritarian tendency in the political structure.

NOTES

1. P. C. Joshi and K. Damodaran, *Marx Comes to India* (Delhi: Manohar, 1975).

2. Mention may be made of an earlier article, "Rise of Foreign Socialists: Their Remarkable Growth in the Continent in Recent Years," reproduced from an English journal in *America Bazar Patrika* (Calcutta: 1903), especially 6.

3. Correspondence between J. P. Bagerhatta and M. N. Roy, quoted in G. Adhikari, ed., *Documents of the History of the Communist Party of India,* Vol. II (New Delhi: People's Publishing House, 1982), 380.

4. Ibid., 591 and 606. The United Communist Party leadership on 18 August 1959 decided to adopt the Kanpur Communist Conference as the date of the formation of the party.

5. N. E. Balram, *Keralathile Communist Prasthanam,* Part I (Malayalam) (Quilon, India: Janayungam Press, 1973), 151.

6. *AKCC Bulletin,* 21 June 1948, November 1950.

7. V. A. Simon, "Katholica thozhilai Union Veendum" (Malayalam), *Golden Jubilee Souvenir Travancore Coir Factory Workers Union* (Alleppey, India: 1972), 237–39.

8. George Kakkanadan, *Suviseshavum Communisavum* (Malayalam) (Trivandrum, India: Prabhatham, 1964), 75.

9. Joseph Vadakkan, *A Priest's Encounter with Revolution* (Bangalore: CISRS, 1974), 88.

10. George M. John, *Youth Christian Council of Action 1938–1954* (Bangalore: CISRS, 1972), 59.

11. C. P. Mathew and M. M. Thomas, *The Indian Churches of Saint Thomas* (Delhi: ISPCK, 1967), 148–49.

12. John, *Youth Christian Council,* 63.

13. T. K. Oommen, "Christianity and Leftist Politics in Kerala," in *Church and Society* (Malayalam), ed. P. T. Thomas (Tiruvalla: CLS, 1976), 141.

14. In 1966–67, the area leased out by churches and their educational and charitable institutions in Kerala for cultivation was about seventeen thousand acres. The churches' relationship with tenants was in the feudal tradition. See M. A. Oomen, *Land Reforms and Socio-Economic Change in Kerala* (Bangalore: CISRS, 1971), 71, 78.

15. V. R. Krishna Iyer, *David Come to Judgement* (Ernakulam, India: Prabhatham, 1959), 107.

16. Quoted in P. D. Devanandan and M. M. Thomas, eds., *Christian Participation in Nation Building* (Bangalore: CISRS, 1960), 29.

17. Ibid., 30–31.

18. J. F. Butler and Chandran Devanesan, *Communism and Christianity*, rev. ed. (Madras: CLS, 1980), 93.

19. P. D. Devanandan and M. M. Thomas, eds. *Communism and the Social Revolution in India: A Christian Interpretation* (Calcutta: YMCA Publishing House, 1953), iii.

20. K. V. Varughese, *The United Front Government in Kerala 1967–69* (Bangalore: CISRS, 1978), 222–23.

21. *CISRS Report for 1974–77* (The Christian Institute for the Study of Religion and Society, P.O. Box 4600, 17 Miller's Road, Bangalore, 560-046 India), 129–35. The purpose of the study was a) to examine to what extent the development of Marxism in India has been influenced by the specific sociocultural situation in India, and b) to find how churches in India have responded to the force of Marxism in thought and action (*CISRS Report for 1972; and 1973*, 60).

22. For a detailed discussion of the political emergency in India, see Saral K. Chatterji, ed., *The Meaning of the Indian Experience: The Emergency* (Bangalore: CISRS, 1978); *Religion and Society* 24:2 (June 1977) and 3 (September 1977).

23. *Religion and Society* 26:3 (September 1979): 1.

24. Ibid.

25. Letter from Father S. Kappen dated 2 November 1978.

26. Interview with K. C. Abraham and Bishop Paulose Mar Paulose.

27. "Towards Marxist Christian Dialogue" (mimeographed).

28. *Search for Man: An Ongoing Project* (Madras: AICUF House, 1980).

29. *The Hope We Share: A New Christian Approach to Marxism* (Barraclepore, India: Dialogue Series, 1983), 126.

30. "People's Struggles in the Context of National History" (Charalkunnu, India: 1979), 2 (mimeographed).

31. "Political Process and Action Groups in India" (New Delhi: Forum for Christian Concern for People's Struggle, 1981), 9 and 10 (mimeographed).

32. Ajit Roy, "A Marxist Critique of Christian Social Service, *Marxist Review* (March 1980): 321.

33. "Excerpt from the CPI-M Central Committee's Report of Political Development" (Bangalore: SAMATA, 1982), 15.

34. *Political Resolution of the Eleventh Congress of the CPI (M)* (Vijayawada, India: 1982), 57.

35. *Review of Political Developments and Party Activities Since Eleventh Party Congress* (CPI Document 1982), 31.

36. *SAMATA* (CISRS-WCSR Documentation) 1 (1982): 14.

37. "A Noteworthy Seminar," *Marxist Review* (19 July 1982): 4.

38. A. B. Shah, "Marxists Vs Christians" (editorial), *The Secularist* (September-October 1980).

39. P. A. Augustine, "A Christian Rejoinder to Marxist Criticism," *Dalit Voice* (February 1982): 3.

40. Bastiann Wielenga, *Marxist Review* (1982): 201.

41. *People's Democracy* (30 May 1982).

SUGGESTIONS FOR FURTHER READING

Adhikari, G., ed. *Documents of the History of the Communist Party of India*. 2 vols. New Delhi: People's Publishing House, 1932.

Chatterji, Saral K., ed. *The Meaning of the Indian Experience: The Emergency*. Bangalore: CISRS, 1978.

Devanandan, P. D., and M. M. Thomas, eds. *Communism and the Social Revolution in India: A Christian Interpretation*. Calcutta: YMCA Publishing House, 1953.

Joshi, P. C., and K. Damodaran. *Marx Comes to India*. Delhi: Manohar, 1975.

Mathew, C. P., and M. M. Thomas, *The Indian Churches of Saint Thomas*. Delhi: ISPCK, 1967.

Vadakkan, Joseph. *A Priest's Encounter with Revolution*. Bangalore: CISRS, 1974.

CUBA
Alice L. Hageman and Paul Deats*

Christian-Marxist dialogue in the so-called Third World differs from that in the First and Second Worlds in that it is not academic but functional, oriented to practice, dealing with institutional relations and administrative issues. The dialogue in Cuba comes out of the revolution.

We will trace briefly the historical background, statements of Fidel Castro Ruz (hereafter "Fidel" as he is affectionately referred to by Cubans) as first secretary of the Central Committee of the Partido Comunista del Cuba (hereafter PCC) and president of the Councils of State and of Ministers, and in turn of the 1976 Constitution and continuing PCC discussion. We will then turn to responses within the churches.

Israel Batista Guerra, Methodist biblical scholar and former teacher in the Protestant Seminary in Matanzas, writes that in Cuba the term *encuentro* is preferred to dialogue, which has too theoretical a connotation. "The theoretical has not been the fundamental fact in our experience. We have lived and moved under the impulse of praxis."[1]

There is a story of Christians and Marxists cutting cane. The Marxist asks, "What is it that makes us different if we are united in a common struggle?" But there are other questions, such as What unites us in the struggle? and Why are some Christians not united in the struggle? Such questions arise not only between Christians and Marxists but also within the PCC and among Christians with different responses to the revolution. Taken seriously they can force both Christians and Marxists more deeply into their own heritage to see what is essential and what is due more to historical circumstances. Batista finds it helpful to clarify two basic presuppositions: that atheism is not intrinsic to Marxist theory, and that a Christian does not necessarily have to be anti-Communist.

Batista does not deny that there is a struggle, probably ideological, between Christian faith and Marxism. Still, he insists that "Marxism as it has

---

*The authors acknowledge with deep appreciation the assistance of Dr. Adolfo Ham Reyes, professor of social ethics at the Protestant Seminary in Matanzas, Cuba, in criticizing drafts of this essay and in obtaining documents.

been put into practice in [Cuba] has been more of a challenge to the church than an adversary." Some Marxist criticism is in error, but some helps Christians deal self-critically with false notions.[2]

José Felipe Carneado, the member of the PCC Central Committee who has primary responsibility for relations with churches in Cuba, has remarked that Protestant churches seemed to have had no ideological problem living with a tyrannical regime prior to the revolution. He does not question that faith *should* inform and criticize ideology, then or now.

We find one illustration of a positive response to the Marxist challenge in the Confession of Faith of the Presbyterian-Reformed Church in Cuba, adopted in 1977 after two years of preparation. It is the only such confessional statement made by a Cuban church since the revolution. Under the heading of "Man as Steward" is this paragraph.

> When Marxists insist on the economic element as the basic and fundamental one for interpreting the meaning of human life in history, they compel the church—by an irony of history—to rethink the biblical criterion of man as "steward."[3]

The revised understanding of stewardship includes dedicated participation of members in public life.

Batista reverses an old question in his final reflections on the role of the churches in Cuba.

> The church in Cuba is a witness to the reality of the churches in socialism. Sometimes people look at us with surprise and ask how it is possible to be a Christian in socialism. This question makes us laugh and we are accustomed to answer it with another: "How is it possible to be a Christian in capitalism?"[4]

HISTORICAL BACKGROUND

Perhaps the single ideological strain to which most Cubans, whatever their other commitments, have given allegiance since the mid-nineteenth century is that of nationalistic patriotism. The fierce desire to have their country free from foreign domination has provided the unifying and motivating force.

José Martí, referred to by Cubans even today as "The Apostle" of Cuban independence, has provided both articulation and the martyr's example for this commitment. Martí, killed in 1895 during the final phase of the wars for independence from Spain, wrote prolifically, and his works command a place of honor equal to Marx, Engels, and Lenin.

Many observers have characterized the Cuban people prior to 1959 as generally indifferent to organized religion. The de facto popular religion was *santería*, a syncretism of Yoruba religion brought by slaves from Africa blended with a Roman Catholic panoply of saints. Those who aspired to "enlightenment" in the nineteenth-century European mold considered themselves free thinkers; some were openly hostile to organized religion.

Roman Catholicism came to Cuba with the Spanish conquest. The first mass was celebrated on Cuban soil in 1494 during Christopher Columbus's second voyage to the New World. The Roman Catholic Church, the officially dominant faith of Cuba in 1959, was established most strongly in urban areas and was virtually nonexistent in the countryside. Its active adherents were drawn largely from among upper-middle- and upper-class segments of the population. It exercised significant influence through an extensive system of private urban schools.

Individual Cubans had sporadic contacts with Protestantism during the latter half of the nineteenth century, often in connection with independence or annexationist activity. However, only after the intervention in 1898 of U.S. troops in the so-called Spanish-American War resulted in a virtual U.S. protectorate of the island did Protestant missions direct their full attention, energies, and resources to Cuba. A proliferation of small churches, mostly related to home missionary societies of U.S. churches, resulted. Dependent on U.S. funds, staffed largely by pietistic U.S. missionaries from the lower-middle class—who shared the rural U.S. belief that charitable acts, personal piety, and good citizenship constituted the best formula for social pro-grams—these imported denominations remained foreign to Cuban life. Nei-ther Catholicism, 75 percent of the 1959 population, nor Protestantism, less than 5 percent of the 1959 population, was able to sink roots deep into popular piety.

Only a minority of active church members participated as self-identified Christians in the struggles against the dictator Batista during the insurrec-tionary period of 1953–58. When in 1959 the revolution triumphed, it brought fundamental social and economic transformation to the country. The churches were ill-prepared to meet the challenge. Their traditional anticom-munism put them into an adversary position with a government which, over a period of two years, moved toward the April 1961 declaration of its Socialist character.

Catholics were largely dependent on Franco's Spain to provide their priests and shape their piety. The Catholic leadership vigorously opposed the increasingly radical measures of the revolution; the anti-Communist reaction was strengthened as the property interests of the middle and upper classes, many of whom were traditionally Catholic, were irrevocably altered. With the worsening of relations between the United States and Cuba, culminating in the January 1961 rupture and the April 1961 Bay of Pigs invasion, Protestants experienced a conflict of loyalty between their identity as Cuban patriots and their ties to the U.S.-based mission boards which had helped shape their religious identity.

Christians left Cuba in large numbers in the early 1960s. The majority of the Christians who remained went into internal exile, looking to the churches as places of refuge. Nationalization of church-administered schools, anxiety about the teaching of Marxist ideology in state schools, expulsion of foreign clergy, prohibition of once-traditional public processions and street-corner evangelism all enhanced a sense of alienation.

One of the low points in relations between the churches and the revolution occurred during the mid-1960s, when agricultural labor "reeducation" camps were established in rural Camagüey province in an effort to deal with the problem of counterrevolutionary attitudes and antisocial activity. Artists, homosexuals, drunkards, prostitutes, pimps, vagrants, criminals—and several priests, pastors, and lay people—were sent to the UMAP (Military Units for Aid to Production) camps. Internments lasted from a few months to more than two years.

The experience of doing manual labor side by side with "lumpen" elements of the society was, for some clergy, an educational experience and produced a stronger commitment to both the revolution and to their faith. The experience further strengthened the orientation of others toward religion as refuge from the new reality with its disruption of previous social norms. The camps were closed in 1968, those directing UMAP were cited for improper activity, and relations between the churches and the revolution have steadily improved since that time. Some consider that, although UMAP was not specifically cited by name, it was one of the "mistakes" of the early years of the revolution to which Fidel referred in his 1975 report to the First Party Congress.[5]

As Christians in Cuba found themselves cut off from former sources of identity and support, they were forced to seek new ways of self-understanding and relation. Protestants mention that their participation in the international ecumenical community helped them break out of their isolation and led them to a more positive interpretation of their situation.

Catholics in Cuba note the impact of the liberalizing forces of Vatican II and the meeting of CELAM (Latin American Conference of Bishops) held in Medellín, Colombia, in 1968, as sources for new perspectives on their situation.[6] During the transition years, Papal Nuncio Cesare Zacchi acted as an intermediary between the Catholic hierarchy and the revolutionary government and developed with Fidel a relation of mutual friendship and respect. He encouraged the faithful to consider that children could participate in the activities of the Young Pioneers and adults could participate in the militia and in volunteer work. By 1969 the Cuban bishops had softened their militant anti-Communist position sufficiently to call for an end to the U.S. embargo.

FIDEL CASTRO'S CONTRIBUTION
TO THE DIALOGUE

Fidel Castro, more than any single other person, has shaped the consciousness of the Cuban people since the revolution came to power. He has explained the circumstances of their lives. He has identified allies and condemned enemies. He has attempted to involve the whole population in the revolutionary process. He is the spokesperson par excellence of the Cuban revolution.

Although Fidel has emphasized different themes at different moments in history, he has been consistent in his attitude toward religious belief and practice. He considers that there is much in common between socialism and the spirit or essence of Jesus' teachings. Early Christians, in their confrontation with imperial pagan Rome, were exemplary human beings, comparable to Communists. Those "honest Christians" who seek the well-being in this world of all humanity are welcome as comrades. Those hypocritical Christians who use anticommunism to justify self-interest and personal privilege are rejected. In July 1960 he stated on national television the basic position that he has reiterated in one way or another throughout the succeeding years: "We understand and firmly believe that there are no contradictions between aspirations for social justice, material progress of the peoples, and spiritual sentiments."

Biblical illustrations and references to church history are scattered throughout Fidel's speeches. In the statement made in his own defense during his trial for participation in the attempt on 26 July 1953 to seize the Moncada Fortress, Fidel utilized the positions of several prominent church fathers in support of his own position that the people have the right to rebel against tyranny.

Confrontation and mutual recriminations between the government and the churches, especially the Catholic Church, were a prominent dynamic during the early years of the revolution. In March 1961 Fidel responded again to charges that the revolution was an enemy of religion. He criticized the clergy for their accommodation with the old order. In effect, he charged that the revolution was being criticized for doing what the church should have done. "Because we have combatted all those evils, they say that they have ideological differences with us. . . . These are the differences that exist between those who remedy all those evils and those who were accomplices to the evils."[7] Fidel also recognized the efforts of some religious workers, for example, those who did medical work under religious auspices. "Those who carry out a human work deserve our respect. All who sacrifice for others deserve our respect."

Even at this time of great conflict Fidel affirmed his position that people should be able to practice religion if they so choose. "Everyone has the right to believe." He also asserted the right of reciprocity. "The same respect that the revolution ought to have for religious belief, those who talk in the name of religion also ought to have for the political beliefs of others."

The attempted Bay of Pigs invasion brought the confrontation to a head, as three Spanish priests who had worked in Cuba came as chaplains to the invasionary forces. On 1 May 1961 Fidel announced that the residence permits of all foreign priests were being cancelled, and all private (including church-administered) schools were being nationalized. Again he raised the question of why, after centuries of accommodation with a variety of regimes, the church was unable to make its peace with this revolution.

> That church existed . . . with the Roman Empire . . . with feudalism . . . with absolute national monarchies . . . with bourgeois national republics. . . . Why is that church not going to live together with a much superior regime of social justice? . . . In its laws and in its social projections, . . . in its defense of the interest of all men of the society, in its struggle against exploitation, this regime resembles Christianity much more than exploitive and cruel feudalism, or absolute monarchies, or the Roman Empire, or the bourgeois republic, or Yankee imperialism resembled it.[8]

Fidel stands squarely within the tradition of Martí in his desire that the revolution be as inclusive as possible. On 4 February 1962, a basic statement outlining the perspectives of the Cuban Revolution, called the Second Declaration of Havana, was presented to the Cuban people following Cuba's expulsion from the Organization of American States. On that occasion Fidel denounced sectarianism and dogmatism and advocated the inclusion of the broadest possible range of the population in the struggle.

> In the antifeudal and antiimperial struggle it is possible to bring the majority of the people resolutely behind goals of liberation. . . . There is a place for all progressives, from the old militant Marxist to the sincere Catholic who has nothing to do with the Yankee monopolists and the feudal lords of the land.[9]

Fidel has insisted on acknowledging the contribution of Christians who have acted out of conviction and has pointed out the challenge that Christian conviction may hold for Marxists. On 16 March 1962, the fifth anniversary of the failed attempt on the Presidential palace in Havana led by Catholic José Antonio Echeverría, Fidel criticized a previous speaker for omitting a sentence from Echeverría's "Testament to the Cuban People" which read, "We are confident that the purity of our intention brings God's blessing in realizing the rule of Justice in our Homeland." Fidel characterized the omission as an act of cowardice.

> Simply because these lines may have been the expression of a formal idiom or of a conviction of comrade José Antonio Echeverría, does it not behoove us to analyze it? Are we going to distort what he believed? Are we going to feel crushed by what he thought, by what he may have believed in regard to religion? What kind of confidence is that in one's own ideas? What kind of a conception is that of history? How can history be conceived as a dead thing, as a decayed thing, as an immovable rock? Could such a manner of thinking call itself Marxism? Could such a fraud call itself socialism? Could such a deception call itself communism? No![10]

By the mid-1960s the direct confrontation had subsided. Meanwhile, major changes had taken place within the Catholic Church elsewhere in Latin America. In January 1968 Fidel addressed fifteen hundred intellectuals gathered in Havana from around the world for an International Cultural Congress. After reading a statement prepared by priests attending the Congress, he acknowledged changes in the posture of at least segments of the church and questioned some dogmatic Marxist perspectives on religion.

> It is unquestionable that we are before new facts, before new phenomena. . . . Marxism needs to develop itself, to come out of a certain stiffening of the joints, to interpret today's realities in an objective and scientific sense, to act as a revolutionary force and not as a pseudo-revolutionary church.
>
> These are the paradoxes of history. How, when we see sectors of the clergy transformed into revolutionary forces, are we going to resign ourselves to see sectors of Marxism transforming themselves in ecclesiastical forces?[11]

Fidel next publicly addressed relations between Christians and Marxists on trips outside the country. During his late 1971 visit to Chile this was a recurring theme. And in his farewell speech of 2 December 1971, he suggested for the first time the possibility of a "strategic alliance" between Christians and Marxists. He noted the points that "the purest precepts of Christianity and the objectives of Marxism" have in common. Recalling that Christianity had originally been the religion of slaves, of poor people, he spoke of the shared concern for the hungry, the sick, the dying, singling out especially those priests who work in the mines or work with miners. He concluded that "when one looks for all the similarities one sees how the strategic alliance between Marxist revolutionaries and Christian revolutionaries is really possible."[12]

Six years later Fidel developed the "strategic alliance" theme further when he met with a group of church leaders in Jamaica. He reiterated his position that "in my opinion, Christ was a great revolutionary." He also referred to his statements in Chile, affirming that "to me it isn't enough to respect each other, we must cooperate with each other in order to change the world." Having asserted that "there are no contradictions between the aims of religion and the aims of socialism," he recalled his use of the term, "the strategic alliance between religion and socialism, between religion and the revolution." He then went on to ask, "where do the contradictions between Christian teachings and socialist teachings lie? Where? We both wish to struggle on behalf of man."[13]

Although the Cuban revolution is officially atheistic, Fidel has indicated that the issue of transcendence, and of life beyond death, is not wholly closed. At the conclusion of his October 1979 speech to the United Nations, delivered as president of the movement of Non-Aligned Nations, he asserted:

> Bombs may kill the hungry, the sick and the ignorant, but they cannot kill hunger, disease, and ignorance. Nor can they kill the righteous rebellion of the peoples—and, in the holocaust, the rich, who are the ones who have the most to lose *in this world,* will also die. (italics added)

In his speech to the Cuban people on 26 July 1980, Fidel went one step further in his characterization of the interrelation between religion and revolution, Christianity and socialism, raising with his people the possibility proposed to him in the previous week's visit to Nicaragua: a unity between Christians and Marxists.

> And some religious leaders in Nicaragua asked us why strategic alliance, why only strategic alliance, why not speak of unity between Marxist-Leninists and Christians?
> I don't know what the imperialists think about this. But I'm absolutely convinced the formula is highly explosive. It exists not only in Nicaragua but also in El Salvador, where the revolutionary forces and Christian forces are closely united.

Fidel carefully distinguishes between the reality of the church of the late 1950s in Cuba, with its own particular history, and the reality of churches elsewhere in Latin America.

> Nicaragua is a country where religious feelings go far deeper than they did in Cuba; therefore, the support given to the revolution by those religious sectors is very important. . . . If the revolution in Latin America were to take on an antireligious character, it would split the people. In our country, the church was, generally speaking, the church of the bourgeoisie, of the wealthy, of the landowners. This is not the case in many countries in Latin America, where religion and the church have deep roots among the people. The reactionary classes have

tried to use religion against progress, against revolution, and, in effect, they achieved their objective for quite a long time. However, times change, and imperialism, the oligarchy, and reaction are finding it more and more difficult to use the church against revolution.[14]

Major changes have taken place in relations between Christians and Marxists during the past twenty-five years, especially in the context of revolutionary movements, in Latin America. Fidel, and the revolutionary process which he represents, has been open to reconsideration of past positions in light of subsequent developments. There has been, and continues to be, an open-ended possibility for dialogue in the midst of shared activity. As Fidel himself pointed out to the International Cultural Congress in 1968:

> No one can say that he has the whole truth; no one can declare today, in the midst of the enormous complexity of the world, that he has the whole truth. We have our truth here, truths which have emerged from our experience, applicable to our conditions; and we have our inferences and our conclusions; but never have we pretended to speak ex cathedra, never have we pretended to hold the monopoly on revolutionary truth.[15]

CONSTITUTIONAL PROVISIONS AND PARTY DISCUSSION

Israel Batista claims that "few revolutionary processes have been as understanding toward the church as has the Cuban revolution." Clearly there have been problems, due to Cuba's underdevelopment or to functionaries who have not always followed conscientiously the policies of the leaders, or even to churches that lagged behind the revolutionary process;[16] or, to mistakes admitted by the PCC or the leaders.

The PCC was not founded until October 1965, almost seven years after the triumph of the Cuban revolution; it did not hold its first congress until December 1975, some ten years later. The PCC brought together three distinct streams of Cuban revolutionary activity: the 26 July movement (in which Baptist Frank País held until his death a major leadership position); the *Directorio Revolucionario* (once led by Catholic José Antonio Echevarría); and the People's Socialist Party (PSP), the only constituent group to have consistently followed Marxist-Leninist ideology. Established in 1925, the PSP found its activities alternately permitted and prohibited. During the periods when the PSP was declared illegal, the small group of PSP adherents was totally isolated and forced into clandestine activity in order to survive.

In addition to the continuing statements by Fidel, the first policy statement is in the "Declaration of the First National Congress of Education and

Culture," 29–30 April 1971. Its section on "Religion" clearly foreshadows later, more explicit policy. Particular attention was paid at that time to the preaching against the revolution and some counterrevolutionary activities by Jehovah's Witnesses and by some Seventh-Day Adventists. Also by this time certain sectors of the Catholic Church were seen as able to separate social and economic problems from those of philosophy, thus opening the way for participation in the practical work of the revolution. In the criticism of both sects and the Catholic Church, there is a strong note of self-criticism by the PCC, especially regarding weakness in party ideological activity and practical policies. The revolution will not be coarsely or clumsily antireligious, but rather it will engage in scientific teaching to raise the cultural level of the people. Teaching is intended to be not atheistic but scientific, referring to Martí's 1883 article, "A Scientific Education," which stresses scientific education even at the elementary level.[17]

The "Constitution of the Republic of Cuba," adopted only in February 1976, deals with religion in Article 54, setting forth three succinct policies.

> The Socialist state, which bases its activity and educates the people in the scientific materialist concept of the universe, recognizes and guarantees freedom of conscience and the right of everyone to profess any religious belief and to practice, within the framework of respect for the law, the belief of his preference.
>
> The law regulates the activities of religious institutions.
>
> It is illegal and punishable by law to oppose one's faith or religious belief to the revolution; to education; or to the fulfillment of one's duty to work, defend the homeland with arms, show reverence for its symbols and fulfill other duties established by the Constitution.[18]

There are tensions between these three sentences, on which discussion continues in the PCC, with at least temporary resolution of the issues reported in *Tesis y Resoluciones* following the First Party Congress in 1975. The following seven paragraphs are an extensive summary of the twenty-eight pages devoted to "On the Policy in Relation to religion, the church, and believers."[19]

Equality of treatment for all religious groups is qualified in the limit placed on expressions which are antisocial or harmful to health (322).

Religion is a "form of social consciousness, a reflection of external reality, earthly in origin," distinguished from other such forms in that it is a fantastic, distorted, and false reflection. Also, religion has a social function; it has been used in most of history by the exploiting classes to protect their power and privilege, to keep the oppressed meek, negating for them the right to violence while justifying its use by the dominant class. Since the rise of socialism, anti-Communists have cynically presented themselves as the defenders of religion and accused the Communists of being its enemies, but half a century of the experience of socialism in power, including the experience in Cuba, "has demonstrated the falsity of these pretensions" (296–98).

The PCC claims that Cuban revolutionary policy and practice are based on principles developed and defended by Martí and by Marx and Lenin. Other factors are also noted: the specific historical condition of the religious question in Cuba, the Cuban experience and that of other countries in building socialism, and changes in the world situation reflected in the churches and among believers. Some groups, including clergy, "assume political postures scarcely conceivable twenty years ago." Also of crucial importance is the situation in Latin America and its churches. Over one-third of the world's Catholics are in Latin America; the Catholic Church there has great influence especially among the poor, and Christian groups are often involved in movements for liberation and revolution (298, 304–10).

There are two aspects of the religious question in Cuba: practice and theory. The following principles are sustained in relation to practice:

a. Liberty of conscience, or the right of citizens to profess whatever religion, or belief, or not to profess any and to maintain materialist and atheist convictions.

b. The right of believers to practice their worship (cult) within respect for the law, public health, and the norms of Socialist morality.

c. Equal consideration with respect to all religions and beliefs. Consequently, neither official religion, nor state religion, nor privileged religion, nor persecuted religion.

d. It is inadmissible that religion or religious beliefs are to be used as a pretext or screen to combat the revolution of socialism, or to contravene or fail to fulfill the laws and the duties of citizens to society and state.

e. Believers, the same as nonbelievers, have the obligation to fulfill the revolutionary and social laws, and, thus, the duties that proceed from them, including military duties, work, and others.

f. Without offending the religious sentiment of believers, each citizen has the right to sustain and to spread his materialist atheist convictions (300–302).

Tactics in dealing with religion as ideology are informed both by the theory of religion and by the estimation of its consequences, quoting Engels: "Persecution is the best way to stimulate undesirable convictions" (299, 309).

There is a recurring caution against an antireligious crusade, coercive means, or a campaign expected to be the work of one day. There is a clear order of priority "based on the presupposition that the struggle for a scientific consciousness—materialist and free from prejudices and superstitions—is subordinated to the struggle to build a new society." The appeal is to Marx and Lenin: "The unity of the truly oppressed class to create a paradise on earth has for us more importance than proletarian criticism of a paradise in heaven." "The task of the Communists is not to convert all people to become atheists but the overthrow of all relations in which man is humiliated, defenseless, despised" (302–3).

Specific attention is paid to the contribution of some Protestant church leaders "of continental personality" who work and speak for the Cuban revolution and for other efforts of national liberation. These examples are set in contrast to the various obstacles posed by Jehovah's Witnesses, obstacles which range from refusal of blood transfusions to failure to fulfill military duties or voluntary labor, with the final judgment that their conduct "possesses nothing of religion and much of counterrevolution," following orders from their North American hierarchy as a "part of imperialist aggression" (315).

The third document comes from the December 1980 Second Congress, with a brief restatement of the earlier resolution. Following the policy of the First Congress on religion, the various parts of the party have achieved a coherent unity of action, providing adequate guidance for the government. Further, the policy has enabled the state to maintain satisfactory relations with the immense majority of religious institutions rooted in Cuba. Still, it is recommended that competent organs of the state "complement and improve the system of legal standards," guaranteeing freedom of conscience. There is a note of approval regarding the international exchange of delegations with religious goals of justice and peace.[20]

CHRISTIANS IN THE ENCOUNTERS

There are a number of ways, informal and formal, in which Christians and church groups encounter Marxists. By 1969 seminarians, pastors, and groups of priests joined in such voluntary labor as cane cutting. Other meetings occur at work or at school, in neighborhood Committees for the Defense of the Revolution (for example, on night watch duty), in the Federation of Cuban Women, or in People's Power (a parallel structure to the PCC, with wide participation). They may discuss party policy or its correct implementation at the local level, including rectifying mistakes. There are negotiations for bringing groups to Cuba or for Cubans to travel to ecumenical meetings elsewhere, which often involve Dr. Carneado.

There is often in Cuban Protestantism an intermingling of faith and ideology and a confusion of religious and ideological options. This confusion finds expression in the perception of some Christians that the revolution seeks to make all Cubans atheists and in their anti-Communist response to that perceived threat. Christian faithfulness becomes confused with anti-Communist ideology. Theo Tschuy, Swiss theologian and pastor, whose 1971 visit was made as a staff member of the World Council of Churches, reflected on earlier visits and observed that there still existed "tension and mistrust," even though subdued, between the revolution and the churches. But he did not have the impression that atheism was as much of an issue in Cuba as it had been ten years earlier.[21]

This change seems to be reflected in the statements by the Catholic bishops of Cuba. On 7 August 1960, the bishops refused to silence their oppositions to "materialist and atheistic communism."[22] Nine years later, on 3 September 1969, a collective pastoral letter again addressed the issue "Contemporary Atheism Is a Reality Which We Cannot Ignore Nor Judge in a Simplistic Manner."

> We have to approach the atheist with all the respect and fraternal charity which the human person deserves by the mere fact of being human. We should not exclude his honesty in taking a position, which can be very sincere, nor should we avoid collaboration in the practical order.[23]

Officially ecumenism began in Cuba with the founding of the Cuban Ecumenical Council in 1941. Adolfo Ham Reyes, President of the Council since 1983, notes a temptation to make the ecumenical idea too narrow. As churches seek to find their identity and their places in the new society, they may be tempted to want to return to the dream of a "Christian society" (before the revolution) or to become a ghetto, surviving as a cell in a society not committed to Christianity. He calls for a larger understanding of ecumenicity so the churches do not simply become a larger ghetto.

Ham pursues a more ideological dilemma. The churches witness to God in a society favoring a scientific interpretation of life; but their witness is through service rather than ideological confrontation. Churches ought to realize that many of their adherents cling to them seeking to evade the changes in society and to take refuge in a "spiritual world" at least subtly hostile to communism. The opposite temptation is for the church to accept its place too uncritically, becoming opportunistically a "revolutionary church" and forgetting the liberating Gospel of Jesus Christ. Ham also insists that he cannot agree with the traditional Marxist dogma that relegates religion to "private practice" or a private affair. This dilemma is between "political Christianity" and "pious privatization."

ILLUSTRATIONS OF THE DIALOGUE
IN DAILY LIFE

Preceding sections set forth some of the historical and ideological dynamics in relations between Christians and Marxists, between church and party, in Cuba. This section indicates some ways in which these relations are lived out on a day-to-day basis.

Access to university study represents a serious policy disagreement between the churches and the revolution. All applicants to the university are asked about their religious beliefs and practices. Church membership disqualifies a student to prepare to teach the humanities (notably philosophy and history) at any level on the ground that the person is "ideologically defective" and lacks the "correct perspective" for teaching.

Some instances of apparent discrimination in other areas of university study stem from inadequate qualification, or even from an unwillingness to take the risk of asserting one's rights. Some young Christians express fear that they would not be admitted to their desired course of study, or that they would not be able to achieve their preferred occupational goal, and so indicate less desirable second choices without ever expressing their real preference. Others decline to challenge an initial rejection, reluctant to struggle to secure guaranteed rights when they appear to be in jeopardy.

There have also been complaints about discrimination against Christians in job placement. There have undeniably been instances of discrimination, perhaps early on in reflection of the hostile confrontation of the early 1960s between Christians and Marxists, or subsequently due to an excess of zeal on the part of party members unduly militant in their advocacy of atheism. There have also been instances of successful challenge to much discrimination, securing jobs sought or restoring positions lost.

Some Christians in Cuba express anxiety about the ideological character of public-school instruction. Many fear that their children will be intimidated or separated from the church by instruction in Marxism-Leninism. In addition, instances of local CDRs (Committee for the Defense of the Revolution) inquiring into the participation of children in religious instruction have been reported. Yet there are also indications that lively discussion can take place between Marxist teachers and children brought up in Christian homes when a child is able to live within the society on its terms and is not fearful about also expressing a religious perspective.

All Cuban males are subject to military service, but some Christians decline to serve in the army. Conscientious objection has no legal status in Cuba; but, in fact, some informal opportunities have existed for alternative service in agriculture and construction since conscription began in 1964.

Although the party has indicated a growing openness to religious practitioners, nevertheless the government does not factor the spread of religious institutions into its future planning. Fidel, when asked during his meeting with church leaders in Jamaica about the omission of new church development from long-range building planning, responded: "Churches are not included in our construction programmes. . . . However, I can assure you that, if a given community were to ask the Revolutionary Government to build a church because the community felt there was a need for one . . . we'd build it."[24]

Some examples of cooperative relations come from very local and informal daily life interchanges. In the Luyanó section of Havana the Popular Power delegate is accustomed to giving his quarterly report to the neighborhood in front of the local Presbyterian church, using the church's electricity for lights and the public address system. Recognizing the church's contribution to Luyanó life, the area Popular Power has assisted parish efforts to obtain materials to make badly needed repairs to the church building. When, in April 1982, the Popular Power delegate learned from the pastor that the two Havana Presbyterian churches would be holding their Good Friday Communion service inside the church at the same time as the scheduled meeting, the delegate offered to move his meeting so it would not interfere with the church service. The change of location took place without comment or opposition from persons in the neighborhood. This stands in contrast to the early 1960s when on occasion some groups deliberately attempted to disrupt church services.

Several church groups participate regularly in voluntary work in the countryside. Students and faculty from the Roman Catholic seminary in Havana spend a month each year doing agricultural work alongside members of the UJC (Young Communist League). Pastors and lay persons related to the Cuban Ecumenical Council spend ten days each winter in theological reflection and voluntary work. In January 1984, 101 persons, including 17 Christians from Nicaragua and 10 members of the UJC, worked in the cane fields of Santiago de Cuba during the day, while at night they engaged in Bible study and reflection on the day's experiences.

Cuban Christians work in Kampuchea, participating since 1980 in a development assistance program funded by Church World Service (U.S.) and implemented with Cuban government support. In 1983 the team consisted of two veterinarians, one Baptist and one Methodist, and two Presbyterian hydraulic engineers. The Cuban Ecumenical Council considers these workers "missionaries"; the Cuban government characterizes them as "internationalists"!

Open hostility between Christians and Marxists has subsided over the past two decades. Although ideological disagreement remains, mutual respect appears to be growing, and actually acceptable means are sought to move through a variety of potential impasses. Insofar as the assertions of "evangelical" atheism are not considered indispensable to the practice of Cuban Marxist theory, and insofar as Cuban churches do not consider Marxist analysis of social and economic relations inherently incompatible with the Gospel of Jesus Christ, in that measure the *encuentro*/dialogue becomes a daily reality.

CONTINUING ISSUES IN THE ENCOUNTER

We have noted several positive factors in the encounter, including themes in the speeches of Fidel, attempts of the party to spell out clear guarantees of religious freedom, and movement in the churches from early hostility and later concern for survival to joining in the struggle for a new society. There are a number of concerns which no longer are at issue. Each "side" accepts the challenge to create the new person in a Socialist society.[25] Each rejoices in the considerable achievements of the new society in literacy, education, and health care. The motifs of internationalism and solidarity find resonance among Christians, despite a residual individualism. Both parties have been open to admitting past mistakes and learning from errors. Witness Fidel, in his Main Report to the Second Congress in 1980.

> Not everything we did was wise; not all our decisions were correct. In no revolutionary process have all actions and decisions been the right ones. Yet, . . . we have not renounced a single one of our . . . revolutionary principles. . . . We have never hesitated to recognize our errors and mistakes and sometimes this requires more courage than risking your life.[26]

But there remain tensions and unresolved issues. One is the unresolved conflict between guarantees of religious belief and practice for churches and citizens on the one hand, and on the other the understanding of Christian faith as at best ideology and at worst superstition, to be countered by the spread of scientific teaching. We have noted the tactical subordination of the second ideological conflict to the more urgent need to unify all Cubans in building the new society. We sense that the ideological conflict is felt most keenly by Christians in regard to the scientific, or Marxist-Leninist, or atheist education for children and youth, and to access to university and jobs.

We noted earlier that in the encounter persons of both traditions might come to reject dogmatic and deterministic interpretations. During lengthy interviews in May 1982 and January 1983, Dr. Carneado discussed the relations between Christians and Marxists in Cuba and throughout the world. He indicated that atheism may not be a fixed dogma and intimated that it is more a historical conclusion than an a priori premise. He noted that practices and policies regarding party membership for Christians differ in various countries of the world; in some countries some persons are active church members as well as active party members. Dr. Carneado further pointed out, however, that party members must accept party discipline; and in Cuba the churches have been historically anti-Communist. Thus it would not appear possible to live under church discipline, which has asserted anticommunism and defense of private property almost as articles of faith, and also accept party discipline. He also suggested that Christians and Marxists share a similar objective—the well-being of the world's peoples; both agree that hunger kills people and should be eliminated. Therefore, he asserts, there is no reason why Christians and Marxists cannot work together to build a new society, one in which hunger, disease, and illiteracy will be eliminated.

We note also an interview in May 1983 by Lee Ranck, editor of *Engage/ Social Action (E/SA)* with Methodist Bishop Armando Rodriguez of Cuba. Asked about the role of the church, Bishop Rodriguez responded:

> Today it is not common to be a Christian. The Communist Party accepts Christians and gives us the opportunity to continue our work. But you can go all over Cuba and not see any sign of Christianity. So, we are not a big group, but we are very united, very faithful.

Later the bishop talked of the challenge to be "real but humble children of God."

> We have learned a lot from the socialists, who work to fulfill the basic needs of the people. Pastoral care becomes the role of the church, so we seek to fulfill the spiritual needs of all our people. Our goal is to work in a humble way to testify to all the Cuban people.[27]

A further issue concerns the constitutional "absolute separation" of church and state and the corollary that religion is a private affair. From Lenin on this is explicitly said to mean "insofar as the state is concerned," thus prohibiting special rights or duties for any group of believers or of nonbelievers. This might mean religious freedom only insofar as there are no political over-tones. A more positive interpretation is that churches may not specifically foster or engage in counterrevolutionary activities.

We suspect that this is an area in which churches and their leaders continue to test whether they have earned the right to be heard, whether they have become sufficiently incorporated into the new society to trust themselves, and to be trusted, to engage in prophetic political criticism.

Batista has affirmed this as a demand upon the churches. Ham has warned of the dilemma of "political Christianity" versus "pious privatization" of the faith.

Finally, the encounter in Cuba has been regarded as *encuentro* rather than dialogue. In the *encuentro* both Christians and Marxists seem to accept as their own the maxim of José Martí, "Hacer es la Mejor Manera de Decir" ("To do is the best way to speak").

NOTES

1. Israel Batista Guerra, "Encuentro Cristiano-Marxista en Cuba," in *Cristo Vivo en Cuba*, ed. Sergio Arce Martinez et al. (San José, Costa Rica: Departamento Ecumenico de Investigaciones, 1978), 81. When titles are in Spanish, the translations are by the authors. See also Israel Batista Guerra, "The Development Challenge: The Role of the Church in Cuba," *Christians' Participation in Development in Socialist Contexts* (Geneva: World Council of Churches' Commission on the Churches' Participation in Development Document No. 18, November 1980, Part 3: "A Just Society"), 15–27.

2. Batista, "Development," 21–23.

3. In *WCC Exchange*, a Bi-monthly Documentation Service from the World Council of Churches (Geneva: WCC) 2 (May 1977): 6. The authors will use inclusive language in the text but will not change the language within quotations.

4. Batista, "Development," 27.

5. Fidel Castro, *First Congress of the Communist Party of Cuba: Report Central* (Havana: Department of Revolutionary Orientation, Central Committee, PCC, 1977). See section titled "Mistakes Made," 144–57, especially this statement:

> We would not be honest revolutionaries if, when rendering an account of the revolution, we did not bluntly tell the First Congress of the Party that we were not always capable of discovering the problems in due time, of avoiding mistakes, of overcoming omissions and acting absolutely in keeping with the working methods that should guide the direction and the functioning of the party. (p. 153)

6. See "Pastoral Constitution of the Church in the Modern World,": 2 December 1965, in *The Documents of Vatican II*, ed. Walter M. Abbott, S.J. (New York: Guild Press, America Press, Association Press, 1966), especially 216–17; and *The Church in the Present-day Transformation of Latin America in the Light of the Council*, Second General Conference of Latin American Bishops, II. Conclusions, 2d ed. (Washington, D.C.; Division for Latin American–U.S. Catholic Conference, 1973).

7. *Religion in Cuba Today: A New Church in a New Society*, trans. and ed. Alice L. Hageman and Philip E. Wheaton (New York: Association Press, 1971), 132. The following three quotations are also from 132.

8. Ibid., 136.

9. *Fidel Castro Speaks*, ed. Martin Kenner and James Petras (New York: Grove Press, 1969), 85.

10. *Religion in Cuba Today*, trans. and ed. Hageman and Wheaton, 137.

11. Ibid., 139.

12. Fidel Castro Ruz, *CUBA-CHILE: Encuentro Symbolico entre dos Procesos Historicos* (La Habana: Ediciones Politicas, Comision de Orientacion Revolucionaria del Comité Central del Partido Comunista de Cuba, 1972), 484–85.

13. "Fidel Castro on Church-State Relations in Cuba," *WCC Exchange* (Geneva) 1 (January 1978): 7–11.

14. *Fidel Castro Speeches*, ed. Michael Tabor (New York: Pathfinder Press, 1981), 321, 320.

15. Fidel Castro, "Speech given at the closing ceremony of the Cultural Congress of Havana, held in the Chaplin Theatre, January 12, 1968," *Ediciones COR* (La Habana) 4 (1968): 42.

16. Batista, "Encuentro," 84; see Batista, "Development," 39.

17. "Declaraction del Primer Congreso Nacional de Educacion y Cultura," *Casa de las Americas*, La Habana, Cuba, Numero 65–66 (March–June 1971): 11–12. See also José Martí, "A Scientific Education," in *On Education*, trans. Elinor Randall, ed. Philip S. Foner (New York: Monthly Review Press, 1979), 121–123.

18. *Constitution of the Republic of Cuba*, trans. and pub. Center for Cuban Studies (220 East 23rd St., New York, N.Y., 10010), March 1980.

19. *Tesis y Resoluciones*. Primer Congreso del Partido Comunista de Cuba 1975 (Ciudad de la Habana: Editorial de Ciencias Sociales, 1978), 295–323. In the following seven paragraphs page references will be given in parentheses in the text.

20. *2nd Congress of the Communist Party of Cuba: Documents and Speeches* (Havana: Political Publishers, 1981), 315–17.

21. Theo Tschuy, "Reflections of Faith and Order in Cuba," World Council of Churches, 16 April 1971 (mimeographed).

22. "Collective Pastoral Letter of the Cuban Episcopacy," 7 August 1960, in *Religion in Cuba Today*, trans. and ed. Hageman and Wheaton, 104.

23. Ibid., 3 September 1969. See note 5, above.

24. "Fidel Castro on Church-State Relations," 16–17.

25. The creation of a new man means the establishment of a new life of community in the new society which has no room for the exploitation of other people's work, for racial discrimination or for the subjection of women as mere objects of consumption, commercial or sexual, and which will not tolerate the exploitation of the legitimate values of family life in the illegitimate interests of a society of class discrimination. (The Presbyterian-Reformed Confession of Faith, *WCC Exchange*, 13.)

26. Main Report, p. 1; see note 20 above.

27. "To Work in a Humble Way," *E/SA (Engage/Social Action)* 2:7 (July–August 1983): 39–40.

28. A banner bearing this maxim dominated the Plaza de la Revolucion at the celebration of the 130th anniversary of Martí's birth in January 1983; this same theme was prominent in the Cuban Ecumenical Council meeting during the same month and the shared work in the countryside of Roman Catholic seminarians and Young Communists.

SUGGESTIONS FOR FURTHER READING

Dewart, Leslie. *Christianity and Revolution: The Lesson of Cuba*. New York: Herder & Herder, 1963.

THIRD WORLD ENCOUNTERS

Dominguez, Jorge L. *Cuba: Order and Revolution*. Cambridge: Harvard University Press, 1978.

Dussell, Enrique. *History and Theology of Liberation*. Translated by John Drury. Maryknoll, N.Y.: Orbis Books, 1976.

Hageman, Alice L., and Philip E. Wheaton, eds. *Religion in Cuba Today*. New York: Association Press, 1971.

Mesa-Lago, Carmelo. *Cuba in the Nineteen Seventies: Pragmatism and Institutionalization*. Rev. ed. Albuquerque, N.Mex.: University of New Mexico Press, 1978.

Randall, Margaret. *Christians in the Nicaraguan Revolution*. Vancouver: New Star Books, 1983.

Silva Gotay, Samuel. *El Pensamiento Cristiano Revolucionario en America Latina y el Caribe*. Salamanca: Ediciones Sigueme, 1981.

Tabor, Michael, ed. *Fidel Castro Speeches: Cuba's Inter-Nationalist Foreign Policy 1975–80*. New York: Pathfinder Press, 1981.

CONCLUSION
Robert G. Thobaben

The aim of this book has been to present a comprehensive and balanced selection of writing on the Christian-Marxist Encounter (CME) in all three worlds insofar as this is possible. It is a controversial topic and the need to select from a large array of writings from scholars in all three worlds demanded that hard choices be made. This is not an apology—only a fact.

As for the contributors themselves, it would be a gross exaggeration to characterize any of them as radically progressive; however, it is fair to label them all as responsible scholars who are dedicated to democracy. They are, as one might expect, in every instance academicians and as such separated from the governing elites in the societies in which they work. Perhaps their greatest virtue is their candor, openness, and honesty in describing the dialogue. One will see in their writing little manipulation of Christian or Marxist symbols or rationalizations of abuses committed in the name of Christianity and Marxism. On the contrary, it is their exposure of myths, excesses, and errors coupled with their obvious yearning for freedom and their capacity for analysis that captures one's imagination. Each has sought to distill what is authentic in the encounter of Christians and Marxists and to strip away in thoughtful description the tradition, ritual, symbol, and custom which only hopelessly confuse the reader. Their task is completed.

However, three things remain to be done: first, to characterize the ebb and flow of the CME in all three worlds since 1960; second, to identify and briefly comment on the agenda for the CME of the future—those issues that plague the world today and should be the focus of the symposium topics and working relations of Christians and Marxists in their future encounters; and finally, to show the relationship to, and significance of, the CME to the study of politics, in all its formal and informal dimensions, and to the discipline of political science particularly.

REVIVAL AND ECLIPSE OF THE CME:
1960–84

Since 1960 one can identify a number of revivals and eclipses in the CME. These changes are, in true Hegelian fashion, a dialectical movement from thesis to anti-thesis to synthesis, that is, ideas and actions of prior stages in the development of the CME have not been totally negated but incorporated into each aspect of the succeeding stage. The metaphor of the dialectic along with this dialectical vision of the CME is helpful in that it sensitizes one to change as opposed to stasis. That is the very nature of the CME. In many ways this change should be characterized as developmental because the direction of the movement denotes progress. What counts is the necessity to conceive, or better to reconceive, the relationships between these two groups in a dynamic manner.

The actual method employed to reach the conclusions about revivals and eclipses in the CME needs some explanation. Initially a horizontal "time line" from 1960 to 1984 was established. Next a vertical "activity line" to measure both quantitative and qualitative dimensions of the encounter was constructed. Then, in reading the contribution of each author, each time one of them commented on a particular time and action in the encounter a "data point" was plotted on one of the three charts (First World, Second World, Third World). Finally, a line was plotted through the "data points" on each of the three charts to trace out a pattern that accurately described both the closeness and the direction of association (in statistical language this would be called a line of regression). These patterns have been empirically determined and what follows is an attempt to report faithfully the nature of those patterns.

First World Encounters

Perhaps the three most important preconditions to the renewal of the CME in the First World were: the action of the Italian Communist Party at the Fifth Party Congress in January 1946 which amended Article 2 of the Constitution so that belief in dialectical materialism was no longer a precondition for membership in the party; Khrushchev's astounding speech to the 20th Party Congress in 1956 denouncing Stalin's excesses; and the overtures of Pope John XXIII in two encyclicals published in the early 1960s (*Mater et Magistra* and *Pacem in Terris*).

Two major revivals and eclipses in the CME occurred in the First World during the mid-1960s and the mid-1970s. The first revival in the mid-1960s involved three separate encounters: a growing and developing series of activities in Italy, the series of four dialogues organized by the Paulus-Gesellschaft between 1964 and 1967, and the parallel dialogue in the United States at various universities (Notre Dame, Temple, Harvard, Santa Clara). Optimism seemed to be the rule of the day. However, the first eclipse occurred shortly after August 1968 when the Warsaw Pact nations invaded

Czechoslovakia. In every instance the quantity and quality of CME dropped. The Italian encounter experienced only a limited eclipse and was the least affected; some activity went on in the United States, but the conferences of the Paulus-Gesellschaft (Austria-Germany) ended. The second revival in the First World is clearly discernible by 1975. The renewed encounter in Italy involved actors at the highest level of decision making in the party (General Secretary Enrico Berlinguer) and the church (Bishop Bettazzi); the Paulus-Gesellschaft organized a series of symposia in Florence, Italy (1975), Salzburg, Austria (1977), and Dusseldorf, West Germany (1978); and in the United States two levels of CME occurred—the first involved participation in a series of seven annual international symposia on peace (to be discussed later), while the second was the organization of three North American Marxist-Christian Dialogues (MCD) held on issues of social justice at Philadelphia (1978), Dayton (1980), and Washington, D.C. (1982). This second revival was probably signaled by the policy of détente between East and West, the signing of SALT I by Nixon and Brezhnev, the end of U.S. involvement in the Vietnam war, the signing of SALT II in Vienna in 1979 between Carter and Brezhnev, and the establishment of Solidarity in Poland.

One other MCD demands mention at this point—the so-called Vienna-Based Dialogue. This encounter involves participants from three groups— The International Institute for Peace (a Soviet-funded group based in Vienna), The Institute for Peace Research of the University of Vienna, and The Institute for International Understanding (U.S.-based group). The two Vienna-based groups began a dialogue in 1971 (during the first eclipse) in Vienna on various issues associated with peace and the avoidance of nuclear war. The U.S.-based Institute began to participate at a symposium held at Rosemont College (Philadelphia) in 1977. To date, the Vienna-Based Dialogue has organized eleven symposia in the last fourteen years (two in the U.S.S.R., two in the United States, seven in Western Europe).

The second eclipse began in 1980, prompted by the Soviet invasion of Afghanistan, the U.S. boycott of the 1980 Olympics, the renewed "Cold War" rhetoric, the Korean airliner incident, and continues to the present time; *but* it is not as serious a blow as the first reversal. The CME in Italy appears to be maintaining itself with no appreciable decline. However, in the United States there seems to be some loss of interest regarding involvement in the Vienna-Based Dialogues, and the Paulus-Gesellschaft has done virtually nothing the last four years. The Vienna-based dialogue continues its uninterrupted series of symposia on peace, but, as noted above, the level of interest (quality) seems to have diminished a bit.

Second World Encounters

One revival and eclipse in the CME occurred in the Second World during the period from 1960 to 1984. Prior to Khrushchev's speech to the 20th Party Congress, relations between Christians and Marxists could only be characterized as confrontational. However, as the process of de-Stalinization developed there was a general deescalation of the conflict, initiation of some reforms in church-state relations, and subsequently a period of constructive dialogue in all three countries. Granted, there was certainly suspicion and tension, but the quantity and quality of contact improved. Contrary to events in the First World, the invasion of Czechoslovakia had little negative impact on the encounter in Poland and East Germany. In fact, as one examines the "data points" the reverse is true. Apparently these two rather unstable regimes were "nerved" by the action of the Warsaw Pact, and with new recognition and acceptance they felt more secure and thus tended to expand contacts with Christians. In any event, the CME in these two countries culminated in the pope's triumphant second pilgrimage to Poland and in Erich Honecker's assumption of the role of chairman of the Martin Luther Committee in East Germany. The only major decline in the Second World countries under review occurred in Yugoslavia in 1971 when Tito "sharply restricted" the process of public dialogue which he saw as a threat. Private dialogue still occurs, but the prospect is not encouraging in Yugoslavia at the moment.

Third World Encounters

The trend in the Third World encounter in Cuba, India, and black Africa is one of almost uninterrupted revival and renewal in the relations between Christians and Marxists. For example, in Cuba in 1960 dialogue was "unthinkable" with "reeducation" camps for Christians and other deviants. From this point on the evolution and development of the CME has moved from "strategic alliance" to "cooperation" to calls for "unity" between the two groups by Castro himself. In both quantity and quality of action, the CME is revived. The same holds true for black Africa. "African Socialism's" CME as expressed over time in the words and deeds of Nkrumah, Nyerere, and Senghor demonstrate commitment to both Marx and Jesus. They have been concerned with the construction of socialism not atheism, and this in a context of Christian values and beliefs. In the states ruled by leaders committed to the principles of "Revolutionary Marxism," the period from 1965 to 1970 was one of almost total alienation between the church and the liberation movements (Angola, Mozambique, Guinea Bissau, Zimbabwe). But from 1970 to the present time one can see a shift in the position of both the

Christian and Marxist groups. Mutual recognition, tolerance, and acceptance of the other's existence is evidenced in numerous actions ranging from formal dialogue and symbolic meetings of the leadership of the two groups to actual cooperation.

In the Third World nations reviewed herein, India represents the only state in which there has been a clear eclipse of the CME. In the period from 1960 to 1980, in Kerala particularly, the CME made some progress. However, since 1980 the encounter is in decline with Communist Party criticism of Christian action groups on numerous occasions and the cancellation of a formal dialogue recently. The dialogue in India today is "not active."

In reviewing the many "data points" and the trends they seem to represent in all three worlds one can only conclude that the CME is alive and well on a worldwide basis. Granted, there have been eclipses in the past and there will be more in the future, but the trend in quantity and quality of action and dialogue between Christians and Marxists is positive. The twenty-first century is only fifteen years away; it will be ushered in by more and more encounters between Christians and Marxists.

TOWARD THE TWENTY-FIRST CENTURY: AN AGENDA FOR THE CME

For many years Karl Marx's work and the life and ministry of Jesus Christ have continuously challenged people. This is still the case today. The social problems of our day are so critical that two-thirds of humanity do not have the basic needs of life (food, clothing, shelter, fuel), while one-third of humankind becomes ever stronger and more powerful. Many people have no money, while some cannot spend the money they have. We have some men who are crushed by their work with no security, while others approach creative activity and the good life. We have, as Nietzsche said, sub-men and super-men. What then should we do? Should we associate ourselves with the miserable of the earth? Have we even begun to cope with alienation in the modern industrial state—regardless of its social system? What can we do about national politics that seems increasingly unable to mediate the basic economic struggle between management and labor? Is it time to redefine the concept of proletariat and bourgeoisie? What is the proper role of the Christian church in the epoch of the "new sovereigns"—the multinationals? These questions and many more cry out for new solutions. Christians and Marxists, in both the philosophical and practical aspects of their encounter, must address these issues and they must do so in a day of rapid change. Think of the changes in cybernetics, automation, exploration of space, penetration of the atom, and the revolution in biotechnology. We are scientifically studying the vast dimensions of space, the infinite complexity of genetics in biology, an ever-growing number of subatomic particles, and automation. How are we to cope with such dramatic technological changes? Can our new environmental and technological conditions and circumstances continue to coexist with the old "truths"? We are living at the dawn of the twenty-first century and it is time, well past time, that the CME addressed these challenges.

Those of us involved in the CME must not be like the gladiators of politics—prepared to refight World War II. The need is for us to keep our eyes on the horizon, the future, if we are to be relevant in this world of rapid change. Paradoxically, participants in the encounter should go "backward" and "forward" in future dialogues. We need to move "backward" in theory to face anew the great philosophical issues of man, God, and history, and in practice to recommit ourselves to self-criticism as well as criticism of others. Today, more than ever before, it is incumbent on Christians and Marxists to reject elegant language, manufactured dialogue, and "whitewashing" of one's own public policy and enter into authentic dialogue and action toward community. We must also go "forward" in theory and forthrightly deal with the political concepts of power, authority, change, justice, and control; while we, in practice, involve ourselves more and more with the power structures of society in order to help construct a more just social order for all people. And we should *never* forget that although our goals are important, the means to achieve them are equally important.

Both theoretical issues and practical struggle for the new day must go hand in hand in the future CME. Practically, we can do "good political work" together on issues such as the nuclear freeze movement, disarmament and arms control, and U.S.–U.S.S.R. détente. *Nothing* could be more important. Theoretically, we should be talking and writing more about the relationship between idea systems and political action because ideas, as well as interests, can be meaningful for good or evil. Christians and Marxists need to clarify their thinking on the significance of ideas to action.

CMEs can be psychologically enfeebling. Anyone who has participated actively in such events has experienced frustration, euphoria, and despair. We must recognize that we are all prisoners of our own orthodoxy to some degree and as such preoccupied with the image of politics rather than its reality. The burden of the past is like a heavy weight on our back that is difficult to dislodge. It is so seductively simple to replace reality with image when one is wearing ideological blinders.

What then are some of the other major theoretical and practical challenges to Christians and Marxists that demand new responses at this dawn of the twenty-first century? What follows is certainly not exhaustive since other issues (such as opening the dialogue to other religious communities, China, reassessment of the role of religion, atheism, and so forth) certainly warrant attention. Nevertheless, the following eight issues seem to illustrate best the variety and scope of the problems that require attention and it is for these reasons that they were selected for brief commentary.

Theoretical Issues

First Issue. Power is the central relational concept of political science. Christians and Marxists should seriously consider the matter of limiting political power. Marxist political thought has failed to develop satisfactory explanations and mechanisms for the control of power as witnessed by the exercise of almost unlimited political power in states such as Poland and the U.S.S.R. Likewise the organized Christian church has often been the dependent of state power rather than its critic.[1] This must change. The church should take a leading role in all countries to bring political power under the control of more and more people. Dictatorships of the right and left stand in contradiction to authentic Christianity and Marxism.

Second Issue. There are myths of Christianity and Marxism that must be renounced lest we become commissars of the Gulag Archipelago or priestly escapists. As Leszek Kolakowski once suggested, we need "more jesters and less priests." Epistemological myths regarding dialectics and logic, metaphysical myths on God's nature, aesthetic myths on art such as Socialist realism, and ethical myths about man's selfish or selfless nature all should be exposed to the harsh light of rational thought. Failure to do so transforms useful paradigms into dogma that necessarily implies inquisition, scientism, inevitability, and the end of humanism. We need models not myths.

Third Issue. Christians and Marxists must adopt a critical but flexible approach to nationalism. In the First and Second World nations they should work to minimize this divisive and limiting ideology that stands in opposition to their internationalist perspective. However, in Third World countries they should openly recognize the virtues of Third World nationalism as it provides the people with self-respect and a sense of worth, begins to corrode notions of racial inferiority, and acts as a link between the tribe and the universal community thus expanding the scope of individual loyalty. This nationalism will cause problems, but Christians and Marxists should support it with their time and money. The process of building a nation from tribal groups is difficult, and it is irrational to expect these people to leap from the tribal to the universal community. The nation is the only transitional form of political organization available to them.

Fourth Issue. Christians and Marxists should face the fact that, as movements, they have lost much of their ethical appeal. Marx's socialism is much more than simply scientific analysis. Granted, Marx did an excellent job of extrapolating trends in history and building a model of social change and development derived from the real world, but his basic concern was how to change the quality of life for human beings. This is the very meaning of Marx's humanism. Marx's theory of alienation in the "Paris Manuscripts" shows clearly his fundamental *moral* concerns regarding the effects of feudalism and particularly capitalism on the particular human individual. What he wrote in his sociology is important, but *why* he wrote it is infinitely more important. Marx's image of man suggested the possibility of moral perfection and goodness.[2] The new man, man as species-being, was his goal. Christians, of course, have no problem with moral concerns—what they must remember is that Christianity is more than mere moral philosophy; it is a world view that has a material dimension. Christian love, as acted out by Jesus, was always associated with human relationships in this world. It behooves those who follow Him to act in the same way and to treat their neighbor, as Buber said, as *"du"* instead of *"Sie."*

Practical Issues

Fifth Issue. A new revolution in biology has replaced the old industrial revolution. Christians and Marxists should cooperate together and assume some responsibility for the nature of this new development. If they abandon their mutual obligation, medical power may replace political power as it exercises decision-making capacity over vital life processes. The CME should be working on issues such as biotechnology, behavior control, genetic engineering, experimentation, and so forth. The immediate consequence will be more rational and human public policy. The latent consequence will be a new trust between Christians and Marxists built upon active work together in a common cause. We border on being masters of evolution. Will the decisions be made by the men of medicine or all men?

Sixth Issue. Meaningful political action without the organized church and party is possible but not probable. Christians and Marxists should recognize this reality and work together to reform, not to eliminate, these institutions. These institutionalized groups provide the necessary structure, organization, and leadership necessary for success in politics. Without them there is a vacuum. The human individual may be effective at the level of political decision making on the school board. However, there is an inverse relationship between the effectiveness of an individual on decisions of public policy and the level of decision making as it moves from local to state to national to international to supranational decision making. The higher the level of decision the less efficacious is the individual. Church and party are necessary "evils." It is difficult to live politically with them. It is impossible to live politically without them. We can and must work together to transform them into more responsive and responsible institutions.

Seventh Issue. Property is here to stay for the foreseeable future, and Christians and Marxists would do well to recognize this fact. Catholic philosophers of the Middle Ages defended property (St. Thomas Aquinas) as did their Protestant counterparts of the Reformation period (Luther). Land reform in the Central American countries so passionately sought by peasants would not negate property but is presupposed in their struggle. Therefore, Christians and Marxists should work together to socialize the functions of property (its decision-making dimension) and leave the title to it alone for the balance of this century at least. Economic democracy should be the goal we struggle to achieve. It is certainly abundantly clear that government ownership, with its attendant bureaucracy, is frequently not an improvement. The separation of ownership from control makes the classic concept of property as a relation almost irrelevant today. Control, not ownership, is the key.[3]

Eighth Issue. Increasing automation implies a degree of alienated labor unknown in the past. Christians and Marxists should be working together to develop at least partial answers to this problem. Automation necessarily implies a widening of the gap between production and consumption and as such is a social "time bomb." Unemployment, one-dimensional man, and staggering environmental changes are built into automation. We are "robotizing" our labor force in the name of industrial growth and the human costs will be great. Even the American work ethic is endangered as the epoch of the labor society draws to a close. Surely this is a topic for cooperative action by Christians and Marxists.

CHRISTIAN-MARXIST ENCOUNTER AND THE STUDY OF POLITICS

The basic argument of this section is that knowledge and understanding of the CME, in both its theoretical and practical dimensions, is absolutely crucial to the study of politics. Indeed, if political science is concerned with the causes, purposes, and effects of political behavior and institutions and with psychological research regarding motivation in man, then it had best attend to the encounters of Christians and Marxists because these people are spokespersons for belief systems that inspire and motivate in varying degree over one-half of the world's population and its ruling elites.

To date, political science has met, in part, the obligation above with respect to Marxism. But religion generally, and Christianity particularly, has certainly not received the same recognition. In fact it has been largely ignored (even denied implicitly and in some instances explicitly) as a major factor in explaining political behavior. The problem for political scientists, and for their students, is that abstinence from discussion of the divine alternative in so-called scientific discussion in classroom, textbook, or conference is not justified, nor is it scientific. Political science has, for too long, "bracketed" the divine alternative, that is, consciously ignored it in the best of cases and unconsciously omitted it in the worst of cases. It is time now for political science to "unbracket" the divine alternative in order to maintain scholarly honesty.[4] Since Christianity focuses on many of the ultimate questions of political theory, political science—if it is to continue saying relevant things about politics—had best correct this serious act of omission. Like it or not, political scientists must abandon the convenient but false dichotomy they have erected between religion and politics. It is not enough to continually talk about the "wall or separation" between the two fields; what is needed now is recognition of their internal relationship in the *real world*. And reality, political reality in particular, simply will not go away by denying or ignoring it.

Of the five major fields of political science, political theory is the oldest and lies at the heart of the discipline. The main components of political theory are concepts. All theorizing and thinking about human behavior begins with concepts and with relationships between concepts—this is fundamental. The work done in political theory reflects the basic and elemental interests of political science as a discipline. Thus it is to this field of political science that we must turn in order to demonstrate the validity of the central thesis of this section.

Political theory involves a rather large number of concepts that have been usefully organized within the framework of three subtopics: concepts of political entities (humankind, the state, community, and so forth), concepts that seek to describe the relationships between entities (power, authority, freedom, justice, property, equality, rights, and so forth), and concepts that address the phenomenon of political change (revolution, evolution, and the like).[5] Although there is a good deal of agreement on what the major concepts of political theory are and on this system of classification in political science, that is the end of unity. From this point on confusion reigns today just as it did twenty-five hundred years ago. This is so because the political association of human beings is involved, intricate, and complex. As a result, the explanations and descriptions of these relationships have reflected this perplexing reality in two great traditions associated with the study of politics—prescriptive and descriptive theory. From Plato to Leo Strauss and from Aristotle to Henry Kissinger, the contradiction between the "ought" of moral prescription and the "is" of empirical description dominates all political thought. Though many theorists claim to have reconciled "right the ethical ought" with "power the political is," few recognize the claim. The struggle goes on with no end in sight. Political theory has been, and is today, divided into political philosophy and political science, and the line between them is ambiguous to say the least. No effort will be made here to cross that Rubicon. What will be attempted is to show how study of the CME can contribute to the development of the major categories and concepts of political theory.

The study of politics in isolation from the study of religion generally and the CME particularly makes no sense at all. In fact, it is nonsense. Naturally, time and space dictate that severe limits be set in this effort to show the significance of the CME for political theory. As such, only five of these concepts will be discussed—humankind, the state, power, justice, change. If even one of these key concepts of political theory is enriched or made more intelligible by an inquiry into the CME, then political science can only benefit as a discipline. The capacity to explain and predict the political behavior of individuals and groups is the *raison d'être* of the discipline.

MAJOR CONCEPTS OF POLITICAL THEORY
AND THE CME

Humankind

The fundamental problem of political theory is that human beings are at the center of the cosmos, and we do not know who they are. Every one of the great political theorists, from Plato and Aristotle to Edmund Burke and J. S. Mill, has constructed his or her political philosophy on a particular theory of human nature and psychology, but all of them are different. Which one are we to believe? Is humankind, as Machiavelli says, egoistic, materialistic, cowardly, and driven by insatiable desires; or is it, as Locke contends, both individually and socially conscious—rational enough to organize its experience to achieve goals? Are the vast majority of us sinners and virtually helpless in the world as St. Augustine contends, or can we use our divine reason, as St. Thomas holds, to do good works and determine and achieve values we deem desirable? Few today subscribe to the notion that human beings can be reduced to the "reality" of economic beings as the dismal discipline of economics suggests. If not politics and economics, perhaps psychology can help us. But consider the following: Freud argues that humankind seeks pleasure, while Adler contends it is power that motivates human beings. Maslow says, on the contrary, that it is "self-actualization" that motivates humankind while Frankl argues persuasively that the driving force in life is a search for meaning *outside* of oneself. The ambiguity of humankind's image in political theory is apparent, and political scientists continue to search for the real nature and identity of human beings in a world of chaos that is becoming ever-more plastic.

Can knowledge and understanding of the CME solve this critical problem for political theorists? Absolutely not! However, it can help them expand, illuminate, and develop their scholarship in this area by becoming familiar with the dialogue of Christians and Marxists on a number of topics—alienation, transcendence, subjectivity, humanism, and praxis.

The problem of humankind is the problem of *alienation*—human estrangement. Marx borrowed the term from Hegel and developed it in the "Paris Manuscripts" and his essay "On the Jewish Question." Here he sought to explain the forms of alienation (economic, political, social, individual) and why humankind was turned against itself and other people. Marx contended that perhaps the most debilitating aspect of human estrangement was religious alienation. For Marx, religion is the illusory reflection in human beings' minds of their own unrealized potential and hopes for the world. As such, the only human response to a transcendent God was awe, worship, and submission to his will that inexorably led to reinforcement of the socioeconomic and political status quo. The alienation of the Jew (or any other religious person for that matter) will not be solved by becoming a Christian, but by becoming an authentic human being—by human emancipation. Marx wants us to understand ourselves as human beings—not men, women, Christians, Muslims, Jews, Americans, blacks, or whites. Think "horizontally" not "vertically," says Marx.

The problem of a person as he or she is (socialist and capitalist being) and a person as he or she might be (as "species being" or "new creation in Christ") is *the* major theme of the CME. Christians and Marxists both seek the new being. Christians contend that if the Marxist dogma that social and economic conditions produce the new being is true, then where is he or she today in the Communist bloc. Surely almost seventy years is enough. They go on to argue that socialism *needs* Christianity and that only faith in Jesus Christ,

His *ideas* and His redemptive and resurrecting power in community, can produce the new man. As evidence they point to the rapid, nay almost instantaneous, transformation of those people who do embrace Christ.[6] The conclusion is that it is not primarily socioeconomic conditions but ideology that inspires, motivates, and impels humankind to go beyond the human predicament of alienation.

If political science purports to explain behavior, it had best direct its attention to two of the most inspirational faith systems in the world today—Christianity and Marxism. It is highly possible that new insights and maturation of political theory will occur through a serious inquiry into the CME. It is certainly probable that failure to do so will result in continued partial and opaque images of humankind.

In Christianity, *transcendence* is traditionally associated with belief in a world beyond—with the supernatural. Today this has changed. Some Christians today, those that subscribe to liberation theology, direct their primary focus not on the transcendent God, the God of Abraham, but on the immanent God, Jesus Christ. The most radical of this faction would even dare to characterize themselves as atheist Christians.[7] For these Christians the kingdom of God is at hand and help is needed. As such, Christians and Marxists in many Latin and Central American countries have joined together as human beings to struggle to overcome what they feel are oppressive and unjust social systems. These Christians and Marxists see the future as unique, and one that must be created. Communism and the kingdom are beyond us, but humankind must play the crucial role in bringing about the new day, the new society, and the new being. For Christians and Marxists humankind can and will transcend itself. Whether this occurs with or without divine help is of little moment to those involved in the struggle to change their lives. These Christians and Marxists work to go beyond, to transcend, humankind and society as they are today.

Subjectivity is, in Christian thought, an expression of transcendence. The idea here is the subjective moment in a human being's life when he or she is "born again" and begins to build a new life of selflessness rather than selfishness, of uprightness instead of greed, of lovingkindness rather than domination. Subjectivity is a new start—a motivating power for change. Change is the rule of life in Marxism, and it is the rule of life in Christianity also, that is, how to think and live a life of change as Jesus did. To Christians, and to Marxists like Ernst Bloch, Jesus Christ shows us what subjectivity means. Jesus' life is what it means to be a human being. Love is the secret of humankind's fulfillment, love of one's neighbor who is "Christ in our midst." Che Guevara once said in effect that if socialism cannot change a person then he finds it of little interest. Christians hold that Jesus is the model of an authentic human being and his message of love was designed to transform the selfish individual and state into the selfless person in community with others. Socialist conditions, they claim, are thus a necessary but not a sufficient condition for emergence of the new human being. The ideas of Jesus are also a necessary, and in the view of these Christians, precondition to the new human being—a precondition that is the first among the two essential conditions.

Humanism is implicit in both Christianity and Marx's writing. Christian humanism is grounded in the incarnation, manifested in love of one's neighbor, and redeemed in material, human history. Marx's humanism is best represented in his early writings and acts as the central reason for all his later works. Marx saw fragmented, alienated, partial humankind and protested against this. He thought he had found the cause of this predicament in the socioeconomic conditions of humankind so he set out to explain how and why this was the case. Humanism is a point of Christian and Marxist convergence. The goal of Marx and Jesus is humanized individuals, and this implies truly human social relations. Some "old" Communists contend that Christians cannot engage in meaningful social activity. This is nonsense. Witness the activity of Christians *within* the Italian Communist Party described by Edward Grace or the action of Christians in bringing about social change today in Central and South America. Historically, is there any one who believes that Martin Luther, Mohatma Gandhi, and Martin Luther King, Jr., were not very important engines of social change and development? Political theorists must understand that for Karl Marx and Jesus Christ humankind is an end in itself—never a means and that revolutionary action is always justified if it seeks to achieve the condition where humankind is free. Much more could be said on this topic, suffice it to say that theorists of politics need to recognize this important common value of Christians and Marxists if they are to begin to explain their common actions in many parts of the world.

Praxis is generally an alien concept in political theory. It is rarely discussed at all. When it is, the vast majority of practitioners equate practice and praxis. Here they err because in both Christianity and Marxism praxis has a special meaning.

Bowerbirds who build their complex nests are practice. A person who builds skyscrapers and great dams is praxis. The former builds by instinct, the latter only after the construction has first taken place in the mind. Praxis is life lived on the dialectical edge of the "razor blade" between thought and action. To Christians and Marxists, a person is praxis in that he or she is a conscious builder of his or her own life. Again, this point of convergence should be understood by political theorists in order to more fully explain and describe Christian-Communist relations. Humankind as praxis is the task of becoming human and transcending alienation.[8]

State

The unresolved questions associated with the state are legion. No short inquiry into these problems can begin to address, much less resolve, the issues. Nevertheless, knowledge and understanding of the theoretical position assumed by Christians and Marxists on some of these major issues can only serve to help political scientists' insights into and mastery over this troublesome concept. Certainly no metamorphosis in this political theory can be expected, but some revision and elaboration may occur. In any event, the ideas of people living in societies that draw inspiration from Marx and Jesus, and representing as they do over one-half of the world's population, must be considered. These ideas affect us all—whatever our personal values and beliefs.

The problems begin in classical political theory. Aristotle sees the state as a natural institution. A human being is a "political animal" and a truly human life is a life lived in political association. In Aristotle's thought hierarchy exists, and the state is superior to the family and individual. Not so with Christians and Marxists. To both of these huge groups of true believers, the state is an artificial and unnatural institution. St. Augustine in the fourth century begins the Christian critique of the state as an unnatural institution and Karl Marx, an unlikely supporter, continues this thesis. To Marx, of course, the state is the political arm of the property owning class and an institution used to reinforce existing property relations. In essence, political theory presupposes the state while Christianity and Marxism are theoretically antistate.

Another great political issue is related to the size of the state.[9] Since most political theory presupposes the state's origin and existence as natural, the next question relates to the size of the state. Should it be small (the city-state), medium (the nation-state), or large (the universal political association of man)? What is the best living arrangement for humankind? Writing in defense of the national interest characterizes the bulk of the literature today. And the growth in United Nations membership since World War II from 45 to over 150 gives witness to the reality of the nation-state as the basic living arrangement for humankind today. Nationalism, the "religion" of the nation-state, may well be the most powerful ideology operative today. Again, Christians and Marxists jointly oppose this world view because they are by nature internationalist. What Jesus and Marx taught was not the organization of man into small, limited groups destined to struggle against each other for particularistic goals, rather they urged humankind to break down the false national barriers that separate them and serve to set human beings against each other internally in class warfare and externally in war.

There is widespread agreement in political theory on what constitutes the nature of the state. Most political scientists list the following objective characteristics as essential: population, territory, government, and sovereignty with the bayonet as the ultimate mechanism of control. In the CME one quickly senses an alternative view. These Christians and Marxists frequently talk and work on issues and programs that reinforce values related to the notion of the community. Here more subjective forces are present, and one hears talk of the end of rigid territory and population lines and the popular control of public policy. The organizing principle of the community is love, and the mechanism of control is not the bayonet but fellowship. In the political community one obeys public policy because it is the right thing to do. This is very different, argue the dialogists, from the obligation to obey the sovereign power of the state based on fear.

Trenchant social analysis demands that political scientists sharpen their inquiry into the notion of political community rather than focus so much effort on the concept of the state. Youths in both East and West condemn their own systems today; we fail frequently in both East and West to relate our means to the ends we seek to achieve; and the role of the state in social and economic relations all over the world necessitates acute insights into different political relations. The ideas emerging from the CME may help in the elaboration of future political theory concerned with the state and community.

Power

Political philosophy is rational thought about power. *Power* is the key concept associated with relationships between entities in political science (power relations between people, between a person and the state, and between states). One of the most useful definitions of power is constructed by Lasswell and Kaplan in their book *Power and Society*. They talk about power in terms of decision making. "G has power over H with respect to the values K if G participates in the making of decisions affecting the K-policies of H."[10] A great deal of excellent theoretical work on power has been done by political scientists—power is a form of influence, and authority is simply power "cloaked in the garments of legitimacy." Power is ruling. Authority is right ruling. Leslie Lipson in *The Great Issues of Politics* relates a number of these concepts in the following manner.

	First	Second	Third
Political Ends:	Protection	Law and Order	Justice
Political Means:	Force	Political Power	Authority

Initially, a person desires security and to achieve this he or she uses collective force. Once security is realized the person desires regularized relations (law and order) and to achieve this he creates political power, that is, some people have the power to manipulate the collective force of the group. Finally, the person wants a just system of law and order (justice) and for this he endows some rules with authority. Most of life is lived at the second level of development.[11]

Up to this point all is well, and we can but applaud the theorists who have worked out such helpful conceptions. But there is one problem associated with the concept of power that the CME may help political science solve. This is the distinction between the formal power relations of governmental institutions and the informal power relations of our major economic and social institutions (family, school, and church). Political scientists naturally focus on the former. The CME tends to concern itself primarily with the latter because its origin and development in the First and Second Worlds and virtually all of its participants have been based in either academia or the pulpit. The historical case for the internal relationship of economics and politics has been most effectively made by James Harrington in *Oceana* (1656) and Karl Marx. Today, everyone recognizes this dimension of power. It is the power relations in our social institutions that need illumination and refinement. Here the CME can assist us.

To be concerned with political behavior is to be concerned with the behavior of both individuals and groups. In the West we have historically tended to focus on individuals and as such discuss politics in terms of individuals. People such as Gandhi, Martin Luther, Pope John Paul II, Martin Luther King, Jr., and so forth are quickly acknowledged as important catalysts of social and political change. Like the case for the intimate relationship between politics and economics, little more needs to be said to establish the validity of this thesis. What is needed, and what study of the CME can provide, are insights into the power relations of our major social institutions—church, family, school. We tend to ignore or dismiss these structures in political science.

The church's relationship with formal power institutions varies in time and space, but it is always there. The state cannot dismiss the power of the church, and the church can ill afford to ignore its relations to the state. Consider the power of the church in Poland, Italy, Romania, and the United States. Perhaps one example might help. Think of the real power position of the church in the United States. There is a church located on virtually every corner in America. This is literally a concrete fact. What would any total-itarian ruler pay to have available such property and organization? Church membership, attendance, and contributions continue to grow. All is volun-tary. Institutions such as the National Council of Churches provide institu-tional links between members of varied faiths. And to a significant degree, the pastors, priests, and rabbis have a weekly forum wherein they can plead, persuade, and cajole their flocks to pursue certain values (both social and individual). What would Hitler or Stalin have paid for such an institutional and bureaucratic apparatus? Add to this the current so-called Electric Church of television—smooth, slick shows, produced and directed by media professionals that influence people's political values and take in millions of dollars at the same time. What political party can begin to match these shows? Is there anyone in political science who takes the position that Jerry Falwell and the Moral Majority are not related to public policy in America? According to George Washington Plunkett of Tammany Hall, the measure of a person's political power is directly related to the number of people who will vote as he or she instructs (Mayor Daley of Chicago was aware of this fact also). If that is true, it is time to see what the pastor and priest are saying. If an example is required, consider Billy Graham and Father Coughlin. It is incumbent on political scientists to seriously study the CME because moral rectitude and respect are bases of political power. What the theologians and philosophers of academia and their practicing counterparts in society, the priests and pastors, are saying and doing merits study. This is not to suggest that occupation of positions in government and control of economic institu-tions are unimportant. What is crucial to remember is that the bases of power are many and that the church has a near monopoly on *some* of these.

Someone once said about internal university politics that it is particularly vicious because the stakes are so low. This may be true, but the political relationships of the state and its educational system are crucial—at least Hitler thought so as his first move was the ideological purification of public and higher education in Germany in 1933. Political scientists sometimes seem to dismiss the political significance of universities and students. How-ever, the events of May–June 1968 in France almost brought down the DeGaulle government, and the protests and unconventional politics of university faculty and students in America during the Vietnam war played a significant role in the downfall of Lyndon Johnson. These were very powerful political rulers, yet they were weakened and enfeebled and ultimately driven from office by young people who possessed no money, few skills, and little respect. What they did possess was knowledge and physical strength ("savage bodies" in the words of Mao Tse-tung) and they used these effectively to achieve their political goals.

There are a host of other activities that involve academics in the public policy process. Some are advisors to politicians while others hold cabinet rank (Henry Kissinger, Zbigniew Brzezinski, Jeanne Kirkpatrick, and so forth). Some write articles for periodicals and newspapers, while others serve as talk-show panelists on television. Then there is the transmission of ideas via the arts. This is a particularly effective way to achieve political goals. Consider the following: paintings such as Picasso's *Guernica;* antiwar books such as *Catch 22, Slaughterhouse 5, The Little Drummer Girl, 1984,* etc.; films such as *Apocalypse Now, Missing, "Z," Das Boot,* and many others; the music of Wagner—believed by Hitler to express the deepest political sentiments of the German people; the use of poetry by the Soviets to express political ideas; mime, theater, dance, and so forth. The point is simply that the arts and politics are internally related.

Finally, the politics of the family must someday become a legitimate topic in political science. The power relations within the family are transforming themselves as we have moved from the extended family to the nuclear family to the one-parent family to the institutional family. The patriarchal society is seriously enfeebled in many Western societies. Family power and income producers have traditionally been directly related. Today that is changing from male dominance to male-female power sharing as more women enter the work force. In Israel we have the institutions of the kibbutzim. The consequence of this on traditional Jewish family life is monumental.[12]

Hopefully the argument has been made. Internal power relations demand much more attention from political scientists today than ever before. Church, family, university, and all the arts express political values and beliefs and as such affect behavior. The CME is unique in that its political activists and participants in dialogue are immersed in these social institutions and activities. They not only affect those who make political decisions, they are today actors in the political process. No reading of the essays in this book could leave any other impression.

Justice

"Is *justice* mere convention, or are things by nature just?" Is there a universal form of justice, a justice that exists outside of history and is good for all men, all times, everywhere, or is justice relative and ultimately only utilitarian in nature? This is the fundamental problem of political theory in dealing with justice. The question of what is justice has been discussed by all the great political philosophers. The only unity to be found is in their disagreement. Witness the following: *Plato* had a vision of a great good, justice that he sought to implement in history. Plato was a universalist and talked about the reality of justice as a form existing outside history, while justice in this world was a mere image of that transcendent reality. For *Machiavelli,* justice was defined by the Prince. Granted, the Prince was always to give the appearance of acting in accordance with the operative ideals of justice, but Machiavelli instructs the Prince to remember his own power position first and forget the rhetoric of universal justice—it did not exist. *Bentham's* theory of justice was utilitarian—the greatest good for the greatest number constituted justice. Justice in public policy was simply a matter of the representative adding of the views of his constituency in terms of quantity and intensity and then voting in accordance with the outcome. *Locke's* notion of justice involved a new expression of natural law. Humankind was possessed of certain natural rights (life, liberty, property), and those social systems that protected these values were just, while those that denied them were unjust. *Marx's* concept of justice was twofold. In the epoch of socialism he suggested "from each according to his ability, to each according to his work." In the era of communism justice was "from each according to his ability, to each according to his need."

The five images of justice above are representative—not exhaustive by far. However, they do illustrate the tremendous lack of agreement in political theory on the topic. How can the study of religion generally, and the CME particularly, help in the refinement of this crucial concept of political theory? First, the *Bible* provides us with a number of concepts of justice that in practice have served man well over the centuries. The Ten Commandments that Moses transmitted to the Jewish people are certainly a good starting point. These have served for over two millennia as the basis of justice for Jews. Additional biblical evidence of the concern with justice can be found in the writings of prophets such as Micah and Amos, who sought to restore social justice in a society that they felt had departed from its basic law. And the Last Judgment of Jesus as portrayed in Matt. 25:31–46 has been interpreted by many as his command to us all to make social justice and love of neighbor concrete in this world or face the possibility of damnation in the next. These themes are analyzed and discussed and their present-day implications drawn out at every CME in which the editors have been involved.

Second, the entire thrust of liberation theology is associated with building a just society. This theology is the topic of numerous books and, of course, is discussed at every CME. If political scientists wish to even begin to understand the revolutionary politics of Central and South America today, they must, as part of that process of understanding, include in their inquiry the CME going on in that area. This new theology includes Marxism as its basic method of social analysis in explaining the claims of the poor for economic and political change. These people seek to liberate themselves from unjust social conditions and from the theological imperialism of the countries in the North Atlantic community. The hope for peaceful-evolutionary transition from oppression to justice ended in Chile with the military *coup d'état* that overthrew Allende in 1973. Despair reigned on this melancholy continent. However, hope has reemerged in the new revolutionary situation, and the theology of liberation is the major expression of that hope. The inspirational value of this theology as a motivating and mobilizing factor for the masses of people in Central and South America should not be ignored by students of politics. The two preconditions for revolutionary change are present in this area of the world—unjust social conditions and the existence of a new ideology that explains to the masses of people where they hurt, why they hurt, and what they can do about it. Jose Miranda's *Communism and the Bible* and Gustavo Gutiérrez's *A Theology of Liberation* are two of the texts that every political scientist in the West should read.

Finally, there is a continuing theme in the literature of political science—an effort to determine the nature of the universal postulates of justice. Perhaps the outstanding effort in this area is by Arnold Brecht in his book, *Political Theory: The Foundations of 20th Century Political Thought*. This is truly a work "of the first magnitude." In it Brecht not only presents a general hypothesis that purports to set down five universal doctrines of justice, he even attempts to prove the likelihood of God's existence using only the tools of the scientific method. This text, recognized as a major contribution, is testimony that the search for those universals goes on in political science. Since this is the case no more useful forum is available to political scientists than the CME. It is here in word and deed that the search for the nature of justice and its implementation in social systems today goes on day after day. The essays in this book on Italy, Poland, and East Germany bear witness to this fact.

Change

Political philosophers have been fascinated with the phenomenon of political change for twenty-five hundred years. The two major types of change, evolutionary and revolutionary change, have been analyzed and described by virtually every one of the great political theorists. Plato sought to prescribe a system that was changeless in his *Republic;* Aristotle devoted a significant part of *The Politics* to an analysis of the conditions associated with revolutionary change; Burke in *Reflections on the Revolution in France* sought to minimize social change in all its aspects; Karl Marx in *The Communist Manifesto* contended that change is the rule of life. Some theorists have constructed cyclical and pluralist forms of evolutionary change while others have been intrigued by insurrection and the great social revolutions of France, Russia, and China. Today, much of the news reported in the media is of wars of national liberation (change) in Africa, Southeast Asia, Central and South America. For good or ill, political change, development, transformation, progress, revolution go on. It is perhaps, the major fact of life for those of us alive at the dawn of the twenty-first century. However, the major questions associated with change remain to be answered—questions such as the following: 1) What are the socioeconomic and psychological conditions of revolutionary and evolutionary change? (2) Why are the inspirational goals of revolution so often betrayed? (3) Who are the leaders of revolutions? (4) What social group or class is the agent of revolution today in developed and underdeveloped countries? (5) Where are revolutions most likely to appear in First, Second, and Third world nations? These and other problems are of major concern to political scientists today.

Historically religion and political change have been intimately related. Consider the following: the Crusades of the medieval epoch; the Reformation and the work of Martin Luther during the sixteenth century; the Peasant Revolution in Germany led by Thomas Müntzer, a Christian priest characterized by Karl Marx (surely a man sympathetic to revolutionary change) as "the most radical fact of German history"; and the rapid expansion of Islam along with the fundamental, deep-seated social changes wrought by this religious development. More currently one might note the role of religion in the attempt at nonviolent revolutionary activity in India under Gandhi and in the United States under the leadership of Martin Luther King, Jr. But violent revolutionary activity still prevails in Northern Ireland, Lebanon, El Salvador, Namibia, Morocco, Iran, and so forth. Political change may well be, as Marx said, "the rule of life." The problem is for political science to understand it and begin to answer the questions raised over time that concern this confusing concept.

One place to begin is with the CME because it is not only a forum for political change in Central and South America, it is an actor in the process via the dialogue and the cooperative activities of Christians and Marxists. It was, at least in part, the work and cooperation between Christians and

Marxists that brought Allende to power in Chile in 1970. It was the coalition politics of Christians and Marxists that helped overthrow the Somoza regime and brought the Sandinistas to power in Nicaragua. It is Christians, such as the assassinated Archbishop Oscar Romero, and Marxists working together in El Salvador that are bringing about significant political change in that part of the Western Hemisphere. The essays in this book on Africa, Latin America, and Cuba demonstrate over and over the role of the CME in the political development of Third World countries. Many people in Third World countries are living out a nightmare. They desperately need hope for "without a vision the people perish."[13] The CME in these areas provides the end (liberation) and the means (revolutionary activity)—the inspiration and the explanation. Perhaps Marx's eleventh thesis on Feuerbach says it best, "The philosophers have only interpreted the world in various ways; the point, however, is to change it."[14] The Christian religion provides the vision of a new day and Marx's methodology the mechanism to achieve that goal.

The disciplines of political science and religion have been fragmented and separated in the West. We need a new holistic approach in both fields if we are to begin to replace confusion and misconception with clarity and comprehension. Familiarity with work in both disciplines can lead to the positing of new, fascinating, imaginative hypotheses. What could be more useful? What could be more helpful than a new, fresh position from which one could inquire into and publish results? It may be that a strange paradox will occur. As each one of us studies the thought and action of the other, as we spend time and energy in trying to understand another's field of concentration, it may well be that paradoxically we will learn the most about our own. This is so not because new answers to old questions will necessarily occur (although this writer believes that will be the case at least to some extent), but because we have created the conditions for a new approach to our own discipline. New facets on old conceptual gems may be revealed. Such is the hope of this writer. It is the opportunity for political science.

NOTES

1. Jose M. Bonino, *Christians and Marxists: The Mutual Challenge to Revolution* (Grand Rapids: Wm. B. Eerdmans, 1976), 58–73.

2. Robert Freedman, *Marxist Social Thought* (New York: Harcourt, Brace & World, 1968), xxvi–xxvii, 65, 253, 276–336.

3. Michael Harrington, *Socialism* (New York: Bantam Books, 1972), 364.

4. Arnold Brecht, *Political Theory: The Foundations of Twentieth-Century Political Thought* (Princeton: Princeton University Press, 1959), 462–64.

5. Thomas P. Jenkin, *The Study of Political Theory* (New York: Doubleday & Co., 1955), 23–61.

6. Josif Ton, "The Socialist Quest for The New Man," *Christianity Today* (26 March 1976): 656.

7. Jean Milet, *God or Christ* (London: SCM Press, 1981), 201.

8. Gajo Petrovic, *Marx in The Mid-Twentieth Century* (New York: Anchor Books, Doubleday & Co., 1957), 171–89.

9. Leslie Lipson, *The Great Issues of Politics* (Englewood Cliffs, N.J.: Prentice-Hall, 1954), 317–49.

10. Harold D. Lasswell and Abraham Kaplan, *Power and Society: A Framework for Political Inquiry* (New Haven: Yale University Press, 1950), 75.

11. Lipson, *Great Issues of Politics*, 61–62.

12. Paula Rayman, *The Kibbutz Community and Nation Building* (Princeton: Princeton University Press, 1981), 192–271.

13. *Religious Socialism* 6:2 (Spring 1982): 3.

14. Karl Marx, "Theses on Feuerbach," *Karl Marx and Frederick Engels: Selected Works* (New York: International Publishers, 1969), 30.

SUGGESTIONS FOR FURTHER READING

Brecht, Arnold. *Political Theory: The Foundations of Twentieth-Century Political Thought*. Princeton, N.J.: Princeton University Press, 1959.

Lasswell, Harold D., and Abraham Kaplan. *Power and Society: A Framework for Political Inquiry*. New Haven: Yale University Press, 1950.

Lipson, Leslie. *The Great Issues of Politics*. Englewood Cliffs, N.J.: Prentice-Hall, 1954.

Milet, Jean. *God or Christ*. London: SCM Press, 1981.

Van Dyke, Vernon. *Political Science: A Philosophical Analysis*. Stanford, Calif.: Stanford University Press, 1960.

INDEX

INDEX

Falwell, Jerry, 210
Fanon, Franz, 138
Farner, Konrad, 2
Fetscher, Iring, 94
Feuerbach, Ludwig, 215
Franić, Frane, 123–24, 127
Frankl, Viktor, 204
Freud, Sigmund, 204
Fromm, Erich, 62–63
Frostin, Per, 150

Gandhi, Indira, 163–64
Gandhi, Mohatma, 206, 209, 214
Garaudy, Roger, 2, 65, 128
Gardavsky, Vitezslav, 2, 65
George, K. C., 159
George, M. A., 159
Gierek, Eduard, 86, 92
Girardi, Giulio, 55
Glemp, Joseph, 82, 95
Gogacz, Mieczyslaw, 93
Gomulka, Wladyslaw, 82, 85, 89
Gotting, Gerald, 103
Grace, Edward J., 13, 206
Graham, Billy, 210
Gutiérrez, Gustavo, 213
Gysi, Klaus, 106

Hagerman, Alice L., 14
Hall, Gus, 64
Ham Reyes, Adolfo, 185, 190
Hardayal, 155
Harrington, James, 209
Harrington, Michael, 67
Hempel, Johannes, 101–2
Heyl, Wolfgang, 102–3
Hitler, Adolf, 210–11
Hodgson, Godfrey, 61
Honecker, Erich, 99, 102–3, 112, 196
Hromádka, Joseph, 3

Jaroszewski, Tadeus, 94
Jaruzelski, Wojciech, 92
Jesus Christ, 197, 205–6, 208
Johnson, Lyndon, 211
John XXIII: and changes in church, 61–62; and *Mater et Magistra*, 194; and *Pacem in terris*, 30, 86, 194; and visit with Adzubei, 3–4

Kakkanadan, George, 159
Kaplan, Abraham, 208–9
Kappen, S., 165
Kaunda, Kenneth: and African socialism, 145–47; and exception to Third World typology, 11; views of, 136–37, 139
Keita, Modibo, 135
Kellner, Erich: and "Dialogue in Freedom and Responsibility," 47; and dialogues, 43, 46–49; as founder of PG, 41; and requirements for dialogue, 51; and Soviet Academy of Sciences, 46
Kenyatta, Joma, 135
Kersevan, Marko, 123, 125
Khrushchev, Nikita, 89, 194, 196
King, Martin Luther, Jr., 206, 209, 214
Kolakowski, Leszek, 83, 199
Kottukapally, J., 165–66
Kowalczyk, Stanislaw, 88, 90, 94–95
Kresić, Andrija, 123, 126
Krusche, Werner, 102
Kuczynaski, Janusz, 84, 88–89, 92, 95

Lasswell, Harold D., 208–9
Lauer, Quentin, 64, 70
Leich, Werner, 99
Lenin, Nikolai, 183
Lens, Sidney, 65
Lipson, Lesli, 209
Lochman, Jan M., 2
Locke, John, 203, 212
Lombardo Radice, Lucio: and Communist Catholic theoreticians, 23, 28, 37; and Italian Communist Party, 19–20; and *Pacem in terris*, 30
Longo, Luigi, 31
Lorenz, Konrad, 44
Luther, Martin: and property, 201; and social change, 206, 209, 214; works of, in East Germany, 99–100, 113

Machel, Samora, 143–44

INDEX